Understanding the Firm: Spatial and Organizational Dimensions

Understanding the Firm

Spatial and Organizational
Dimensions

Edited by

Michael Taylor (University of Birmingham)
and Päivi Oinas (Erasmus University)

OXFORD
UNIVERSITY PRESS

Great Clarendon Street, Oxford OX2 6DP
Oxford University Press is a department of the University of Oxford.
It furthers the University's objective of excellence in research, scholarship,
and education by publishing worldwide in

Oxford New York

Auckland Cape Town Dar es Salaam Hong Kong Karachi
Kuala Lumpur Madrid Melbourne Mexico City Nairobi
New Delhi Shanghai Taipei Toronto

With offices in

Argentina Austria Brazil Chile Czech Republic France Greece
Guatemala Hungary Italy Japan Poland Portugal Singapore
South Korea Switzerland Thailand Turkey Ukraine Vietnam

Oxford is a registered trade mark of Oxford University Press
in the UK and in certain other countries

Published in the United States
by Oxford University Press Inc., New York

© Oxford University Press 2006

The moral rights of the authors have been asserted
Database right Oxford University Press (maker)

First published 2006

All rights reserved. No part of this publication may be reproduced,
stored in a retrieval system, or transmitted, in any form or by any means,
without the prior permission in writing of Oxford University Press,
or as expressly permitted by law, or under terms agreed with the appropriate
reprographics rights organization. Enquiries concerning reproduction
outside the scope of the above should be sent to the Rights Department,
Oxford University Press, at the address above

You must not circulate this book in any other binding or cover
and you must impose the same condition on any acquirer

British Library Cataloguing in Publication Data

Data available

Library of Congress Cataloging in Publication Data
Understanding the firm: spatial and organizational dimensions/edited
by Michael Taylor and Pivi Oinas
p. cm.
Includes index.
1. Industrial organization (Economic theory) 2. Institutional economics.
I. Taylor, Michael, 1946 Feb. 28- I I. Oinas, Pivi.
HD2326.U535 2006
338.5—dc22   2006019918

Typeset by SPI Publisher Services, Pondicherry, India
Printed in Great Britain on acid-free paper by
Biddles Ltd., King's Lynn

ISBN 0-19-926079-6   978-0-19-926079-9

1 3 5 7 9 10 8 6 4 2

Contents

List of Tables and Figure   vii
List of Contributors   viii

Part I. Theorizing the Firm—Introduction   1

1. Fragments and Gaps: Exploring the Theory of the Firm   3
   Michael Taylor

Part II. The Boundaries of the Firm   33

2. The Many Boundaries of the Firm   35
   Päivi Oinas
3. Guns, Firms, and Contracts: The Evolution of Gun-Making in Birmingham   61
   Michael Taylor and John Bryson

Part III. Collective Agency and Narratives on Performance   85

4. The Firm: Coalitions, Communities, and Collective Agency   87
   Michael Taylor
5. The Corporation, Shareholder Value Added, and the Power of Financial Management Narratives   117
   Phillip O'Neill

Part IV. The 'Political' Firm and the State   147

6. Distortions in Industrial Geography: Triangulating Among Industrial Firms, Financial Firms, and the State   149
   Ann Markusen

Contents

7. Firms as Political Actors in Processes of Capital
   Accumulation and Regional Development   169
   Ray Hudson

Part V. The Firm in Place   189

8. Studying the New Economy: An Activity Specific
   Approach to the High-Tech Firm   191
   Mia Gray
9. Learning Firms in Learning Regions: Innovation,
   Cooperation, and Social Capital   214
   Bjørn T. Asheim

Part VI. Theorizing the Firm—Afterword   235

10. Theorizing the Firm in Economic Geography   237
    Päivi Oinas

Index   255

List of Tables and Figure

Tables
3.1. Birmingham's group contracting matched against Chesterman's criteria for a firm — 71
4.1. Ownership structure of South Hampshire electronics firms, 1998–9 — 100
5.1. The shift in BHP and BHP Billiton's financial management strategy — 131
5.2. Diversification in BHP Billiton: the world's largest resources company — 131
6.1. Changes in DoD prime contract awards by select states and region — 158
6.2. Employment in defence-related manufacturing in four US aerospace regions, 1989–94 — 159

Figure
5.1. Industry consolidation in the world's minerals and petroleum industries, 1997–2001 — 136

List of Contributors

Professor **Bjørn T. Asheim**, Department of Social and Economic Geography, University of Lund, Sweden, and Centre for Technology, Innovation, and Culture, University of Oslo, Norway.
(bjorn.asheim@keg.lu.se)

Professor **John Bryson**, School of Geography, Earth and Environmental Sciences, University of Birmingham, UK.
(j.r.bryson@bham.ac.uk)

Dr **Mia Gray**, Department of Geography, University of Cambridge, Cambridge, UK.
(pmg27@camb.ac.uk)

Professor **Ray Hudson**, Department of Geography, University of Durham, Durham, UK.
(ray.hudson@durham.ac.uk)

Professor **Ann Markusen**, Project on Regional and Industrial Economics, The Humphrey Institute of Public Affairs, University of Minnesota, USA.
(amarkusen@hhh.umn.edu)

Dr **Päivi Oinas**, Department of Applied Economics, Erasmus University Rotterdam, The Netherlands.
(oinas@few.eur.nl)

Professor **Phillip O'Neill**, Director, Urban Research Centre, University of Western Sydney, Sydney, New South Wales, Australia.
(phillip.oneill@newcastle.edu.au)

Professor **Michael Taylor**, School of Geography, Earth and Environmental Sciences, University of Birmingham, UK.
(m.j.taylor@bham.ac.uk)

Part I

Theorizing the Firm—Introduction

1
Fragments and Gaps: Exploring the Theory of the Firm

Michael Taylor

1.1 Introduction

Theorizing the firm in economic geography is fundamental to understand how local economies and communities function and evolve in a globalizing economic environment. Firms, we would contend, are at the very heart of modern-day life. They come in a seemingly infinite variety—from transnationals to small firms, corporations to branch plants, to subsidiaries and joint ventures, subcontractors to franchisees, sole proprietorships to partnerships, and manufacturers to service providers and retailers. For the most part we view them as the creators, destroyers, and repositories of jobs—the creators and destroyers of people's livelihoods, lives and dreams. But, deciding just what a firm is, is neither a simple nor a straightforward task. As Loasby (2001) has outlined, there is a range of legal categories of firms (up to forty in some national classifications) and a range of definitions of firms for purposes of regulation (e.g. labour regulation and taxation). Simultaneously, there is an array of types of interlock between firms, together with limits to managerial discretion and degrees of autonomy within firms. These layers of complexity make firms' boundaries fluid and very hard to define. And yet, it is possible to agree with Taylor (1984) that firms are vital to the functioning of modern economies as, 'the loci where social and economic forces meet and are played out' (p. 8), a sentiment recently reiterated by Moran and Ghoshal (1999). They are the vehicles of wealth creation in modern society.

Indeed, if we are to begin to understand the processes shaping international, national, regional, and local economies, it would now seem more important than ever to understand what a firm is. Processes of internationalization and globalization have made understanding the growth and evolution of multinational and transnational corporations a central issue, not least because the global reach of these corporations is constantly widening and deepening. The speed of this change, together with the rapid industrialization and growth of the Indian and Chinese economies, adds urgency to the development of an understanding of what firms are and how they operate. At the same time, the competitive advantage of places is now seen as increasingly dependent on enterprise, entrepreneurship, and the local embedding of firms in networks of trust that are said to occur in place-based clusters, regional innovation systems, innovative milieu, and 'new industrial spaces'. Understanding local processes of enterprise and entrepreneurship in both corporations and small firms, together with processes of new firm formation, are now major research questions in themselves, along with related issues of opportunity recognition, risk taking, and people 'being enterprising'. The local integration of small firms in agglomerations, yielding benefits of externalities and untraded interdependencies, has thrown into prominence firms' interconnections and idiosyncrasies, along with their competencies, capacities, and capabilities, and their weaknesses, limitations, and vulnerabilities. Now, even the subsidiaries of transnational corporations are said to need to be embedded in these local economic systems to gain access to local, place-specific knowledge to enhance their own performance (Yeung 1998).

To develop a fuller appreciation of how individual enterprises and local economies prosper and decline, it is essential to appreciate how the many different types of firm that comprise modern economies mesh together commercially one with another, and also with the markets and institutions of which they are part (Moran and Ghoshal 1999). Central to this task is the development of an understanding of how individual firms both exercise and cope with the inequalities of powerfulness and powerlessness that bind them together in the pursuit of wealth (Taylor and Thrift 1983; Taylor 1995, 1999, 2000).

Against this background of the dynamic complexity and plurality that business forms (and firms) can assume, there is a constant search within academic research for the processes that create and maintain both enterprise and enterprises in capitalist societies: a search for a theory of the firm. The search for such a theory is, unsurprisingly, contentious. That contentiousness depends largely on what question is being asked. Neoclassical economists substitute parsimony and timeless ahistoric rationalism for realism, to ask, 'What firms *should* we have?' Tractability of this complex problem is achieved through assumption—indeed, a string of assumptions that some might call heroic. Many in management science, and the social sciences more generally, see economies as socially constructed and ask in the context of the theory of the firm, 'what firms *do* we have?' or, '*can* we have?' with ancillary questions of 'when' and 'where' (see Weeks and Galunic 2003). Grappling with this complex reality brings to this stream of work imprecision, poorly defined core concepts, problems of replication, and a tendency to accrete layers of theorization with only modest verification (see the detailed discussion in Barney 2001, and Priem and Butler 2001*a*, 2001*b*).

As an introduction to the volume, this chapter attempts to pick a path through this constantly expanding field of debate to develop a context within which the separate chapters of the volume can be placed. It begins by exploring the complete contracts and incomplete contracts theories of the firm in economics that have adopted a particular approach to theory building centred on 'what should be' rather than 'what is'. Reactions to this approach, centred on 'what is', have built on the resource-based, behavioural and evolutionary ideas on the theory of the firm pioneered respectively by Penrose (1959), Cyert and March (1963), and Nelson and Winter (1982). Section 1.2 of the chapter explores these foundations. In Section 1.3, the more recent theories, or rather fragments of theories, of the firm are explored that tackle the question of why we have the firms we have. The competitive heterogeneity version of the resource-based theory of the firm is examined along with the knowledge-based theory, evolutionary theory, and the more idiosyncratic and weakly developed 'relational' theory. Section 1.4 identifies the principal limitations of these current lines of thinking on the theory of the firm. It highlights their inadequate treatment of time, entrepreneurship, and demand. It is these readily identified gaps in the fragments of thinking that make up the current theory of the firm which are used to introduce the separate contributions of the volume.

1.2 Complete and Incomplete Contracts Theories of the Firm

As the theory of the firm developed in economics, intense abstraction was used as a methodology to explore and explain the processes associated with three basic questions. These questions were: (*a*) why does the firm, as a form of organization, exist, persist, and prevail in exchange economies?; (*b*) what determines the size and boundaries of the firm?; and (*c*) what processes shape the firm's internal workings and external interactions (Foss 1999; Maskell 2001)? For Maskell (2001), the theories of the firm developed in economics to explore these questions fall into two broad groups. The first group comprises theories that adopt a 'complete contracts' approach, making the assumption that within a trading economy all economically significant contingencies can be foreseen and incorporated into contracts between parties. The second group comprises theories that adopt an 'incomplete contracts' approach, and begin from the more realistic position that it is impossible or too costly to specify unforeseen contingencies so that contracts between parties are necessarily open-ended or incomplete.

The complete contracts approach sees *a firm* as a production set that transforms one set of commodities into another, and *a market* as a coming together of firms and consumers to exchange commodities, with those exchanges mediated by contracts (Milgrom and Roberts 1988). In addition, it makes a number of key assumptions. It assumes that all decisions are made to achieve maximum economic efficiency—an increasingly relevant goal as the pressures of globalization mount (Taylor and Asheim 2001). It adopts equilibrium assumptions that deny the significance of time and path-dependence for the functioning of firms. And, it assumes that in all decision situations human agents are fully informed and, thus, omnisciently rational. The effect of these assumptions is to remove human agency from the theoretical calculus. The rationalism that underpins them leaves the firm completely described by its production function (Archibald 1971), to all intents and purposes turning it into a phantom that appears by name but lacks substance (Coase 1994). The approach, '... cannot (and does not attempt to) explain the firm as a planned entity involving hierarchical direction and authority that makes entrepreneurial decisions and is sometimes genuinely surprised by changes in the surroundings' (Maskell 2001: 334). Indeed, it leaves the boundary between the firm and the market quite ambiguous.

The incomplete contracts approaches also see firms as contractual entities but moulded by the costs of using a market-based price mechanism. These are the transaction cost views of the firm built on the seminal work of Coase (1937), and include ideas on governance (focused on bounded rationality, opportunism, and asset specificity—see Williamson 1975, 1985, 1991), and property rights (the rights to use and control assets—see Hart and Moore 1990, and Hart 1995). To establish working contractual relationships within an economy involves a wide array of costs, including search costs and information costs, bargaining and decision costs, together with policing and enforcement costs (Coase 1960; Dahlman 1979; Maskell 2001). The goal of every economic agent is, therefore, to economize on these costs such that:

... transactions that involve uncertainty about their outcome, that recur frequently and require substantial 'transaction-specific investments'—of money, time or energy that cannot easily be transferred—are more likely to take place within hierarchically organized firms. Exchanges that are straightforward, non-repetitive and require no transaction-specific investment will take place across the market interface. Hence transactions are moved out of markets into hierarchies as knowledge specific to the transaction (asset specificity) builds up. When this occurs, the inefficiencies of bureaucratic organization are preferred to the relatively greater costs of market transactions. (Powell 1990: 297)

Equally, when the 'information overload' faced by managers expands in magnitude, complexity, or diversity to the extent that it exceeds their competence and compromises the firm's efficiency, transactions may be moved to the market. Williamson elaborated and extended these ideas and added 'bounded rationality', 'self-interest', and 'asset specificity' to the equation. Boundedly rational behaviour (founded on less than complete information) and the self-interest of economic agents were seen to make contracts incomplete by definition, at the same time spawning opportunistic behaviour. That opportunism was, in turn, reinforced by asset specificity (when the value of an asset was much less outside its current context). Under these circumstances, retaining functions within the firm rather than contracting them within the market was seen as economically rational behaviour that set place-, time-, and sector-specific boundaries around the operations of the firm.

This highly influential transaction cost view of the firm, while tempering economism with elements of behaviouralism has, nevertheless, come in for strong criticism. It may offer an alternative to highly stylized, neoclassical, complete contracts ideas, but it also shares many of that perspective's limitations. According to Weeks and Galunic (2003), the three core assumptions of the transaction cost view are bounded rationality, 'opportunism', and 'functionalism'. The *bounded rationality* assumption is questioned because, as Foss and Klein (2005) have remarked, '... it is a sort of background assumption that while necessary, never really assumes a central role' (p. 7). Loasby (2001) following Foss (2001) has gone so far as to remark that this, '... "thin" conception of bounded rationality results in a "firm" that is so exiguous as to be barely visible'

(p. 276). Indeed, the full process aspects of the concept of bounded rationality (along with their operational implications) are not incorporated into the transaction cost model. As a consequence, Dow (1987) has pointed out that this 'thin' use of the concept brings inconsistency to the transaction cost theory. It is inconsistent to assume bounded rationality to explain incomplete contracts and then to assume that the same agents make rational choices about contracts and governance structures. Hart (1990), in fact, has maintained that the concept of asymmetric information between economic agents is a more elegant and tractable way of incorporating incomplete information into the theory of the firm. The *opportunism* assumption that is the basis of motivation in the transaction-cost view has been extensively criticized because it finds little support in empirical research. For Foss and Klein (2003), however, drawing on Ghoshal and Moran (1996) and Osterloh and Frey (2000), it is not that the opportunism assumption is wrong and that economic agents are not opportunistic, but that opportunism is assumed to be essentially extrinsic; that motivation is driven by forces external to the individual, especially the expectation of monetary reward. Moran and Ghoshal (1996) identify intrinsic motivation too—an individual's 'feelings for the entity'. But, neither intrinsic motivation, nor a blend of intrinsic and extrinsic motivation, is recognized in the transaction-cost argument. More problematic still is the *functionalism* that lies at the heart of the transaction cost argument: that if costs can be economized, they will be economized (Weeks and Galunic 2003). Advocates of this view of the firm maintain that not only *should* transaction costs be economized but that they *are* necessarily economized because of the Darwinian selection mechanism of competition. Williamson and Ouchi (1981) even suggest ten years is the maximum time needed for that process to occur. The question is, how are transaction costs recognized by firms? And, to maintain that those costs are always accurately recognized flies in the face of the bounded-rationality assumption.

Notwithstanding the implausibility of the assumptions underlying the transaction cost perspective on the firm, it remains fundamentally a stylization that does little more than convert behavioural characteristics into measurable costs, with every firm striving to achieve an efficiency goal. It is a view of what firms we should have, rather than what firms we do have, leavened with a few behavioural traits that barely penetrate the essence of the calculus. Taylor and Asheim (2001) argue that this means, first, that the transaction cost view of the firm still treats the firm as no more than a production function. Second, it completely ignores the reciprocal nature of inter-firm relationships. There are two or more parties involved in business transactions. Firms do not simply assemble and react to information: that information is embodied. Third, the perspective neglects the 'processual' nature of inter-firm transactions that involves the building of trust and reciprocity over time through repeat business. Finally, extending this last point, the transaction cost view of the firm is fundamentally static. It is, by inference alone, *in* time, but it is not *of* time.

1.3 Towards an Alternative Conceptualization of the Firm

The alternative, more strongly socialized approach to theorizing the firm begins with the question of why we have the firms we have. It derives from mounting dissatisfaction with the complete contracts and incomplete contracts theories of the firm. Its emergence as a set of integrated ideas is, however, both fragmented and incomplete. It constitutes more the basis of a theory rather than a complete and testable theory in itself, and comprises a number of variants that all find their origins in three strands of thinking. These strands are: the resource-based ideas exemplified by the work of Edith Penrose (1959); the behavioural ideas most fully elaborated by Cyert and March (1963) and the evolutionary ideas proposed in the work of Nelson and Winter (1982), for example. Obviously, these are not the only authors in each of these fields. They are simply the most prominent.

The first strand of thinking derives from Penrose's interpretation of the firm as a set of resources mobilized to cope with the pressures of the external commercial environment. In comparison with previous theory, she shifted the focus on the firm from the external conditions and pressures that were thought to shape it, to its internal conditions, resources, and capabilities. For Penrose, the firm was, '... an administrative organization designed to make profitable use of a pool of resources under its jurisdiction' (Dunning 2003: 5). It was a vehicle of value creation that could fuel economic growth. The resources themselves were seen much as Schumpeter (1934) had seen them, as '... the things and forces within our reach' (p. 14), or as '... all existing assets, both tangible and intangible, whose services can be used productively' (Moran and Ghoshal 1999: 392). These were resources that could be substituted one for another and combined to achieve an optimal pattern of firm expansion (Rugman and Verbeke 2002). To achieve such optimal growth was seen to involve balancing the exploitation of existing resources and the development of new resources. Here learning in management teams was recognized as an important process, but a process that was path dependent and dynamic. Also, in the Penrose view, firms possessed excess resources, and their human capital was not entirely specialized. As such, they had the capacity (the organizational slack) to diversify to achieve growth, with that growth limited and constrained only by managerial capacities (Rugman and Verbeke, 2002).

What was provided in this view of the firm was a description of the strengths and weaknesses of firms as they meet the environment within which they operate. It is a perspective on *value creation* in firms rather than *value appropriation*, as Rugman and Verbeke (2002) among others have been at pains to point out. It is *not* about the creation of competitive advantage within firms—firms 'isolating' their advantages so they can be used as a source of above average rents. This is an aspect of the resource-based view (RBV) that emerged strongly only in the 1990s. Also, in common with later RBV ideas, Penrose's approach is essentially a supply-driven approach centred on the strengths and capacities of individual firms. The demand side of the equation–the 'task environment' and the 'domain' of the structural contingency view of the firm—remain exogenous. Nevertheless, Penrose's ideas provide an essential foundation and springboard for a range of related theoretical perspectives that continue to grapple in ever increasing detail with the issue of why we have the firms we have.

The second strand of new thinking drew on behavioural ideas, and was most fully articulated in Cyert and March's *Behavioural Theory of the Firm* (1963). Though these ideas were novel and different, it must also be emphasized that they did not seek to replace conventional economic theory. To quote Cohen and Cyert (1965), 'The behavioural theory is viewed as supplementing the conventional theory of the firm. ... [T]he behavioural theory of the firm should be viewed as focusing on a different set of questions concerning the internal decision-making structure of the firm' (p. 330). By this interpretation, the firm is a site of decision-making in the face of conflict, uncertainty, problem-stimulated search, learning, and adaptation. The firm is conceptualized as sitting within a network of transactions—in Cyert and March's terms a 'coalition'—which is a framework of relationships with, 'managers, workers, stockholders, suppliers, customers, lawyers, tax collectors, regulatory agencies etc.' (Cyert and March 1963: 27). Most have little interest in the specific objectives of the firm as long as they receive satisfactory side-payments (sufficiently high wages, and dividends, satisfactory products, good treatment of creditors). Conflict then arises mainly within the firm among its managers as it pursues its collective goals. The most important of these goals have been identified in relation to production, inventory, sales, market share, and profits. It is postulated that individual managers will prioritize these goals differently depending on their area of responsibility, and each will attach aspiration levels to each goal reflecting past performance against targets. When goals are not met, search behaviour is instigated initiating learning and adaptation. However, change based on search and learning does not occur rapidly because of 'organizational slack'. Organizational slack arises when 'coalition members' are paid in excess of their opportunity costs (wages, profits, and dividends are higher than necessary, prices are too low or creditors are paid too quickly, for example). When necessary, however, that 'slack' can be used as a cushion against rapid change.

The mechanisms that underpin the behavioural theory of the firm have been summarized by Curwen (1976) in the following way:

The firm has an aspiration level with respect to each individual goal. Although the goals are inconsistent it is possible to satisfy them all simultaneously provided that the firm is satisficing rather than profit maximising. The holding of excess inventories does not necessarily conflict with the profit goal, although it will clearly do so when the profit goal is not being achieved. In the latter event, search behaviour will be initiated and continued until some source of slack has been identified and eliminated, thus increasing profits in line with aspirations. However, no attempt is likely to be made to eliminate more slack than is strictly necessary in order to meet profit targets. The firm sub-optimises at all times. (pp. 146–7)

What this approach provides is a set of linked mechanisms to explain how decisions are made within firms when futures are vague and opaque, how resources are deployed, and how knowledge is created and used.

The third strand of thinking which has contributed to the emergence of the RBV of the firm is drawn from evolutionary economics and is illustrated by Nelson and Winter's seminal work (1982) on the firm and economic growth that added an evolutionary dimension to behavioural views. These authors began from the position that economic change involves the combination of firm-specific, endogenously generated factors with exogenous pressures for change generated in the environments within which firms operate. In line with Penrose's ideas, firms were seen as repositories of competencies and resources and as a device for learning and accumulating both. Firms then evolved and changed by building on their prior competencies and resources. In Nelson and Winter's view (1982), there were three elements that shaped this process and its success or failure: routines, search, and the selection environment, with routines being pivotal.

Routines were the ways of doing things and the ways of deciding what to do that were built into all forms of organization, including firms (Nelson and Winter 1982: 400). They were all that is regular and predictable about business behaviour. They were based on experience and were, therefore, idiosyncratic. Moreover, routines limited the flexibility of firms and organizations to respond to external pressures. They could generate both appropriate and inappropriate actions, thus making change a risky but essential strategy for firms to adopt. *Search* involved firms constantly looking for new routines and new technologies to cope with external pressures. Firms by this view were constantly looking for new solutions, threats, and opportunities, which necessitated keeping their management routines under constant evaluation leading potentially to their modification and replacement (see the discussion on innovating routines in Pavitt 2002). That modification and replacement came through processes of incremental and cumulative learning, once again placing learning at the heart of business strategy and development. The *selection environment* comprised everything that affects a firm's well-being; conditions outside the firm in a particular industry or sector and the behaviour of other firms. This was the environment that was not only the arena within which the firm sought opportunities but it was also the arena within which the firm was itself selected.

The vital role of firms' routines in this path-dependent process of change was very clearly explained by Nelson and Winter (1982):

> In our evolutionary theory, these routines play the role that genes play in biological evolutionary theory. They are a persistent feature of the organism and determine its possible behavior ... ; they are inheritable in the sense that tomorrow's organisms generated from today's ... have many of the same characteristics, and they are selectable in the sense that organisms with certain routines may do better than others, and, if so, their relative importance in the population (industry) is augmented. (p. 14)

This is an approach to the firm reiterated in Hodgson (1988) in which the firm is seen as a protective enclave from market competition where skills and information build rules, routines, and habits that are part of a durable organizational structure. Routines and habits are seen as gene-like and able to reproduce the firm. They also act as a buffer between the firm and speculative markets where commitments are more tenuous and short-lived.

In summary, while each of these three strands separately adds issues of resources, behaviour, and path-dependent evolution to thinking on the theory of the firm, they also share several common traits. First, they all relax the rationality assumptions of the complete contracts and incomplete contacts theories of the firm, and they more fully connect with behavioural ideas rather than simply paying lip service to them (March and Simon 1958; Cyert and March 1963; Curwen 1976; Higgins and Savoie 1995). Second, in these three approaches, maximizing behaviour based on perfect knowledge has been replaced by satisficing behaviour based on imperfect information and uncertainty. Third, learning and knowledge transfer are seen as central to the success or failure of individual firms.

1.4 The Resources-based Theory of the Firm

The three strands of work on the theory of the firm outlined in the previous section have acted as a starting point for a suite of socio-economic approaches to the firm, beginning with the RBV (the conventional label for the resource-based view) and its derivatives. These derivatives include the knowledge-based, the competence-based, and the evolutionary and cultural views of the firm, and they have been incorporated in fragmentary fashion into the emerging relational views of economic geography which more directly addresses issues of space and place in this behavioural, resource-based perspective. However, it is in strategic management that these views have emerged most strongly. But, focused on the reality of competitive rent-seeking behaviour, they have shifted subtly and significantly from the ideas in this area of research that were originally espoused by Edith Penrose.

The perspectives that build on Penrose's ideas on the firm have shifted the ground of theorizing in significant ways. Most importantly, they have become prescriptive rather than descriptive, focusing on the processes creating 'competitive heterogeneity' in current populations of firms, with competitive heterogeneity defined as, '... enduring and systematic performance differences among relatively close rivals' (Hoopes, Madsen, and Walker 2003: 890). Heterogeneity, however, does not mean that all firms have to be different one from another, only that some have to be different. To Rugman and Verbeke (2002: 770), this version of the RBV of the firm has four central tenets:

1. The firm's goal is to achieve sustainable, above average rents compared to rivals;
2. Resources are not equally available to all firms, and their combination into competencies and capabilities is a precondition for sustained superior returns;

3. Superior returns are sustainable to the extent that they are valuable to customers, non-substitutable and difficult to imitate. The resulting heterogeneity among firms is reinforced by both path-dependence and first-mover advantages and 'isolating mechanisms';
4. Innovation is a source of sustainable superior returns.

At its core, this view of the firm sees resources being used to create isolating mechanisms and, therefore, to generate rents when they are assembled into combinations that cannot easily be substituted or imitated. Resources in this view are also broadened to include capabilities. Resources themselves are seen as observable assets that can be branded and traded. Capabilities, in contrast, are regarded as intangible, not observable, and can be valued and exchanged only as part of the entire unit of which they are part (of a marketing capability or a management system, for example). Hoopes, Madsen, and Walker (2003: 891) identify three general isolating mechanisms, though many more specific mechanisms have been identified. The first mechanism operates through *property rights*, and includes patents. The second is *high learning and development costs*, which also deter competitors. The third isolating mechanism is *ambiguity* about a rival's capabilities, which impedes imitation. Interpreted in this way, the resources, assets, and capabilities available to a firm are used as purposive, competitive weapons (Rugman and Verbeke 2002: 773).

However, Hoopes, Madsen, and Walker (2003) argue that barriers to imitation may not be the only mechanism that can create competitive heterogeneity. They draw on an extensive literature to demonstrate four other and potentially just as important mechanisms. The first is buyer switching-costs, which also affect buyer loyalty. The second is market segmentation, which creates differences in the prices that firms can charge. The third relates to processes operating within networks. On the one hand, strong network relationships have the potential to give firms access to lower cost inputs. On the other, lack of engagement with those networks can raise barriers to firms' operations in terms of access to and costs of inputs. Finally, regional differences in factor markets can generate competitive heterogeneity. These are geographically based sources of heterogeneity that are most obvious in either low wage regions and countries or the place-based embedded networks of clusters.

Moran and Ghoshal (1999) extend the RVB further to emphasize value creation in firms in addition to value appropriation, and to argue that neither firms nor markets by themselves can achieve adaptive efficiency. They argue that theories of the firm need to move beyond ideas of market failure and, '... recognise the positive role of organizations in the process of identifying and exploiting new resource combinations' (p. 408). It is not resources themselves that create value, but the abilities of people working within firms to access, deploy, exchange, and combine resources that is the well-spring of value. They also argue that:

> Firms or markets alone, left untempered by the countervailing forces of the other form of organisation, subject us to institutional straightjackets—one an iron cage of bureaucracy; the other, a treadmill of ever-tightening competition. Neither offers sufficient freedom to perceive, experiment with, and evaluate new ways to create and to realize value. Institutional pluralism (i.e., a rich variety of institutional forms and sizes) helps to overcome the institutional straightjacket. Both markets and firms are needed for adaptively efficient economic development. Operating together, in a dynamic state of creative tension, they provide the necessary checks and balances to bring about adaptive efficiency. As development ensues, institutional pluralism and the dynamic tension made possible by a variety of firms (rather than by a multitude of atomistic, independent actors) matters even more. (Moran and Ghoshal 1999: 406)

Nevertheless, they concede that, notwithstanding the argument that they make, we still have no clear and complete picture of the conditions that make adaptively efficient structures. These, only time will reveal.

Ghoshal, Hahn, and Moran (1999) have built on and extended this focus on the role of people in the RBV of the firm by emphasizing the role of managerial competence. This competence, they argued, makes firms agents of discovery and progress. Managerial competence they saw arising from two sources; entrepreneurial judgement and organizational capability. Entrepreneurial judgement was the ability to perceive new resource combinations and exchanges. It is, in essence, vision and imagination built on an initial stock of knowledge and insight coupled with the ability to learn, innovate, and evaluate opportunities. Organizational capability was the ability to carry out these new combinations, an ability built on insights into the behaviour and capabilities of the people whose cooperation is needed for a particular combination of resources to achieve commercial viability. Clearly, managerial competence is also a source of competitive heterogeneity, and Ghosal, Hahn, and Moran (1999) argue that:

> ... the notion of 'managerial competence' provides a plausible explanation of the apparent disproportionate distribution of large firms in the most productive economies. ... 'managerial competence' leads to the evolution of those institutional innovations that promote and sustain the continued growth of both prosperous nations and large firms in those nations. (p. 143)

However, to achieve growth in environments where there is high managerial competence (i.e. prosperous countries) makes it essential for, '... firms to attract, develop and retain high levels of managerial competence within their organisational boundaries' (p. 144), reinforcing competitive advantage in much the way envisaged by Porter (1990, 1998).

The knowledge-based view of the firm adopts a related but somewhat different perspective on resources—that the principal intangible resource of the firm is the competence of its people. It is a view of the firm championed and elaborated particularly by Kogut and Zander (1992, 1995, 1996, 2003*a*, *b*). By this view, firms are, 'social communities that serve as efficient mechanisms for the creation and transformation of knowledge into economically rewarding products and services' (Kogut and Zander 2003*b*: 516). They are the sites of situated learning, and they provide an identity for their members (Kogut and Zander 1992) in the form of a shared culture of coding, language, and cognition, conventions and rules of decision-making, together with convergent expectations among their members. Weeks and Galunic (2003) have argued that firms exist because they are better and more suited than markets in applying valuable knowledge to business. In other words, firms exist because they are efficient and effective; internally efficient, externally effective. This is very different to the transaction-cost view of the firm. It does not assume opportunism (Kogut and Zander 1992) or functionalism (if costs can be economized they will be economized) or market failure. This is not to deny that contractual hazard plays a part in why firms as an organizational form exist, it simply asserts that knowledge, and the evolution and sharing of knowledge are a more powerful explanation (Kogut and Zander 2003*a*: 511). The firm is not a monolith or the 'black box' of the complete contracts and, to a lesser extent, the incomplete contracts perspectives. It can comprise a number of subcultures in the manner of Lave and Wenger's 'communities of practice' (1991).

In this knowledge-based view, the firm is, in effect, a 'learning firm' (Lundvall and Johnson 1994) in which, 'the firm's capability to learn reflects the way it is organised' (Lundvall and Johnson 1994: 39). Flat structures with strong worker involvement and loyalty are said to create collective rather than individual learning (see Taylor and Asheim 2001). They liberate tacit knowledge and are the key to inventiveness and innovation—well-recognized sources of competitive advantage.

As proposed by Kogut and Zander (2003*a*), the firm in this knowledge-based view also has defined boundaries based on the situatedness of knowledge and learning. 'Cooperation within an organisation leads to a set of capabilities that are easier to transfer within a firm than across organizations and constitute the ownership advantage of the firm. These capabilities consist as well of the capacity to grow and develop through the recombination of existing elements of the firm and its members' (Kogut and Zander 2003b: 517). Indeed, 'identification [a feeling of "belonging" to the firm] *correlated* with a firm's boundaries enhances communication and learning' (p. 512). Firms, therefore, are free to get it right and to get it wrong, to establish appropriate or inappropriate boundaries that can just as easily be multinational as regional or national. And, their capacity to 'get it right' or 'get it wrong' changes over time through evolving, path-dependent processes of learning, knowledge transfer, and knowledge leakage.

Weeks and Galunic (2003) have further extended knowledge-based ideas on the firm, coupled with notions of firm evolution, in their theory of the cultural evolution of the firm. They suggest that the Kogut and Zander view of knowledge viewed essentially as 'knowledge transactions' is unnecessarily complicated. It suggests that people contemplating setting up a firm are:

... trying within the limits of their bounded rationality, to estimate the net present values of the rent streams accruing from various knowledge trajectories as they decide whether to come together as a firm and, if so, to arrive at the optimal design for the firm culture they want to create. (p. 1314)

For these researchers, '... firms are best thought of as cultures, as social distributions of modes of thought and forms of externalization' (p. 1344). Those cultural modes of thought are identified as ideas, beliefs, assumptions, values, interpretative schema, and know-how, which they describe collectively as 'memes'. They summarize their ideas in the following way:

... cultures ... [are] ... social phenomena, ... patterns of symbolic communication and behavior that are produced as members of the group enact the memes they have acquired as part of the culture. Memes spread from mind to mind as they are enacted and the resulting cultural patterns are observed and interpreted by others. The uncertainties of interpretation and the possibilities of reinterpretation and recontextualization create variations in the memes as they spread. Over time, firms evolve as a process of the selection, variation and retention of memes. (p. 1344)

The shared identity of a firm's members is, by this interpretation, generated through the culture of the firm that is built over time. Agency and power, not fiat, mould the evolution of that culture, and while it can include, please, and benefit some, it can equally exclude, displease, and disadvantage others. Firms exist in this cultural evolutionary view because those that enact a particular selection of memes gain benefits from the process, with the benefits and the beneficiaries changing through time. Clearly there are parallels between these views and the functionalist views of the complete contracts and incomplete contracts theories of the firm, but it substantially broadens the reasons why firms are set up and exist beyond efficiency, opportunism, and market failure. It also allows for the possibility that firms exist now for reasons completely different from those for which they were created.

Outside the Strategic Management discipline, these resource-based and knowledge-based views of the firm underpin the emerging 'relational' and discursive views of the firm in economic geography. The approach echoes some of the aspects of Weeks and Galunic's cultural evolutionary perspective (2003) (Schoenberger 1997; Thrift 1998; O'Neill and Gibson-Graham 1999; and the discussion in Taylor and Asheim 2001; Yeung 2002; Bathelt and Glückler 2003). Here firms are seen as bringing together diverse social relations: the interpersonal, family relationships, and social ties. This is the firm as discourse—a discourse of managerialism centred on information, knowledge, and talk. For Bathelt and Glückler (2003), understanding the geography of economic growth and change, 'is based on an understanding of intentions and strategies of economic actors and ensembles of actors and the patterns of how they behave' (p. 125). Bathelt and Glückler (2005) see firms in the Penrose sense, as combinations of resources: bundles of competencies exercised by people with shared understandings that generate idiosyncratic and firm-specific bundles of services. As in the RBV, the principal asset of the firm is knowledge—the 'know what', 'know who', 'know why', and 'know-how' that is not only problematic to trade and transfer, but which is also 'sticky' and spatially sensitive, having distinctive spatialities of both creation and transfer.

The approach does, however, move beyond the firm, seeing firms not as individual entities but as parts of larger structures of social relations involving competing, controlling, and complementary organizations and groups. Those structures are, in turn, sites of shifting power relations and sources of social capital that both offer opportunities and impose constraints on individuals and groups in pursuit of their economic goals. But, for Yeung (2005) the firm and, indeed, individual actors and organizations are not causal in their own right. Instead, causal power is vested in their 'relational geometries'. In short, the firm is an irrelevant analytical category just as Walker (1989), writing from a structuralist perspective, suggested fifteen years ago.

As it currently stands, this relational perspective from economic geography is no more than an heuristic, a description of collections of relationships that by Yeung's admission (2005) is fragmented and fuzzy. Unlike the theories and views of the firm in Economics and Management Science it offers no processes through which combinations of people, assets, competencies, and knowledge arise, prosper, decline, fail, or evolve and change, just that power and relationships exist. It has, for example, no processes such as the isolating mechanisms of the RBV which, coupled with issues of inimitability, create heterogeneity, enable competitive rent-seeking and cast resources as 'competitive weapons'. Though it has the potential to throw a new light on the firm it is currently no more than process-less description that is neither in time nor of time. It is a non-operational set of generalities about some indeterminate object that is somehow 'economic' and everything to do with 'knowledge'.

1.5 A Collection of Fragments: Gaps in the Theories

The perspectives on the firm outlined and discussed in the previous sections of this chapter are all concerned with the central questions of what firms are and how they develop. Clearly, it is a major, but still incomplete project. Indeed, in some respects it is no more than a disparate collection of fragments of thinking on three basic issues:

- Why firms exist;
- What determines the boundaries between firms and markets; and
- What determines firms' internal organization.

It has been suggested that the chronology of work in this field has seen a progressive deepening of thinking (Taylor and Asheim 2001). The processes of the rationalist, equilibrium theory of the firm assumed a more subtle form in the transaction cost, incomplete contracts theories, while the resource-based, knowledge-based, and evolutionary perspectives began to unpack processes operating within firms as they currently exist. Relational views have moved outside the firm to engage with network relationships and market structures offering potential insights into the debate on the boundaries between firms and markets.

But, despite this deepening of understanding, these theories and elements that might contribute to a more nuanced theory of the firm all share a number of important problems and shortcomings that detract from their explanatory power.

Principal among these problems is that, to a greater or lesser extent, all the approaches reviewed here *deal inadequately with time*; and this shortcoming has serious knock-on effects (Priem and Butler 2001a, 2001b). The rational choice, complete contracts theories are neither 'in time', in the sense used by Hicks (Loasby 2001), nor 'of time', in the sense that they focus only on intertemporal equilibrium. The transaction costs theory, founded on incomplete contracts, shares this limitation. As Loasby has remarked (2001):

> An economy 'in time' is an economy subject to Knightian uncertainty (Knight, 1921), [the impossibility of predicting or ascribing probabilities to investment and decision-making outcomes]; in these conditions, as Knight observes, co-ordination is not a matter of efficient *ex-ante* allocation but a continuing managerial task of problem-solving and learning. (p. 276)

Beginning with the work of Edith Penrose (1959), the RBV of the firm and the other, more recent approaches begin to address the issues of problem-solving and learning within firms but they still suffer the limitations imposed by being based on bulked-up microprocesses (see Massey 1999). In this sense, these approaches are of time but still not in time. They incorporate issues of change, evolution, and sequential processes of learning, innovation, action, reaction, and managerial decision-making, but essentially as the micro-adjustments that are all too easily aggregated into functionalist linear trajectories of change. This 'bulking-up' of microprocesses is well illustrated in Ghoshal, Hahn, and Moran (1999). They argue that the learning process within the firm takes time and this:

> ... effectively limits the rate at which a firm can internalise resources into its organisational structure—the rate of the firm's growth. Yet, even though management as a factor poses a dynamic limitation to the speed at which a firm can expand, it simultaneously creates new incentives to apply this firm-specific management knowledge to new profitable opportunities, partly because of the temporary under-utilisation of existing management. (p. 130)

What is more, if the propositions are accepted of the knowledge-based theory of the firm, as the most recent variant of the RBV, then the proprietorial control of knowledge and the issue of inimitability must lead inevitably to unremitting ownership concentration, tending towards monopoly. Though such concentration is evident in the trajectory of capitalist economies, so too is the persistence of enterprise niches and the persistence of organizational types into periods of time that no longer match with the conditions that created those types and styles of organization. Stinchcombe (1965) has demonstrated this persistence of organizational forms in the historical record, when styles of enterprise organization are appropriately seen in time, and it is an essential aspect of the enterprise segmentation model proposed by Taylor and Thrift (1983). The implication is, therefore, that the bulked-up managerial microprocesses of current theories of the firm offer little empirical insight into historical sequences of changing organizational forms in time.

Indeed, adding time into the theory of the firm radically alters the three basic questions that underpin it. According to Rathe and Witt (2001) the questions become:

- What guides the creation of a firm organization?
- How do firms, and the markets within which they operate, co-evolve, and how is the boundary between them affected?
- What regular paths of internal, organizational development can be identified, and what contingencies determine which of the paths is likely to be taken?

Recast in this way, these questions highlight three further shortcomings in current thinking on the theory of the firm: its failure adequately to conceptualize the boundaries of the firm, regarding them as multiple, indistinct, and fuzzy; its failure to incorporate *entrepreneurship* and processes of new firm formation; and its failure adequately to incorporate the dynamics of demand as it shapes firm and/or market boundaries.

In the context the *boundaries of the firm*, it is argued by some that in a new era of flexible accumulation and flexible specialization (Piore and Sabel 1984) the boundaries of the firm have become increasingly indistinct. Now, with firms quasi-integrated into local networks to counter problems associated with globalization, trust is seen to substitute for a formalized control system both within firms and between firms (Brusoni, Prencipe, and Pavitt 2001). The fuzziness of firms' boundaries is said to be expressed in the emergence of internal markets within firms, in emergence of quasi-firms, and in the appearance of hybrid firms, for example (see the critique in Hodgson 2002). To Araujo, Dubois, and Gadde (2003) firms now have multiple boundaries, that are more or less permeable depending on the nature of the relationship they have with their customers, suppliers, and competitors. What then is a firm? If it has no boundaries with other firms and institutions it is, in effect, an irrelevant analytical category. And, yet firms continue to trade, make profits and losses, employ people, self promote, and have major social and environmental impacts. Understanding their boundaries is a major question for theory.

The theories reviewed in this chapter all assume, implicitly, that the creation of firms lies outside their scope and both predates and is disconnected from the theorized processes of resource allocation and decision-making that shape their survival and growth. The acts of entrepreneurship that lead to firm start-up are, to all intents and purposes, divorced from the theories, even though continuing entrepreneurial processes are central to the firms' progress, expansion or contraction. In the transaction cost model this situation is at its starkest. Here decisions have to be made about the firm and/or market boundary before the firm exists—a particular benefit of static equilibrium assumptions!

However, entrepreneurship is itself a problematic concept. In Schumpeterian terms, the entrepreneur is an innovator who introduces new resource combinations that disturb an existing set of economic relations. In Kirznerian terms, he or she is an opportunist who generates profits from their superior foresight—their 'nose' for money-making ventures. Nooteboom (2004) who, among other things, has questioned whether it is a quality possessed only by an individual or whether it is a quality of a group has also highlighted the vagueness surrounding the concept of entrepreneurship.

A number of researchers, however, have recognized the failure of the theory of the firm to incorporate any concept of entrepreneurship. In recognizing this omission, Rathe and Witt (2001) point to the 'critical points' of enterprise development that face entrepreneurs. They follow Bhidé (2000) by suggesting that, '... many entrepreneurs seize small opportunities in a Kirnerian fashion by means of opportunistic adaptation. If they want to build larger, longer-lived enterprises they have to change the nature of their business. This requires a change from projects with high uncertainty and low investment to ventures with longer time horizons and higher investment which require ... strategic planning ... [and] ... managerial input' (p. 341). To leave entrepreneurship out of the theory of the firm therefore removes the first vital transition from the purview of theory. However, Penrose (1959) like Chandler (1962) recognized later critical points in the development of the firm that required the temperament and ambition of the entrepreneur. While also critical of the omission of entrepreneurship from the theory of the firm, Foss and Klein (2005) argue that entrepreneurship is more than Schumpeterian and/or Kirznerian creativity, innovation, and alertness to profit opportunities because none of these activities must necessarily take place within a firm. Instead, they argue that entrepreneurship is, 'judgemental decision-making under conditions of uncertainty', and, '... because markets for judgement are closed, the exercise of judgement requires starting a firm; moreover, judgement implies asset ownership' (p. 15). The logic of this argument is itself problematic, but it represents a specific attempt to incorporate entrepreneurship into the transaction cost theory of the firm.

The inadequate treatment of demand and the pressures of the market are particularly evident in the resource-based, knowledge-based, and evolutionary theories of the firm. Here the problem is not so much omission as the distractive preoccupation of these theories with the internal workings of the firm. With the firm characterized as a collection of assets and production and organizational capabilities, the focus of the more recent institutional theories of the firm is on internal processes of coping to meet the pressures and demands of the external commercial and governance environment and the demands of the market. And, central to these processes is 'learning' within the firm. The external contingencies of the firm's immediate 'task environment' (the external agents with which it currently interacts) and 'domain' (the external agents with which it might potentially interact) figure only weakly in the calculus of these theories. This contrasts strongly with the structural contingency model of organization and/or environment interactions that was popular in the 1980s (see the detailed review in McDermott and Taylor 1982). These contingency views, however, left little room for firms' responses to these pressures to be heterogeneous and for that heterogeneity to persist. The relational view of the firm, as exemplified in the work of Yeung (2005) does place greater emphasis on the external environment of the firm, though concerned almost exclusively with large corporations and transnational corporations (TNCs). However, this focus too is idiosyncratic and privileges social contacts and the interplay of interpersonal relations above the immediately commercial. As such it tends to interpret these relationships as benign and facilitating the free interchange of information between firms—precisely the opposite view of the control of knowledge in the knowledge-based theory of the firm.

1.6 The Chapters

The chapters in this volume begin to address these gaps in the theory of the firm from an economic geography perspective. They do so under four headings:

- The boundaries of the firm viewed from a theoretical and an empirical perspective;

- The collective agency of the firm, embracing issues of entrepreneurship, coalition formation, and the discursive, performative nature of the firm;
- The political firm, financial markets, and the state, broaching important external contingencies that affect the nature and functioning of the firm; and, continuing this theme from an essentially geographical perspective
- The firm in place.

A key issue in the theory of the firm is to understand the nature of the boundaries of the firm, and this issue is addressed in Part II. The chapters by Päivi Oinas, Michael Taylor, and John Bryson adopt two very different approaches to addressing this question. Päivi Oinas discusses the issue from an essentially theoretical perspective, using a number of key references in the economic geography literature to initiate a discussion of the assertion that firms' boundaries are multiple, fuzzy, and indistinct because they are enmeshed in market and network relationships embedded in a broader social environment. In this discussion, she draws the important distinction between the firm as an *economic institution*, grounded in the laws and regulations of its particular institutional environment, and the firm as a *business organization*, interacting with other organizations on a daily basis involving the flow of goods, services, information, knowledge, and other influences across its boundaries. As an economic institution a firm's boundaries are delineated and precise. As a business organization its boundaries are necessarily permeable. But, that permeability is not fuzziness or indeterminacy. Michael Taylor and John Bryson explore the boundaries of the firm from an historical, empirical perspective using early nineteenth-century Birmingham's gun-making trade to develop their argument. They, too, are critical of the notion that under conditions of flexible specialization firms boundaries are indistinct, permeable, and fuzzy. Their analysis of Birmingham's intensely flexible group contracting system shows, contrary to expectations, that the boundaries between the micro-firms involved were set by contract, and those contracts were strongly enforced. However, by the mid-nineteenth century this system was in serious decline, and factory production was in the ascendancy. Firms' boundaries had changed radically, and the question for theory is why? The explanation offered by these authors is that the *direct pricing* of contracts, that was extremely time consuming in the group contracting system, had become too cumbersome and had been progressively replaced by *proxy pricing*, reducing former system members to paid labour and putting the control of proxies into the hands the new entrepreneurs, who had been the 'factors' and market-makers in the former system. The clear message from the two chapters in this section is that for economic geographers to contribute to a fuller understanding of the boundaries of the firm and the ways they change, they need to explore more deeply institutional processes and the nature and implications of contracts of all types.

In Part III, two chapters deal with the issue of the firm as collective agency, engaging with Rathe and Witt's question (2001) of why we have the firms we have. Michael Taylor opens his argument with the contention that the theory of the firm has neglected the key role played by coalitions of people who run, strategize, and control firms, and the collective agency they exercise. He argues that the theory of the firm needs to move beyond the stylization of the firm as a legal unit cast in a timeless world, to embrace issues of power inequalities and personal wealth creation. Processes of enterprise are seen as more than the legally defined enterprise. They are seen as the activities of temporary coalitions of individuals, that are more than the 'stylised shell' of the legally defined firm, and that are shaped by processes of dynamic inequality. Those coalitions are seen as more than communities of practice. And, it is argued that only when the processes of collective agency are unpacked will we be able to more adequately theorize the firm. Phillip O'Neill also focuses on processes that operate internally and externally to create, re-create, and shape the firm. His analysis begins from the position that communities have agreed meanings about what a firm is, derived from common understandings among language users. His concern is with large corporations, and he examines the nature of the modern firm through the case study of BHP Billiton and the way financial management narratives are driving contemporary corporate structures (an issue echoed by Ann Markusen in Chapter 6). He sees the firm defined in a pragmatic sense so that owners and managers can understand what the firm is. This understanding is achieved through 'talk'—the narratives of legal, financial organizational, and production and/or investment activities (involving distinctive logics, vocabularies, and modes of calculation). He views the firm as a performative entity and argues that what is meant by 'the firm' appears and fades according to which narrative of the firm interacts with which of the firms' interest groups. Knowing these narratives is critical to knowing the geographies of accumulation as distribution pursued by corporations. Nevertheless, though powerful, those narratives are uncertain and volatile. What is important about these two chapters is that they move the discussion of what the firm is beyond the confines of the legally defined firm, a necessity, it might be argued, if the theory of the firm is to be understood as dynamic.

Fragments and Gaps: Exploring the Theory of Firm

The two chapters of Part IV open a discussion on the external contingencies of the firm through an examination of what can be termed 'the political firm' and its relationship and interactions with the state. The chapters, by Ann Markusen and Ray Hudson, bring an essentially geographical dimension to the discussion. Ann Markusen begins from the standpoint that the firm in economic geography is often treated as a generic unit, with a focus on the industrial or service firm, its links with suppliers and relationships with competitors and customers. Yet little attention has been paid to the financial firm, whose returns accrue to the buying and selling of assets, including entire firms, and the underwriting of industrial firms' assets. Indeed, little attention has been paid in economic geography as a whole to the supply of funds as opposed to the use of funds. The central argument of the chapter is that financial firms, seeking short-term returns, have the potential to induce long-term spatial restructuring of industrial and service firms that would otherwise not have occurred. The chapter examines in detail the differences in motivation, behaviour, and competence between financial and industrial firms, and argues that financial firms have been ascendant both in industrial firm decision-making and in state policy, with important consequences for the geographical distribution of industrial activity. Using the case of the aerospace industry, the chapter shows how the contemporary geography of this industry in the USA is shaped by this nexus of conflict between the two types of firm and the influence each has on the intermediary role of the state. Ray Hudson uses the context of the emergence of new forms of regional policy in north-east England in the 1920s and 1930s to extend this theme of 'the political firm'. The core of his argument is centred on asymmetric power relationships in capitalist societies within which the state emerges as a mediating mechanism. The state, he argues, cannot satisfy the interests of all firms simultaneously, while at the same time firms seek to influence the content, form, and implementation of state policies. Using a range of theoretical perspectives, he explores the necessity for firms to act politically, and the limits of their political action. The chapter emphasizes the role of firms in policy creation, and in defining the content, scope, and the boundaries of those policies. It is also pointed out, however, that this involvement can bring quite unintended consequences.

The discussion of Part IV is continued in the two chapters of Part V by Mia Gray and Bjørn Asheim, but with a focus on the impact of place on the operations and functioning of firms. Mia Gray argues that to understand firm behaviour and decision-making it is essential to break down the firm into its functional parts—development, production, and realization (including marketing) processes—and to appreciate the strategic choices and locational opportunities for each separate functional part. This is because each function may require and display its own strategy separate from those of other functions, not least because each function can have its own barriers to entry of very different heights. The argument of the chapter is illustrated by case studies of bio-pharmaceutical firms. The economic geography literature makes the implicit assumption that such high-tech firms need to agglomerate in new industrial spaces. Mia Gray's analyses shows otherwise. Firms in her case studies exhibit agglomeration in some functions alongside decentralization in others. Firms in the same sector may adopt different strategies; each activity in a firm may adopt a different strategy; and strategies may differ by product within the same firm. In short, place impacts within firms in very complex ways. Bjørn Asheim's chapter is concerned with the achievement of place-based endogenous growth and the role of the learning firm in a post-Fordist, globalized world. His focus is the achievement of learning-based competitiveness. Interactive learning between firms is suggested as having the capacity to promote and sustain that competitiveness and the growth of local economies. Building organizational capabilities is seen as a way of fostering trust, building social capital in networks of private sector firms, and public sector organizations to achieve that interactive learning. However, the conditions to achieve such learning-based growth are not found everywhere. Typically, it is argued, they are confined to well-off regions in developed countries with coordinated market economies rather than liberal market economies. Nevertheless, learning firms in learning regions are thought to offer the prospect of long-term, growth-oriented capitalism.

In the final part Part VI, Päivi Oinas initiates a discussion on the challenge economic geographers face as they begin to engage with the theory of the firm and the substantial body of critical thought that already exists in this area.

References

Araujo, L., Dubois, A., and Gadde, L.-E. (2003). 'The Multiple Boundaries of the Firm', *Journal of Management Studies*, 40(5): 1255–77.

Archibald, G. C. (ed.) (1971). *The Theory of the Firm*. London: Penguin.

Barney, J. (2001). 'Is the Resource-based "View" a Useful Perspective for Strategic Management Research? Yes', *Academy of Management Review*, 26: 41–56.

Bathelt, H. and Glückler, J. (2003). 'Towards a Relational Economic Geography', *Journal of Economic Geography*, 3: 117–44.

—— —— (2005). 'Resources in Economic Geography: From Substantive Concepts Towards a Relational Perspective', *Environment and Planning A*, 37: 1545–63.

Bhidé, A. (2000). *The Origin and Evolution of New Business*. Oxford: Oxford University Press.

Brusoni, S., Prencipe, A., and Pavitt, K. (2001). 'Knowledge Specialization, Organizational Coupling, and the Boundaries of the Firm: Why Do Firms Know More Than They Make?', *Administrative Science Quarterly*, 46: 597–621.

Chandler, A. D. (1962). *Structure and Strategy*. Cambridge, MA: Harvard University Press.

Coase, R. H. (1937). 'The Nature of the Firm', *Economica*, 4: 386–405.

—— (1960). 'The Problem of Social Cost', *Journal of Law and Economics*, 3: 1–44.

—— (1994). *Essays on Economics and Economists*. Chicago and London: Chicago University Press.

Cohen, K. and Cyert, R. (1965). *Theory of the Firm: Resource Allocation in a Market Economy*. Englewood Cliffs, NJ: Prentice-Hall.

Curwen, P. (1976). *The Theory of the Firm*. London: Macmillan.

Cyert, R. M. and March, J. G. (1963). *A Behavioral Theory of the Firm*. Englewood Cliffs, NJ: Prentice-Hall.

Dahlman, C. (1979). 'The Problem of Externality', *Journal of Law and Economics*, 22(1): 141–62.

Dow, G. (1987). 'The Function of Authority in Transaction Cost Economics', *Journal of Economic Behaviour and Organization*, 8: 159–82.

Dunning, J. (2003). 'The Contribution of Edith Penrose to International Business Scholarship', *Management International Review*, 43: 3–19.

Foss, N. (ed.) (1999). *Theories of the Firm: Critical Perspectives in Economic Organisation*. London: Routledge.

—— (2001). 'Bounded Rationality in the Economics of Organization: Present use and (some) Future Possibilities,' *Journal of Management and Governance*, 5: 401–25.

—— and Klein, P. (2005). 'The Theory of the Firm and Its Critics: A Stocktaking and Assessment', DRUID Working Paper No. 05–03.

——, Lando, H., and Thomsen, S. (2002). 'The Theory of the Firm', in B. Bouchert and G. de Geest (eds.), *The Handbook of Law and Economics*. Aldershot, UK: Edward Elgar, pp. 1–27.

Ghoshal, S., Hahn, M., and Moran, P. (1999). 'Management Competence, Firm Growth and Economic Progress', *Contributions to Political Economy*, 18: 121–50.

Hart, O. (1990). 'Is "Bounded Rationality" an Important Element of a Theory of Institutions', *Journal of Institutional and Theoretical Economics*, 146: 696–702.

—— (1995). *Firms, Contracts and Financial Structure*. Oxford: Clarendon Press.

—— and Moore, J. (1990). 'Property Rights and the Nature of the Firm', *Journal of Political Economy*, 98: 1119–58.

Higgins, B. and Savoie, D. (1995). *Regional Development Theories and Their Application*. New Brunswick, NJ, and London: Transaction Publishers.

Hodgson, G. (1988). *Economics and Institutions: A Manifesto for a Modern Institutional Economics*. Cambridge: Polity Press.

—— (2002). 'The Legal Nature of the Firm and the Myth of the Firm-market-hybrid', *International Journal of the Economies of Business*, 9(1): 37–60.

Hoopes, D., Madsen, T., and Walker, G. (2003). 'Guest Editors' introduction to the special issue: Why is There a Resource-based View? Towards a Theory of Competitive Heterogeneity', *Strategic Management Journal*, 24: 889–902.

Kogut, B. and Zander, U. (1992). 'Knowledge of the Firm, Cognitive Capabilities and the Replication of Technology', Organization Science, 3: 383–97.

—— —— (1995). 'Knowledge, Market Failure and the Multinational Enterprise: A Reply', *Journal of International Business Studies*, 26(2): 417–26.

—— —— (1996). 'What Firms Do? Coordination, Identity and Learning', *Organization Science*, 7(5): 502–18.

—— —— (2003*a*). 'A Memoir and Reflection: Knowledge and an Evolutionary Theory of the Multinational Firm 10 Years Later', *Journal of International Business Studies*, 34: 505–15.

—— —— (2003*b*). 'Knowledge of the Firm and the Evolutionary Theory of the Multinational Corporation', *Journal of International Business Studies*, 34: 516–29.

Lave, J. and Wenger, E. (1991). *Situated Learning: Legitimate Peripheral Participation*. Cambridge: Cambridge University Press.

Loasby, B. (2001). 'Forum "Knowledge, Evolution and the theory of the firm"—Introduction', *Journal of Management and Governance*, 5: 275–85.

Lundvall, B.-Å., and Johnson, B. (1994). 'The Learning Economy', *Journal of Industry Studies*, 1(2): 23–42.

March, J. and Simon, H. (1958). *Organizations*. New York: Wiley.

Maskell, P. (2001). 'The Firm in Economic Geography', *Economic Geography*, 77(4): 329–44.

Massey, D. (1999). 'Space-Time, "Science" and the Relationship Between Physical Geography and Human Geography', *Transactions of the Institute of British Geographer*, New Series, 24: 261–76.

McDermott, P. and Taylor, M. (1982). *Industrial Organisation and Location*. Cambridge: Cambridge University Press.

Milgrom P. and Roberts, J. (1988). 'Economic Theories of the Firm: Past, Present and Future, *Canadian Journal of Economics*, 21: 444–58.

Moran, P. and Ghoshal, S. (1999). 'Markets, Firms and the Process of Economic Development', *Academy of Management Journal*, 24(3): 390–412.

Nelson, R. and Winter, S. (1982). *An Evolutionary Theory of Economic Change*. Cambridge, MA: Harvard University Press.

Nooteboom, B. (2004). 'Governance and Competence: How Can they be Combined', *Cambridge Journal of Economics*, 28: 505–25.

O'Neill, P. and Gibson-Graham, J. K. (1999). 'Enterprise Discourse and Executive Talk: Stories that Stabilize the Company', *Transactions of the Institute of British Geographers*, 24: 11–22.

Osterloh, M. and Frey, B. (2000). 'Motivation, Knowledge Transfer and Organizational Form', *Organization Science*, 11: 538–50.

Pavitt, K. (2002). 'Knowledge About Knowledge Since Nelson and Winter: A Mixed Record', SPRU Electronic Working Paper #83.

Piore, M. and Sabel, C. (1984). *The Second Industrial Divide: Possibilities for Prosperity*. New York: Basic Books.

Porter, M. (1990). *The Competitive Advantage of Nations*. New York: Free Press.

—— (1998). *On Competition*. Boston, MA: Harvard Business School Press.

Powell, W. (1990). 'Neither Market nor Hierarchy: Network Forms of Organization', *Research in Organizational Behaviour*, 12: 295–336.

Priem, R. and Butler, J. (2001a). 'Is the Resource-based "View" a Useful Perspective for Strategic Management Research?', *Academy of Management Review*, 26: 22–40.

—— —— (2001b). 'Tautology in the Resorce-based View and the Implications of Externally Determined Resource Value: Further Comments', *Academy of Management Review*, 26: 57–66.

Penrose, E. (1959). *The Theory of the Growth of the Firm*. New York: Wiley.

Rathe, K. and Witt, U. (2001). 'The Nature of the Firm—Static Versus Developmental Interpretations', *Journal of Management and Governance*, 5: 331–51.

Rugman, A. and Verbeke, A. (2002). 'Edith Penrose's Contribution to the Resource-based View of Strategic Management', *Strategic Management Journal*, 23: 769–80.

Schoenberger, E. (1997). *The Cultural Crisis of the Firm*. Cambridge, MA: Blackwell.

Schumpeter, J. ([1934] 1978). *The Theory of Economic Development*. Oxford: Oxford University Press.

Stinchcombe, A. (1965). 'Social Structure and Organizations', in J. March (ed.), *Handbook of Organizations*. Chicago, IL: Rand-McNally, pp. 142–93.

Swedberg, R. (2000). 'The Social Science View of Entrepreneurship: Introduction and Practical Applications', in R. Swedberg (ed.), *Entrepreneurship: The Social Science View*. Oxford: Oxford University Press, pp. 7–44.

Taylor, M. (1984). 'Industrial Geography and the Business Organisation', in M. Taylor (ed.), *The Geography of Australian Corporate Power*. Sydney: Croom Helm.

—— (1995). 'The Business Enterprise, Power and Patterns of Geographical Industrialisation', in S. Conti, E. Malecki, and P. Oinas (eds.), *The Industrial Enterprise and Its Environment: Spatial Perspectives*. Aldershot, UK: Avebury.

—— (1996). 'Industrialisation, Enterprise Power and Environmental Change: An Exploration of Concepts', *Environment and Planning A*, 28: 1035–51.

—— (1999). 'The Small Firm as a Temporary Coalition', *Entrepreneurship and Regional Development*, 5: 1–19.

—— (2000). 'Enterprise, Power and Embeddedness: An Empirical Exploration', in E. Vatne and M. Taylor (eds.), *The Networked Firm in a Global World*. Aldershot, UK: Ashgate, pp. 199–234.

—— and Asheim, B. (2001). 'The Concept of the Firm in Economic Geography', *Economic Geography*, 77: 315–28.

—— and Thrift, N. (1983). 'Business Organisation, Segmentation and Location', *Regional Studies*, 17: 445–65.
Thrift, N. (1998). 'The Rise of Soft Capitalism', in A. Herod, G. Ó. Tuathail, and S. Roberts (eds.), *An Unruly World? Globalization, Governance and Geography*. London and New York: Routledge.
Walker, R. (1989). A Requiem for Corporate Geography', *Geografiska Annaler, 71B*: 43–68.
Weeks, J. and Galunic, C. (2003). 'A Theory of the Cultural Evolution of the Firm: The Intra-organizational Ecology of Memes', *Organization Studies*, 24(8): 1309–52.
Williamson, O. E. (1975). *Markets and Hierarchies*. New York: Free Press.
—— (1991). 'Comparative Economic Organization: The Analysis of Discrete Structural Alternatives', *Administrative Science Quarterly*, 36: 269–96.
Williamson, O. (1985). *The Economic Organizations of Capitalism*. New York: Free Press.
—— and Ouchi, W. (1981). 'The Markets and Hierarchies and Visible Hand Perspective', in W. Joyce (ed.), *Perspectives on Organizational Design and Behaviour*. New York: Wiley, pp. 347–70.
Yeung, H. (1998). 'The Social-spatial Construction of Business Organizations: A Geographical Perspective', *Organizations*, 5: 291–309.
—— (2002). 'Producing the Firm in Industrial Geography III: Industrial Restructuring and Labour Markets', *Progress in Human Geography*, 26(3): 366–78.
—— (2005). 'Rethinking Relational Economic Geography', *Transactions of the Institute of British Geographers*, New Series, 30: 37–51.

Part II

The Boundaries of the Firm

2

The Many Boundaries of the Firm

Päivi Oinas

2.1 Why Boundaries? Don't You Know They are Just Fuzzy?!

Our common-sense conception of any commonly known social entity is that it is identifiable and definable. This suggests intuitively that its boundaries are known. But, in the case of the firm, it has been claimed that its boundaries are increasingly fuzzy. Does this mean that we are losing our grasp on what the firm is, or is it that there is a range of different rhetorics on the meaning of 'the firm'?

Indeed, in discussion of the firm, we are at the meeting place of a number of different rhetorics. Think, for instance, of the rhetoric of the business world (and the business press) concerning the processes bringing about peerless products and services with first-class resources—competent managers and employees, technology, materials, and so on—embraced by the magic of the corporate logo and the figure of the powerful CEO. (Just think how, for years, we were led to envision Jorma Ollila as the scrupulous but understanding father figure behind Nokia's engineers as they doggedly strove to design fashionable and technically robust communication devices, or how Carly Fiorina was portrayed as the face of HP struggling to recreate itself.) It is *The Corporation*—or its image—that is paraded in front of us in this rhetoric: the corporation with a strong identity and a clear sense of goals; '*Our Corporation*' for happy employees; the *Trusted Producer* for loyal consumers; the *First-on-the-Market* for strategy analysts and competitors and/or imitators, the *Innovator* for technology (or competitiveness) freaks; the *Job Creator* for policymakers.

Then, we have the academic and policy rhetoric of the firm as the key agent in processes of economic growth and development. This 'growth engine' is analysed with the help of statistical data; its managerial, innovative, learning, or labour processes are investigated via questionnaire surveys, interviews, and participant observation.

These two rhetorics do not question the notion of the firm. It is implicitly assumed that it is clear what we are talking about when we refer either to particular firms or to 'the firm' as a social form.

Moreover, there is the rather more recent academic and business rhetoric that is concerned with the fuzziness of the boundaries of the very same object of analysis. With increased (real, imagined, or desired) inter-firm or personal 'networking'—relations between firms allowing goods, services, information, knowledge, plans, beliefs, stories, rumours, gossip, etc. to flow across firms' boundaries—it is said that firms' boundaries have become fuzzy or blurred. In Nooteboom's words (2000: 109–10),

> increasingly, the boundaries of the firm have become fuzzy and permeable, and the distinction, in the field of management and organization, between 'internal' and 'external' organization has become problematic and can be counterproductive.

It may be warranted to claim that the literature focusing on the tightly knit inter-organizational and social networks among firms has served as a key source of evidence of the claim that firms' boundaries have indeed become fuzzy. Included in this literature is work on the spatial organization of economic activity, suggesting that industrial districts or clusters offer environments that support inter-firm interactions and the monitoring of each others' activities. While all this is very relevant, the fuzziness claim creates a problem if we want to understand what the firm is. Firms do *exist*, as they own assets and produce goods and services; they are managed, they employ people, they are regulated and monitored by government decision-makers, they affect our views of the world and our behaviours. Yet, apparently, they do not have clear boundaries. But then, if they do not have clear boundaries, it is not clear *what* is producing the goods and services we consume. It is not clear what employs us. What creates our identity as employees? What owns the machines we use at work? What are policymakers targeting? What are analysts scrutinizing with their statistics? Indeed, what are firms; how does one recognize them; where do they begin and end? If indeed the boundary is fuzzy, how do we know we are not confusing parts of *a particular firm* with *some other firm* or *something else in a firm's environment*?

The statement that firms' boundaries are fuzzy—or 'blurred', or 'permeable'—is not entirely wrong. But it is without doubt problematic. Consider first, what it means to claim that firms' boundaries are fuzzy. Intuitively, it would seem to suggest one of two possibilities:

- either, that it is possible to identify an entity which we call 'the firm', but that it is not possible to tell exactly where it ends and where something else, some other entity, begins (and vice versa), that is, the dividing line remains fundamentally inexact;
- or, that we believe that there is actually a dividing line between the firm and its external environment but we just cannot uncover it.

The problem with the first formulation is that we do not know what we are talking about when we talk about the firm; we are not able to pin down the essence of the capitalist firm. The problem with the second formulation is that it is difficult to maintain that a boundary exists if we are not able to point it out. Neither is particularly satisfactory. This is especially so as to understand the firm as a social entity—its generic identity, its theoretical essence—is often taken to imply that we should be able to account for (a) the existence of firms, (b) the organization of firms, and (c) the boundaries of firms (Holmström and Tirole 1989). The idea that theories of the firm should address these issues is often reiterated in the literature without much further reflection as to how well it suits different theoretical traditions (e.g. Foss and Klein, forthcoming; Ioannides 1999; Maskell 2001). What does this mean? Thinking of a range of existing economic theories of the firm, it would have to mean that once a particular theory attempts to explain why a firm *exists* (i.e. what purpose does the kind of social entity that the firm is, serve; what is its *raison d'être*), it should explain what becomes *organized* inside the firm and how,[1] what remains outside, and why its *boundaries* are placed where they are. All theories that aim to explain these issues make assumptions, and they provide different partial perspectives to the firm. Attempts to develop theories of the firm have been made in different disciplines, but there is no shared understanding among scholars as to how exactly those different theories relate to each other in answering variations of the above questions, and whether they

---

[1] Note that 'organization' tends to be understood narrowly in economics. Langlois (1988: 35) provides an example: 'the explanation of the organization of firms' means 'the problem of explaining the boundaries of the firm—explaining *the extent of internal organization or vertical integration*' (emphasis added). In other words, the 'theory of the firm' in economics follows in Coase's footsteps and mainly asks: around which activities are firms' boundaries set, i.e. what is the scope of the firm? Within economics, then, broader organizational structures and processes, discussed in other subdisciplines, are commonly disregarded (see Gibbons 2005: 210).

Many Boundaries of the Firm

might complement each other so as to jointly bring about a comprehensive understanding of the firm, including its boundaries.

My aim in this chapter is to explore the boundary problem in the light of recent discussions in economic geography literature. A few relatively well-known passages in the literature provide starting points for a discussion on the firm boundary with an emphasis on allegations about its fuzziness. The discussion opens up an avenue to address central issues in understanding what the firm is; it helps us grasp pressing problems in theorizing the firm.

The argument of the chapter proceeds as follows. Following the introduction, Section 2.2 explores how the boundary question and the fuzziness argument have featured explicitly or implicitly in recent debates in economic geography to reveal different aspects of firms' boundaries. The problem of boundary identification is seen as closely associated with a lack of clarity in conceptualizations of firms, and a brief clarification is attempted, focusing on two often conflated aspects of the firm; the firm as a business organization and the firm as an economic institution. Section 2.3 discusses various boundaries of the firm that are implicitly or explicitly suggested by the literature: the boundary with the broader social environment, with local economic systems, with other firms in networks, with employees, and with the market. The conclusion, Section 2.4, suggests that a future more encompassing theory of the firm, which casts the firm as a multidimensional social entity, might draw these different definitions together, obviating the problem of 'fuzzy boundaries'.

The broad approach to the firm that informs the discussion in this chapter takes seriously many of the themes that economic geographers have developed in their discussions since the 1980s. The firm in this literature is depicted as enmeshed not only in markets and in network relationships, but also as being embedded in a broader social environment, and acting as an agent for societal change (see Oinas 1997). The prevailing perspective in economic geography can be broadly called institutional and evolutionary in that it attempts to portray economic activities, especially activities carried out in firms, as part and parcel of broader societal dynamics (Dicken and Thrift 1992; Amin 1999; Martin 1999; Scott 2000; Dicken and Malmberg 2001).

2.2 In What Sense 'Fuzzy' Boundaries?

In economic geography, the extensive literatures on agglomerations, industrial clusters and districts, on the one hand, and networks, on the other, can be seen as having implicitly reinforced the view that firms' boundaries are fuzzy. Storper's perspective on industrial districts in the Third Italy is representative of much of the thinking, seeing the regional production systems of industrial districts as *integrated wholes*:

> The point of departure of virtually all the detailed studies of the NEC Italian production systems—by both admirers and detractors—is that they should not be regarded as collections of small firms, but rather something akin to multiproduct organizations, and that the internal institutional arrangements of the systems are deeply inscribed in broader social arrangements (or what economists might call the 'institutional environment'). (Storper 1997: 139)

Saxenian's study (1994) of Silicon Valley, in which she established the cultural foundations for the competitive superiority of Silicon Valley over Route 128 in the early 1990s, was a key study that had a lasting impact on economic geographers' thinking. She described many aspects of the 'blurred' boundaries between firms and their external environments, emphasizing the role of social networks in facilitating flows of technological knowledge among innovating engineers in different firms. In her account, Silicon Valley was depicted as a coherent whole, as in the comment made to her that, '[t]here are a lot of people who come to work in the morning believing that they work for Silicon Valley' (a quote in Saxenian 1994: 37). In addition, in Silicon Valley's innovation oriented enterprising lifestyle, 'personal and business life is borderless' (Saxenian 1994: 68). That the area's business system became successful was due to the region's *industrial culture* which key firms in the region had implanted at an early stage (Oinas 1995).

The boundary question is also implicit in conceptualization of economic action as *embedded*, '... in concrete, ongoing systems of social relations' (Granovetter 1985: 487). At an abstract level, the notion of embeddedness has been woven into economic geographers' discourses (e.g. Martin 1994: 43; Taylor and Leonard 2002). Amin and Thrift criticized the popular use of 'embeddedness', however, asserting that the economy is too often seen as 'a separate sphere which is then, in some sense, institutional, collectivized, embedded in the social' (Amin and Thrift 1994b: 259). Such a misguided usage of the embeddedness metaphor, in their view, is 'in danger of reproducing the split between the economic and the social that its usage was intended to avoid'. To say that economic *action* is embedded in *social relations* merely makes us see 'economic action as social action' (Amin and Thrift 1994a: 12). Without qualifications, this view denies the existence of a boundary between the economy and the rest of what is social.

Boundaries are explicitly blurred in Dicken and Thrift's suggestion (1992: 285) that business organization should be redefined. They adopt Cowling and Sugden's definition (1987: 60) that a 'firm is the means of coordinating production from one centre of strategic decision making'. A firm conceived in this manner 'need not coincide with a "legal firm". Indeed, it may encompass many legal firms' (Cowling and Sugden 1987: 62). In this conception, the term 'firm' is actually *a network* potentially consisting of several legal firms *controlled from one centre* (Dicken and Thrift 1992: 285). That is, the firm is an assembly of networking firms with one control centre; the firm boundary is set at the point where centralized control ceases.

Dicken and Malmberg (2001: 351) develop this idea further. They follow Badaracco (1991: 314) in proposing a view of the firm as 'a dense network at the center of a web of relationships'. 'The central domain of the firm blends slowly into its surrounding environment as ownership, hierarchy, control, power, social bonds, classic contracting, and other boundary-defining devices diminish in significance or are shared with other organizations' (Dicken and Malmberg 2001: 351). '[T]he gradual attenuation of these relationships reaches a point at which the firm exercises neither power nor influence. Here, the genuinely external environment of the firm begins' (Badaracco 1991: 314). Dicken and Malmberg also point out that firms' boundaries frequently *change* owing to outsourcing, collaborative relations, and transnationalization. In short, boundaries are either unstable, or they do not exist at all.

In contrast to this line of argument, Markusen (1999: 878) has asked, 'Can firms' boundaries be fuzzy, even in theory?' Her judgement on the issue is that, actually, firm boundaries are not fuzzy at all:

Capitalist firms, whether large or small, operate in a highly regulated, environment in which property-rights, stock ownership, bank loans and other equity investments are very carefully watched and tended to. *The boundaries of a firm are, ultimately, not at all fuzzy*—they are written down in *asset, cost and revenue statements* that owners and managers, whether private or public, scrutinize carefully every quarter. If the bottom line is not positive for most quarters, or in the case of a start-up within a few years, firms will cease to exist. Firm survival rates may be low and personnel turnover high, but *as organizations and institutions, firms are clearly bounded*. (Markusen 1999: 878, emphases added)

Thus, for Markusen, asset ownership and property rights seem to determine firms' boundaries. The quote also seems to suggest that firms are equally clearly bounded 'as organizations' and 'as institutions' (an issue I return to below.)

Many Boundaries of the Firm

What we seem to learn from the economic geography literature—apart from Markusen—is that there is a range of issues that suggests that firms' boundaries are fuzzy, and that on several grounds we cannot, or need not, draw boundaries around the firm. Those issues involve:

- *inter-firm relations*—Dicken and Thrift; Dicken and Malmberg
- *transnationalization*—Dicken and Malmberg
- *firms' relations with their specific regionally integrated production systems*—Storper; Saxenian
- *regional culture*—Saxenian
- *flows of knowledge via social networks*—Saxenian
- *closely tied personal and business lives*—Saxenian; Dicken and Malmberg
- *embeddedness in surrounding society*—Amin and Thrift
- *external control*—Dicken and Thrift; Dicken and Malmberg
- *ownership and contractual relations*—Dicken and Malmberg vs. Markusen

The boundary problem, as reflected in the items of this list, is far from simple and deserves detailed scrutiny. We have to begin by unravelling the conceptions of boundaries explicit and implicit in the views listed above. The relevant questions are: a boundary of what; a boundary with what; and then, in what sense a boundary?

Dicken and Malmberg (2001) unintendedly hint at a way of actually identifying firms' boundaries. For them, the boundary is defined on a range of dimensions; 'ownership, hierarchy, control, power, social bonds, classic contracting, and other boundary-defining devices' (p. 351). However, the implication of this statement is not drawn; namely that different 'boundary-defining devices' do not merely make firms' boundaries 'fuzzy' in some indeterminate manner. Rather, each should be discussed in its own right in a theoretically informed manner. When we refer to the boundary of the firm we have to specify *which* aspect of the boundary we are talking about.

To structure the discussion on these matters, I suggest that economic geographers' implicit and explicit problems concerning the existence of firms' boundaries can be clarified by discussing boundaries in five contexts:

1. boundaries with the broader social environment (institutional environment)
2. boundaries with local economic systems
3. boundaries with employees
4. boundaries with network partners
5. boundaries with markets

There is an existing broad interdisciplinary literature on theories of the firm (e.g. Langlois, Yu, and Robertson 2002*a*, *b*, *c* gives a flavour of the span of the literature) but none of the theories is able to unite explanations so as to cover so many different aspects of firms and their boundaries. However, before discussing these items a number of observations need to be made on the very entity whose boundaries are being questioned—the firm.

2.3 The Firm

Among the numerous definitions of the firm, Whitley's characterization (1987: 126) of the firm provides an informative entry point:

> Rather than reducing them to epiphenomena of market processes or class conflicts, firms need to be conceptualized as interdependent, semi-autonomous economic agents which are able to control and direct the uses of resources by virtue of delegated property rights in ways which make a difference to economic and social outcomes.

In this formulation Whitley regards firms as *social* agents (cf. Dicken and Thrift 1992; Amin and Thrift 1994*a*, *b*; Thrift 1994) but he emphasizes equally that they are *economic* agents. Highlighting the control of resources and property rights, it is much in line with Markusen's concerns as cited above. Besides control of resources and property rights, Whitley's formulation emphasizes semi-autonomy and interdependence, that is, it refers to issues that potentially blur firms' boundaries.

In addition to issues related to economic agency, firms are *organizations* which can be characterized as 'goal-directed, boundary-maintaining, and socially constructed systems of human activity' (Aldrich 1979; Aldrich 1999: 2–5). Thus, the manner in which firms 'direct the uses of resources' (Whitley, above) are related to firm-specific goals (which does not eliminate internal conflict in goal setting; see Langlois and Robertson 1993: 33). And it is a generic and institutionally imposed feature within capitalist institutional environments that the goals of private firms relate ultimately to survival in market competition (Markusen 1999: 878). That firms are 'boundary-maintaining' (Aldrich 1999) is motivated by their need to create enough internal coordination to facilitate goal-directed collective action, and by their need to maintain distance from competitors—though this does not, *as yet*, eliminate the possibility of fuzziness.

Firms rely on various external actors for complementary resources either via the market or through network relationships. This is the interdependence Whitley refers to. There is also a broader sort of interdependence that relates to the socio–politico–cultural environments in which firms operate. What firms are like and how they are organized internally and in their external relations is a firm-specific matter, yet it is linked to the institutional environments in which they develop (e.g. Whitley 1992: 7; Morgan 2005a). This is emphasized by organization theory's *open systems perspective*: 'Organizations are systems of interdependent activities linking shifting coalitions of participants; the systems are embedded in—dependent on continuing exchanges with and constituted by—the environments in which they operate' (Scott 1992: 25; see also Granovetter 1985).

From interdependence follows what Whitley refers to as semi-autonomy. That firms are semi-autonomous means that their external relations in effect may bring some degree of external control to their operation. This has to do with the double-edged sword business organizations have to deal with, namely that they *seek to achieve autonomy* (independence) and at the same time they *seek to reduce uncertainty* by creating and maintaining interdependent ties with external actors (Pfeffer and Salancik 1978). This makes issues of *governance*—that is, 'the management of interdependence' (Fligstein and Freeland 1995: 22)—a particularly thorny and multifarious task which firms try to tackle while struggling to reach the goals set by their strategies. Those strategies may be *deliberate* or they may just *emerge* out of firms' practices and out of their reactions to competitive impulses (Mintzberg and Waters 1985; Mintzberg 1994).

So, are we able to identify the boundaries of such an externally interdependent and only semi-autonomous but still 'boundary-maintaining' entity? To do so requires several implicit elements of Whitley's characterization of the firm to be unpacked. The fact that firms are 'economic agents' is a result of their emergence as a kind of institution during the evolution of the broader institutional environments typical of market economies in their various forms. Their nature *as economic institutions* is subject to variation only to the degree that it is allowed by the legal and political institutions of the jurisdictions in which they are registered. The characteristics particular firms assume, however, may be very different. Their goals and internal functioning *as organizations* may remain very distinct from each other, and their modes of coordinating relations with other firms may differ considerably.

Firms—with the exception of the one-person owner-manager type—are organizations, but all organizations are not firms. Or, what concerns organizations, concerns firms as well, but it is not the organizational feature of firms that defines them as firms. A firm is primarily a distinctive capitalist economic institution. Therefore, what a firm is and where its boundaries are should be determined by the higher order institutional framework (laws and regulations) that enable the of specific lower order institutions to exist (i.e. firms).[2]

The above is a simple point but it has important implications for the quest to understand whether or not firms have boundaries and whether or how we can identify them. Dicken and Malmberg's list (2001: 351) of 'boundary-defining devices' is helpful here. Some of the items on their list—ownership, classic contracting, control (control as regulated by the law and thus formal in nature)—relate to firms *as economic institutions*, largely in line with Markusen's suggestion (1999: 878). Others more clearly fall into the domain of items spanning the boundaries of firms *as organizations*: hierarchy, power[3] (not formally established use of power), social bonds, and 'other boundary-defining devices' (examples of such other devices could be, for instance, informal collaborations of various kinds, trust, sharing of information and knowledge, cultural influences, etc.).

To sum up, we have discussed two aspects of the firm, each raising different issues concerning firms' boundaries:

(a) *The firm as an economic institution*: firms' boundaries are determined by property rights and contractual considerations, grounded in laws and regulations particular to specific institutional environments. The economists Putterman and Kroszner (1996: 8–9) observe:

Asking where the boundaries of the firm lie raises some difficult theoretical issues. But most authors have relatively simple notions of control and of ownership in mind when deciding where one firm ends and another begins. Few if any question that a company having multiple plants producing the same or even different products should be treated as a single firm so long as the right to the residual earnings and to hire and fire the managers of subunits belongs to a central managing organ that either itself 'owns' or is responsible to the owner or owners of the overall entity.

---

[2] Hodgson (2002) shows how a legal conception of the firm was taken for granted by leading economists such as Smith, Marshall, and Commons but, from the 1920s to the 1970s, the legal conception was abandoned as the treatment of the firm as a production function gained ground within economics (Coase 1937, having been a rare exception in this period).

[3] Dicken and Malmberg list the terms power, control, and hierarchy. As concepts they are closely related, but for the sake of simplicity, I classify these terms here so that *control* refers to the formal—and thus legally recognized—right to command the use of resources based on property right considerations; *power* refers to informal uses of power within and between organizations. Hierarchy can be related to both power and control in these senses, but because these distinctions are not fundamental for the argument of this chapter I list it here as a matter related to organizational practices, and thus will not raise it in the context of discussing firms' boundaries.

(b) *The firm as a business organization*, the boundaries of which are crossed by flows of goods, services, information, knowledge, cultural influences, etc. as part of its day-to-day operations. A key author within organizational institutionalism, Scott, regards organizational boundaries as arbitrary:

We have previously noted the open systems assertion that the boundary separating the organization from its environment is somewhat arbitrarily drawn and varies with the flows or activities being examined. (Scott 1992: 145–6)

As organizations, firms are not isolated from their environments, and thus, their boundaries are permeable. But does this make the boundaries fuzzy, unidentifiable or non-existent? These questions are tackled in more detail in the following section, where firms' boundaries with various external entities are discussed.

2.4 Boundaries with What?

Essential to the successful operation of firms is their interaction with external agents; competing, controlling, and complementary organizations as well as individuals in different roles. In different combinations, these counterparts constitute the institutional environment, the local economic system, networks, employees, and the markets in which firms operate. The discussion that follows aims to identify the boundaries of firms associated with their relations to these external entities and agents.

2.4.1 The Boundary Between the Firm and the Broader Social Environment (the Institutional Environment)

The economic geography literature has, to a large extent, accepted the conceptualization of economic action as 'embedded' in social relations, but it has put little effort into answering the question, '*What* exactly is embedded in *what*?' (Oinas 1997). In viewing 'economic action as social action' Amin and Thrift (1994a: 12), attempted to sidestep this question and render it unnecessary. However, while economic action indeed represents one kind of social action that is carried out as part of a variety of social relations, it is not *any* social action. Swedberg, Himmelstrand, and Brulin (1990: 66) criticized Polanyi's notion of embeddeness precisely for being 'a concept of the economic system where the economy just fades into the rest of society at some undetermined point', and they called for clear lines to be drawn between the economy and the other subsystems.

What might this mean in the context of discussing 'business organisations, [that] are [...] "produced" through a complex historical process of embedding' (Dicken and Thrift 1992: 287), and whose boundaries are allegedly fuzzy? The notion of embeddedness provides a perspective on the firm where emphasis is put on *what is shared* with the environment (features in an institutional environment such as customs and practices, cultural values, beliefs and traditions, principles of a political system and their conventional implementation, power relations, common goals as in networks, and the like). When specific social features or aims remain the same across a firms' boundary, no boundary appears to be in place. This is the effect of the perspective: what is focused on as a consequence of the theoretical lens that has been chosen. The notion of embeddedness as such a theoretical lens provides an important insight into the nature and operations of the firm. However, in itself it provides no aid in understanding firms' boundaries (other than that the firm, as a separate, identifiable entity, is implicitly presumed in suggesting that 'the firm' is 'embedded').

If *the firm* is the economic actor that is embedded, and what it is embedded in is Granovetter's 'concrete, ongoing systems of social relations' (1985: 487), the thorny question arises as to how one defines a boundary between the firm and a host of other social entities in different societal spheres and spatial scales. As 'systems of social relations' is a broad category, and potentially involves the rest of what is social outside of the firm, it may in principle refer to relations with *known actors*—in *dyadic* relations (Granovetter 1992: 33) or in *networks* (Granovetter 1985)—as well as relations with *broader social structures* or *institutions,* or what Ingham (1996: 267) calls 'large-scale social systems' (Oinas 1998). It is not possible to discuss all these social relations in concert and thus to identify unambiguously the boundary between the firm and the environment in which it is embedded. Therefore, the discussion that follows moves to the more specific firm–environment interface.

2.4.2 *The Boundary Between the Firm and Local Economic Systems*

Local systems of production and innovation have fascinated the economic geography research community in recent years. The creation of firm competitiveness has been seen as fundamentally supported by interactions in industrial districts, industrial agglomerations, clusters, regional innovation systems, learning regions, and creative cities, for example. If firms are regarded as operating seamlessly with other agents in such circumstances, and if the system and its individual firms are regarded as mutually dependent on each other for survival, it is tempting to think that there are no boundaries between them. The unit of analysis becomes *the system*, and there is no need for its constituent parts to have separate identities. Implicitly, this has been a dominant line of thinking in much of the economic geography literature.

With the deeper understanding of the dynamics and interactions within local production systems that has emerged in recent years, it has become clear that we need to view these systems more closely. Three aspects of local systems throw light on this situation, and enable the formulation of an argument on firms' boundaries in the local systems.

First, the fact that firms are not only tied to their local environments, but maintain extra-local relations and make extra-local direct investments, means that they also have the capacity break-off from their local systems. This neither breaks the system nor creates a significant fracture (or boundary) inside the externally operating firms. Insulated and isolated local systems are not sufficient to cater for all the external resources needed by firms—a fact that itself proves the strength of firms' boundaries.

A second aspect of local systems is rivalry. While the literature has largely focused on collaborative and benevolent relations in local systems, it has been increasingly recognized that rivalry and political power plays are also a central aspect in them (Bathelt and Taylor 2002; Malmberg and Maskell 2002). Producers of the same or similar products or services share a competitive and/or technological environment and they may be rivals in product or services markets but locally they benefit from a shared resource base (e.g. a skilled labour pool, supply of raw materials or suppliers, industry-specific social capital, and so on). Rivals may interact with each other and even collaborate, but typically not on matters that are of strategic significance to their competitiveness (Oinas 2002). They may collaborate to develop a sufficient local resource base (e.g. for infrastructure, education, training, and public support) or they may even combine efforts to develop basic technologies that they can then build upon individually to implement their own, specific strategies in particular product markets or in geographically differentiated markets (Oinas 2002). To do this means that firms attend very carefully to their boundaries vis-à-vis rivals in local systems. Thus, how firms act strategically both to close their boundaries for specific purposes and to open them up for others needs to be better understood (see Scott 1992: 83).

Third, there is the very real issue of close and confidential relations between agents in local systems. These relations often involve *indivisibilities* (Storper 1997: 270), for example in the form of mutually specific assets and/or interdependent decision-making under conditions of uncertainty. At the system level, this suggests tight coordination at the cost of maintaining tight boundaries around the system's constituent parts. Intuitively, this problem of indivisibilities appears to erode the distinctiveness of firms' boundaries. However, since it relates to network relations more generally, this issue will be discussed in the next section.

2.4.3 Boundaries Between Firms Within Networks

The 'hybrid' forms of economic organization, that are neither market relations nor business organizations (Powell 1990), are an issue that has been extensively addressed in the business and economics literatures in the past twenty years. The arguments by Dicken and Thrift (1992) and Dicken and Malmberg (2001) and others about boundary fuzziness understandably stem from this phenomenon. Here I discuss a number of issues related to inter-firm relations in networks—with 'networks' being used here as an umbrella term for a variety of relatively enduring relationships between firms with some shared goals negotiated among or imposed upon network members.[4]

First, however, it is necessary to reflect on the idea that firms' boundaries are 'changing'. With phenomena such as the dismantling of large vertically integrated corporate structures and their replacement by vertically disintegrated network structures, or the search by smaller firms for complementarities from a range of network partners as a strategy for product development, market extension, internationalization and growth, it has become commonplace to suggest that by so doing firms' boundaries are changing (e.g. Dicken and Malmberg 2001: 351; Foss 2005: 13). Integration within a firm widens the boundary and disintegration shrinks it. 'Changing' a boundary in this sense does not make it fuzzy, however; simply more or fewer activities are included within the boundaries. Changes, even frequent ones, do not imply fuzziness.

Dicken and Thrift (1992), however, saw networks as involving a fundamental blurring of boundaries. By adopting Cowling and Sugden's conceptualization (1987) of the firm as 'the means of coordinating production from one centre of strategic decision making' (p. 285) they concluded that a firm is actually *a network* potentially consisting of several legal firms *controlled from one centre* (Dicken and Thrift 1992: 285). This view is highly

---

[4] For the argument in this section we need not solve the definitional problem concerning the point at which and under what conditions repeated interactions become network relations.

problematic, however, because it confuses the key concepts of network and firm (cf. Oinas 1998: 34–6).

As to the idea of firms as networks and networks as 'firms', it is true that *firms* are increasingly *organized in a network-like manner* (cf. Dicken and Thrift 1992: 286) and, since networks can be reasonably characterized as *coordinated entities* (as firms are), they are recognizable forms of organizing economic activities. (There are even other similarities between intra-firm relations and inter-firm networks: for instance, they may incorporate various combinations of characteristics such as hierarchy/power; formality and informality in relations; stability or change; setting and achieving shared goals; complementarity; reciprocity; collaboration; trust; internal competition.) However, analogous characteristics do not make networks and firms the same thing. In the set of institutions in which firms and networks are embedded, the legal firm remains the locus of analysis (Hodgson 2002). Independent networked firms do not formally own each others' assets (cross-ownership is a possibility but that is then formally established). Networks are not legal entities that become bankrupt, only networked firms do. It follows that on formal grounds related to the firm as an economic institution, networking does not make firms' boundaries fuzzy.

How about the issue of control within networks? It is true that, for example, a weak supplier of a resourceful firm may face tight external control. *De jure* independence, however, provides the dependent firm in principle with the right to widen its customer base which may enable it to lower its external dependence. Sometimes this is not possible, as in the case of what the economics literature calls the 'hold-up' problem: when an investment made by one party is entirely relation-specific and is thus of zero value in any other relationship (Klein, Crawford, and Alchain 1978). But even in the case of hold-up, if a supplier fails to supply the goods or service for which it has been hired, and the contract is ended, it will fail *as an independent firm*—and the contractor suffers the consequences *as another independent firm* (often having to make the needed investment itself). It follows that external dependence does not blur boundaries.

And does coordination or control from one centre make a difference here? One firm's ability to gain control over other firms' resources in a network is often based on its possession of scarce resources, as diverse as know-how, financial resources, technology, or access to social capital via extensive networks (Pfeffer and Salancik 1978; Burt 1992). These resources may be differently distributed among network members, and thus networks may be asymmetrical but also relatively symmetrical in terms of power and influence (see also Dicken and Thrift 1992: 285–6; Oinas and

Packalén 1998). This means that even if it is a clear possibility that control is ultimately concentrated in one centre, it is often also distributed in complex ways. This is suggested by the 'differing degrees of networked inter-relationships of power and influence' in corporations and the fact that both corporate organizations and networks consist of 'a web of power and influence' (Dicken and Thrift 1992: 286–8). Note also that while the centre of strategic decision-making within networks may be a (large) corporation (Dicken and Thrift 1992: 288)[5] it may also be a *unit* of one (supported by the resources of the larger corporate whole). Also, a firm or unit may exercise power over a *unit* of another corporation but this does not mean that it controls the entire corporation. We can conclude that control over a network of firms from one corporate centre is a special case but, nevertheless, by intervening in another firm's decision-making, unequal power relations seem to have the potential to *blur firms' boundaries*. However, in the legal notion of the firm, the right to control and command corporate assets is the key to *defining the firm* (cf. Dicken and Malmberg 2001: 251). We arrive at conflicting conceptualizations. A way out is to accept the legal definition of the firm (Masten 1993; Hodgson 2002) as an economic institution and at the same time acknowledge that the boundaries of the firms' organization are porous. A firm or a corporate unit can exert external control over another firm: they may influence managers or employees that have a (legal) employment relation with the controlled firm or make demands concerning the use of assets that are (legally) owned by the controlled firm.

Finally, at any rate, the boundary has to be recognizable so as to be able to say that external control is used. A 'blurred boundary' renders such an statement meaningless.

If inter-firm power and control do not blur the boundaries between firms and networks, are there other aspects in the organization or operation of networks that might do so? A widely recognized aspect of networks is that they are not necessarily established on the basis of a formal agreement. Various informal network arrangements may continue for long periods of time while the threat of losing reputation or trust substitutes the need to sign formal contracts. Agreements may be implicit when they are understood similarly among parties sharing goals or due to con-

---

[5] Units in a corporation, organized internally so as to resemble a network, may be involved in a power struggle inside the corporation concerning intra-corporate strategic resource allocation. In a tight situation, however, the decision made by the top management team is the principal one. Internal authority relations make a difference. A unit is not able independently to choose to belong to another corporation (employees can, but that is again another question): a management-buyout of a unit is not possible without approval from the top. The idea of *one* centre of control may, thus, apply better to firms than to networks, and is likely to prove itself especially in extreme situations.

vention. Collaborations where assets and/or knowledge are genuinely shared—Storper's 'indivisibilities'—present a problematic case. Consider the details. If a firm, Alpha, releases a piece of information, ideas or advice to a second firm, Beta, does the situation make it difficult to identify the boundaries of these firms? Not really. As part of the act of sharing, a formal or informal, explicit or implicit agreement details (or estimates) what the gains are for each party. The property rights to assets remain unchanged (or, if they change, that is a separate procedure). And, if (intellectual) property rights are violated, legal structures can be drawn upon to punish violators. Information and knowledge have the characteristic that they can be the property of many actors at the same time—the fact that it *crosses* firm boundaries does not blur the boundary as such. When knowledge is unintentionally leaked across firm boundaries to other firms, it is an unfortunate incident, not a blurring of boundaries. Again, to be able to identify an unfortunate leakage implies that it is possible to identify, first, the boundary itself and, second, the very incidence that something has leaked *over* it.

One could also refer to reputation or pre-established social relations that are often the basis of trust in close collaborations, as something that might blur firms' boundaries. Again, while the boundaries of *organizations* may blur because of intensive social relations, as *economic institutions* firms' boundaries are determined by the employment contracts of the individuals involved in social relations across firms' borders.

To reiterate, boundary-crossing joint activities may bring firms intimately together so that they share each others' resources and even understand a great deal about the basis of each other's competitiveness. If one of the firms is more powerful than the other (e.g. by dominating the market, by being a dominant contractor, or by possessing superior business-specific knowledge) the use of power can be an issue. However, in terms of the boundary problem and the theory of the firm, this remains an instance of boundary crossing, not blurring. Firms' boundaries do not blend or blur into their surrounding environment as Dicken and Malmberg (2001) have argued. They do not stretch to encompass network boundaries, through the interconnectedness of activities and people or through sharing resources or for reasons of control.

2.4.4 *The Boundary Between the Firm and Individuals: Employment Relation and Identification*

Individuals and their behaviour in firms are subject to the employment contracts they agree to when they begin work. For Hodgson, '[t]he boundary of the firm is made up of points in time at which the "legal person" of the firm concludes legal (written or unwritten) contracts with individuals or other legal persons. [... A]n employee (unlike a slave) is only "inside" the firm during the periods, and under the circumstances, specified in the employment contract' (Hodgson 2002: 44). This represents the classic Coasian (1937) view where employment *contracts* grant employers the authority to command. In this view, the scope of command defines the boundaries of firms (Schlicht 1998: 221). Many authors still refer to authority as a key feature of firms (Williamson 1975, 1985; Whitley 1992: 6–7; Schlicht 1998). It should be noted, however, that, with the increased autonomy of individual agents, especially in various knowledge-intensive activities, authority is gaining a broader meaning. It does not refer only to 'commanding specific actions'; it may also relate to *requiring results to be produced*, not to the specific ways of reaching the results (Simon 1991: 31; Foss 2002: 19).

The conception of individuals in the contracts perspective on the theory of the firm is obviously limited. The *contract-based employment relation* employees have with their employers as economic institutions, as legal entities, is very different from *membership* in an organization which is an equally crucial aspect of being an employee. Employment contracts do not ensure that employee identities fit corporate identities in a manner that is beneficial for the internal functioning of firms and their employees. Individual characteristics, as well as organizational leadership and culture matter more in this regard. Building on the sociological tradition, Aldrich (1999: 116) makes a distinction between members of organizations as *users* and *supporters*. 'User' employees engage in self-seeking individualistic behaviour, seeking personal benefit from their affiliation, whereas 'supporters' behave in a manner that sustains organizations and their goals, and they are subject to organizational authorities—even if they are not emotionally committed to an organization (Aldrich 1999: 116–17, 133). Organizations develop *coherence* as members' activities begin to involve them more deeply in organization-specific *communities of practice* (Aldrich 1999: 128, 142). Without full involvement in the knowledge systems and sociocultural practices of communities, members will not be able to take part in the utilization of the relevant knowledge and skills (cf. Lave and Wenger 1991: 29; Aldrich 1999: 143). Communities of practice increase homogeneity within organizations through their selection practices (Aldrich 1999: 126).

Schlicht discusses such patterned social interaction in firms in terms of custom. 'Each firm forms an island of custom in the ocean of the market'

(Schlicht 1998: 207). For him, firms are custom-driven entities and, as in much institutionalist thinking, the role of custom is to coordinate action in the entity where a custom applies. It brings *clarity* to the shared cognitive schemata among (e.g. employee) groups (Schlicht 1998). For Schlicht, firm-specific customs have an explicitly emotional basis and they are instrumental in forming firm-specific individual and collective employee identities. Identification and emotional commitment may vary in strength (cf. Aldrich 1999: 116–17). It follows that to the degree that identification and emotional commitment are the basis for pinpointing organizational boundaries, the varying degrees of commitment and identification make it more difficult to identify firms' boundaries. In this regard, the boundaries of firms as organizations appear to be considerably fuzzy.

Things get murkier when organizational cultures are introduced. Martin (1992) distinguishes three views of organizational culture, those of integration, differentiation, and ambiguity. The *integration* view emphasizes organizational coherence, in line with the ideas of Schlicht and Aldrich. The *differentiation* view introduces the possibility of conflict, and the *ambiguity* view acknowledges the changing cultural cognitions and behaviours of members. The differential and changing identification of organizational members may be due to external identifications that might give rise to the argument about blurring the cultural boundaries of firms (as discussed in detail below). What seems an obvious conclusion at this point is that, in the context of firms as organizations, firms' boundaries are not tight but they allow employees to identify themselves with goals that do not coincide with those of the firm (even if such a position may not enhance career prospects). However, as employees of economic institutions, those same employees are required to perform minimally *as if* they accept those goals and the authority of the employer (whatever mode that authority might take).

The focus on individuals gives rise to an additional consideration on inter-firm relations (cf. the previous section). Even though firms lend their name to the activities that are undertaken within them, in the actual practice of inter-firm relations, firms do not interact with each other as complete wholes. In order for firms to interact with external actors they have to be able to relate to their environments in different ways on different 'fronts'. They do this through specialist people, often in specialist departments—people who can create an appropriate activity-specific fit with external actors (financial experts for dealing with the financial world, specialists experienced in arts and design for dealing with designers, etc.). From the point of view of individuals and groups, interaction with environmental entities means that they develop capabilities that make possible the flow of information and knowledge that is crucial for their operation. Is it possible to defend a view that firms' boundaries are genuinely blurred by individuals who identify with a group of collaborators in a firm that is a network partner instead of the firm that employs them? Identification with a 'community of practice' or an 'epistemic community' (e.g. Nooteboom 2000; Wenger and Snyder 2000; Amin and Cohendet 2004) may certainly make individuals supporters in the community to a degree that it may at times be questioned whose goals are being served. Their actions may relate to the development of, say, technology in a manufacturing network, or fashionable artistic approaches in the world of advertising. Memberships in such inter-firm communities of practice influence individuals' belief systems and potentially their loyalties. This will affect their behaviour, and thus, the outcome of their actions in their employer firms. As it was expressed by Aldrich (1999: 159), '[o]rganizational boundary maintenance depends, in part, on how strongly members feel about the ties linking or separating them from people in other organizations'.

Yet again, such identification or behaviour *as such* does not blur the employment relations that individuals have with their firms. However, if extra-firm community membership leads to violating the goals of the employer firm—by, for example, using firms' resources for purposes that are not acceptable to the firm or deceitfully releasing strategic information or knowledge to another firm via an extra-firm community—the firm has the authority to stop such behaviour and/or dismiss the individual involved. Such action indicates where a boundary is from the point of view of the firm. It is significant that this may be a highly firm-specific question; some firms are inwardly oriented and highly secretive, others, due to the nature of their activity, are much more tolerant of the external engagements of their employees, and may even encourage them. Such behaviour may be due to (regional) industrial cultures (see Saxenian 1994). Sometimes, decision-makers in corporate headquarters only legitimize the action of individuals and communities after the event, even re-defining corporate boundaries more flexibly when the activities of communities at the interface of several firms work for the benefit of all parties.

This discussion shows that sometimes considerable effort has to be put into boundary identification. Issues related to identification may blur some aspects of the boundaries of firm *organizations*. Through short- or long-term employment contracts, crafted in line with firm-specific strategic goals, firms *as economic institutions* are able to delineate clear boundaries with regard to the activities carried out by their employees.

2.4.5 *The Boundary Between the Firm and the Market*

While economic geographers have made claims about the impossibility (or lack of necessity) of identifying firms' boundaries in general, they have not engaged in any significant discussions on whether there is an identifiable boundary between the firm and the market.

In general terms, at least, the boundary between a firm and the market would seem to be the simplest of all aspects related to firms' boundaries. Market exchanges always involve a contract, and that contract lays down the principles based on which the ownership of whatever is being exchanged or hired passes on from one party of the contract to the other. However, markets are not anonymous. Their functioning is often influenced by reputation and social networks involving various actors in the market (managers, experts, employees, customers, retailers, other intermediaries), who may have a significant effect on what purchasing decisions are made and how. However, '[i]n all exchanges there is an implicit or explicit legal contract, leading to the transfer of property rights' (Hodgson 2002: 45), whatever the forces that potentially influence the negotiating and formulating of contracts. This is where the boundary of the firm rests in relation to the market.

This simple conclusion does not suggest that economists would be unanimous about where and on what grounds the boundary is set. Economists have discussed the firm/market boundary since Coase (1937) prominently posed the 'make or buy' question. The economists' concerns related to firms' boundaries, however, are different from our concerns here, namely: boundaries 'simply' delimit what is 'inside' (e.g. Masten 1998: 54). It is not asked whether the boundaries are fuzzy or not; the issues on the geographers' agenda are not raised.

2.5 The Challenge: Theorizing the Multidimensional Firm

Economic geographers' writings on the firm suggest various dimensions of the firm boundary, and jointly they provide a very broad perspective on the firm. By inspecting these various dimensions it has been possible in this chapter to show that the firm boundary is identifiable—not blurred or fuzzy. This suggests that it is possible to theorize the firm, a key institution in market economies, as a coherent entity. It also raises expectations concerning a desirable theory of the firm, a theory that economic geographers among other social scientists would find useful. We need theories that explain how, why, and where firms maintain boundaries in relation to different external entities. This is not to say that this kind of theory development is not in place. On the contrary, this is exactly what theories of the firm do—and many theories even attempt to explain aspects of firms that are not among economic geographers' objects of study. What we do lack, however, is a way of theorizing the firm in such a comprehensive manner that would allow the inclusion of the various aspects or dimensions of the firm in a joint explanatory structure.

The fact that some observers continue to refer to firms' boundaries as fuzzy may be related to the deficiencies in contemporary theorizing. To claim that a firm's boundary is fuzzy suggests that the particular theory used by the observer making the claim is incapable of explaining an aspect of firms' external relations that the observer has identified; it falls beyond the explanatory scope of the theory being used. When an observer does not have the explanatory tools to explain an aspect of the firm's boundary, it may seem fuzzy. In contrast, a comprehensive theory of the firm, regarding the firm as a multidimensional social entity, would be able to encompass all aspects of firms' boundaries, thereby helping us evade the apparent problem of fuzzy boundaries.

A full account of the boundaries of the firm is developed along with a full account of the firm in general. A comprehensive theory of the firm should be able to portray the firm both as a social organization and an economic institution. By so doing a theory should be able to *fix firm boundaries* on (at least) all of the 'fronts' discussed here: in relation to the market, networks, employees, local economic systems, and the broader social environment. The theory should explain why a firm exists rather than dissolves into its many environments; why it maintains boundaries at its various interfaces with the environment. The development of such a comprehensive theory is not imminent because theorists are bound by disciplinary traditions or schools of thought, and seldom cross disciplinary boundaries. Current theories look at firms from different perspectives and are, therefore, only partially helpful in explaining their organization and operation, and their boundaries. The challenge to develop a more broadly based and comprehensive theory for the social sciences is considerable.

References

Aldrich, H. (1979). *Organizations and Environments*. Englewood Cliffs, NJ: Prentice-Hall.
—— (1999). *Organizations Evolving*. London: Sage.

Amin, A. (1999). 'An Institutionalist Perspective on Regional Economic Development', *International Journal of Urban and Regional Research*, 23(2): 365–78.
—— and Cohendet, P. (2004). *Architectures of Knowledge. Firms, Capabilities, and Communities*. Oxford: Oxford University Press.
—— and Thrift, N. (1994a). 'Living in the Global', in A. Amin and N. Thrift (eds.), *Globalization, Institutions and Regional Development in Europe*. Oxford: Oxford University Press, pp. 1–22.
—— —— (1994b). 'Holding Down the Global', in A. Amin and N. Thrift (eds.), *Globalization, Institutions, and Regional Development in Europe*. Oxford: Oxford University Press, pp. 257–60.
Badaracco, J. (1991). 'The Boundaries of the Firm', in A. Etzioni and P. R. Lawrence (eds.), *Socio-economics: Towards a New Synthesis*. Armonk, NY: M. E. Sharpe, chapter 17.
Bathelt, H. and Taylor, M. (2002). 'Clusters, Power and Place: Inequality and Local Growth in Time-Space', *Geografiska Annaler*, 84B(2): 93–109.
Burt, R. (1992). *Structural Holes. The Social Structure of Competition*. Cambridge, MA: Harvard University Press.
Coase, R. (1937). 'The Nature of the Firm', *Economica*, 4: 386–405.
Cowling, K. and Sugden, R. (1987). 'Market Exchange and the Concept of a Transnational Corporation: Analysing the Nature of the firm', *British Review of Economic Issues*, 9(20): 57–68.
Dicken, P. and Malmberg, A. (2001). 'Firms in Territories: A Relational Perspective', *Economic Geography*, 77(4): 345–63.
—— and Thrift, N. (1992). 'The Organization of Production and the Production of Organization: Why Business Enterprises Matter in the Study of Geographical Industrialization', *Transactions of the Institute of British Geographers*, 17: 279–91.
Fligstein, N. and Freeland, R. (1995). 'Theoretical and Comparative Perspectives on Corporate Organization', *Annual Review of Sociology*, 21: 21–43.
Foss, N. J. (2002). ' "Coase vs. Hayek" : Economic Organization and the Knowledge Economy', *International Journal of the Economics of Business*, 9(1): 9–35.
—— (2005). *Strategy, Economic Organization, and the Knowledge Economy*. Oxford: Oxford University Press.
—— and Klein, P. (forthcoming). 'The Theory of the Firm and its Critics: A Stocktaking and Assessment', in Jean-Michel Glachant and Eric Brousseau (eds.) *New Institutional Economics: A Textbook*. Cambridge: Cambridge University Press.
Gibbons, R. (2005). 'Four Formal (izable) Theories of the Firm?', *Journal of Economic Behavior and Organization*, 58: 200–45.
Granovetter, M. (1985). 'Economic Action and Social Structure: The Problem of Embeddedness', *American Journal of Sociology*, 91(3): 481–510.
—— (1992). 'Problems of Explanation in Economic Sociology', *Networks and organizations. Structure, form and action*, in N. Nohria and R. G. Eccles (eds.), Boston, MA: Harvard Business School Press, pp. 25–56.

Hodgson, G. M. (2002). 'The Legal Nature of the Firm and the Myth of the Firm-Market Hybrid', *International Journal of the Economics of Business*, 9(1): 37–60.

Holmström, B. and Tirole, J. (1989). 'The Theory of the Firm', in R. Schmalensee and R. D. Willig (eds.), *The Handbook of Industrial Organization*, vol. 1. Amsterdam: North Holland, 61–133.

Ioannides, S. (1999). 'Towards an Austrian Perspective on the Firm', *Journal of Austrian Economics*, 11(1/2): 77–97.

Ingham, G. (1996). 'Some Recent Changes in the Relationship Between Economics and Sociology', *Cambridge Journal of Economics*, 20: 243–75.

Klein, B., Crawford, R., and Alchian, A. (1978). 'Vertical Integration, Appropriable Rents, and the Competitive Contracting Process', *Journal of Law and Economics*, 21: 297–326.

Langlois, R. (1988). 'Economic Change and the Boundaries of the Firm', *Journal of Institutional and Theoretical Economics*, 144: 635–57.

Langlois, R. N. and Robertson, P. L. (1993). 'Business Organization as a Coordination Problem: Toward a Dynamic Theory of the Boundaries of the Firm', *Business and Economic History*, 22(1): 31–41.

—— Yu, T. F.-L., and Robertson, P. (2002a, b, c). *Alternative Theories of the Firm*, Vols. I, II, III. Cheltenham, UK: Edward Elgar.

Lave, J. and Wenger, E. (1991). *Situated Learning: Legitimate Peripheral Participation*. Cambridge, UK: Cambridge University Press.

Malmberg, A. and Maskell, P. (2002). 'The Elusive Concept of Localization Economies: Towards a Knowledge-based Theory of Spatial Clustering', *Environment and Planning A*, 34: 429–49.

Martin, J. (1992). *Cultures in Organizations. Three Perspectives*, New York: Oxford University Press.

Martin, R. (1994). 'Economic Theory and Human Geography', in D. Gregory, R. Martin, and G. Smith (eds.), *Human Geography. Society, Space, and Social Science*. Minneapolis, MN: University of Minnesota Press, pp. 21–53.

—— (1999). 'The New "Geographical Turn" in Economics: Some Critical Reflections', *Cambridge Journal of Economics*, 232: 65–91.

Maskell, P. (2001). 'The Firm in Economic Geography', *Economic Geography*, 77(4): 329–44.

Masten, S. E. (1993). 'A Legal Basis for the Firm', in O. E. Williamson and S. G. Winter (eds.), *The Nature of the Firm*. Oxford: Oxford University Press, pp. 196–212.

—— (1998). 'The Three Great Puzzles of the Firm', in Steven G. Medema (ed.), *Coasean Economics: Law and Economics and the New Institutional Economics*. Dordrecht, The Netherlands: Kluwer, pp. 51–63.

Markusen, A. (1999). 'Fuzzy Concepts, Scanty Evidence, Policy Distance: The Case for Rigour and Policy Relevance in Critical Regional Studies', *Regional Studies*, 33(9): 869–84.

Mintzberg, H. (1994). *The Rise and Fall of Strategic Planning*. New York: The Free Press.

—— and Waters, J. A. (1985). 'Of Strategies, Deliberate and Emergent', *Strategic Management Journal*, 6: 257–72.

Morgan, G. (2005). 'Introduction: Changing Capitalisms? Internationalization, Institutional Change, and Systems of Economic Organization', in G. Morgan, R. Whitley, and E. Moen (eds.), *Changing Capitalisms?* Oxford: Oxford University Press, pp. 1–18.

Nooteboom, B. (2000). *Learning and Innovation in Organisations and Economies*. Oxford: Oxford University Press.

Oinas, P. (1995). 'Roundtable on AnnaLee Saxenian's *Regional Advantage* (1994)', *Economic Geography*, 71(2): 202–4.

—— (1997). 'On the Socio-spatial Embeddedness of Business Firms', *Erdkunde*, 51(1): 23–32.

—— (1998). *The Embedded Firm? Prelude for a Revived Geography of Enterprise*. Helsinki: Acta Universitatis Oeconomicae Helsingiensis, p. A-143.

—— (2002). 'Competition and Collaboration in Interconnected Places: Towards a Research Agenda', *Geografiska Annaler*, 84B(2): 65–76.

—— and Packalén, A. (1998). 'Strategisten yritysverkkojen neljä tyyppiä—täydennys aluekehityksen tutkimukseen' (Four Types of Strategic Interfirm Networks—An Enrichment of Research on Regional Development), *Terra*, 110(2): 69–77 [*in Finnish*].

Powell, W. W. (1990). 'Neither Market, nor Hierarchy: Network Forms of Organization', *Research in Organizational Behavior*, 12: 295–336.

Pfeffer, J. and Salancik, G. (1978). *The External Control of Organizations. A Resource Dependence Perspective*. New York: Harper & Row.

Putterman, L. and Kroszner, R. S. (1996). 'The Economic Nature of the Firm: A New Introduction', in L. Putterman and R. S. Kroszner (eds.), *The Economic Nature of the Firm*. Cambridge: Cambridge University Press, pp. 1–31.

Simon, H. A. (1991). 'Organizations and Markets', *Journal of Economic Perspectives*, 5: 25–44.

Schlicht, E. (1998). *On Custom in the Economy*. Oxford: Clarendon Press.

Saxenian, A. (1994). *Regional Advantage. Culture and Competition in Silicon Valley and Route 128*. Cambridge, MA: Harvard University Press.

Storper, M. (1997). *The Regional World: Territorial Development in a Global Economy*. New York: Guilford.

Scott, A. J. (2000). 'Economic Geography: The Great Half-century', *Cambridge Journal of Economics*, 24: 483–504.

Scott, W. (1992). *Organizations. Rational, Natural, and Open Systems*. 3rd edn. Englewood Cliffs, NJ: Prentice-Hall.

Swedberg, R., Himmelstrand, U., and Brulin, G. (1990). 'The Paradigm of Economic Sociology', in S. Zukin and P. DiMaggio (eds.), *Structures of Capital. The Social Organization of the Economy*. Cambridge: Cambridge University Press, pp. 57–86.

Taylor, M. and Leonard, S. (eds.) (2002). *Embedded Enterprise and Social Capital*. Aldershot, UK: Ashgate.

Thrift, N. (1994). 'On the Social and Cultural Determinants of International Financial Centres: The Case of the City of London', in S. Corbridge, R. Martin, and N. Thrift (eds.), *Money, Power and Space*. Oxford: Blackwell, pp. 327–55.

Wenger, E. and Snyder, W. (2000). 'Communities of Practice: The Organizational Frontier', *Harvard Business Review*, 78: 139–45.

Whitley, R. (1987). 'Taking Firms Seriously as Economic Actors: Towards a Sociology of Firm Behaviour', *Organization Studies*, 8(2): 125–47.

—— (1992). 'Societies, Firms and Markets: The Social Structuring of Business Systems', in R. Whitley (ed.), *European Business Systems. Firms and Markets in their National Contexts*. London: Sage, pp. 5–45.

Williamson, O. (1975). *Markets and Hierarchies*. New York: The Free Press.

—— (1985). *The Economic Institutions of Capitalism*. New York: The Free Press.

3

Guns, Firms, and Contracts: The Evolution of Gun-Making in Birmingham

Michael Taylor and John Bryson

3.1 Introduction

The purpose of this chapter is to explore the implications for the theory of the firm of the interplay between firms, markets, governance, and technology. The structure and boundaries of the firm are examined in the circumstances of flexible specialization using the historical case study of the gun-making trade in nineteenth-century Birmingham. The last thirty years have been widely recognized as a new era of flexible specialization and a shift away from the Fordist mass production that reached its zenith in the decades following the Second World War. In this new era, firms are said to have changed, because the commercial environment within which they operate has changed, and is now strongly socially constructed. Under these changed circumstances, the path to economic growth in local economies is seen to depend on close inter- and intra-firm relations and co-operation to foster learning and knowledge creation and transfer, to generate technological change, and to create competitive advantage. In line with this shift, some approaches to the theory of the firm contend that the boundaries of the firm are, of necessity, increasingly indistinct, permeable, and fuzzy. The question asked in this chapter is whether, on the basis of Birmingham's historical record in gun-making, this restyling of firms' boundaries is necessarily a condition of flexible specialization. Early nineteenth-century Birmingham's group contracting system was intensely flexible and specialized (Sabel and Zeitlin 1985). However, there is evidence to suggest that strong contracts as much as trust, reciprocity, and cooperation between firms were essential to the workings of the system.

3.2 Flexible Specialization and the Boundaries of the Firm

Flexible specialization has strong historical antecedents. Sabel and Zeitlin (1985) argued in their seminal paper on historical alternatives to mass production that:

... high skill, universal-machine economies, which in many ways anticipate current developments, emerged in various regions of western Europe and North America towards the end of the eighteenth century. Areas using this manufacturing system—we call it flexible specialization—continued in many cases to be technologically vital well into this [the twentieth] century; when they stagnated ... the reasons had to do with social stalemates and unfavourable background conditions, not the exhaustion of technological possibilities. (p. 134)

These authors identified three systems of flexible specialization: the *municipality* (a self-organizing locality of small shops coordinated by merchants); *paternalist welfare capitalism* (large factories organized as artisans' workshops under a single roof); and *the federated family firm* (a loose reliable alliance of specialized medium and small manufacturing firms built on family ties). Birmingham gun-making is an example of the municipality form of flexible specialization in the early nineteenth century (see also Allen 1929; Berg 1993; Zeitlin 1997; Behagg 1998). We argue here that the historical evidence on the nature of firm boundaries and interrelationships that can be drawn from this industry can be used to throw light on the future and the dynamics of the phase of flexible specialization being experienced at the present time.

The resurgence of flexible specialization after the mid-1970s has been associated with accelerating processes of economic globalization. As a consequence, the focus is now squarely on firms: why they exist, what determines their boundaries, and what shapes their internal organization (Rathe and Witt 2001). The theory of the firm is now more important than ever. Indeed, globalization processes have thrown into prominence the actions and activities of multinational and transnational corporations in all sectors of the economy as they both orchestrate and react to the shifting global commercial milieu. The same processes have thrown a new light on the growth, significance, and susceptibilities of small and medium sized enterprises (SMEs) and their activities in regions, places, and localities. An emerging era of flexible specialization sees them striving to cope with and take advantage of the erosion of old certainties and the imposition of new, more ephemeral ones. Simultaneously, governments are trying to foster firms through a cocktail of neoliberal policies to attract foreign direct investment and to simulate the development of small firms in 'clusters' to secure jobs and growth.

The current discourse on mass customization, flexible production, and flexible specialization emphasizes the importance of knowledge and learning in what have been labelled 'coordinated economies' (Lundvall and Borras 1999; Soskice 1999; Asheim 2001; Asheim, Chapter 9 of this volume). Now it is argued that firms need to be quasi-integrated into local networks to overcome the problems associated with globalization, lean production, and flexibilization. Trust has been seen as a substitute for formalized control systems both within firms and between firms (Brusoni, Prencipe, and Pavitt 2001). In other words, in the world of inter-firm relations trust has replaced contracts, and a moral landscape has replaced a legal one. Trust it is argued can be built through proximity and knowledge sharing. Non-economic factors are now seen to be as important if not more important than the adoption of techno-economic strategies to enhance firm performance. The upshot from this reinterpretation of economic relations in a new 'flexible world' is that the boundaries of the firm are now seen to have become increasingly indistinct. This fuzziness is said to be expressed in internal markets within firms, in quasi-firms, and in hybrid firms, for example (Hodgson 2002). To Araujo, Dubois, and Gadde (2003), it is also that firms now have multiple boundaries, their boundaries being variably permeable depending on the nature of the relationship they develop with their customers, suppliers, and competitors. Economic geographers have not really addressed this complex set of issues seeing firms as merely 'relational' (Yeung 2004).

The emphasis in these approaches is on the dynamics of firms and their capacities to generate, retain, attract, and accelerate competitive advantage. From this perspective, firms are change agents: not only sources of potential growth, but also equally potent sources of decline and economic decay. The principal issue of theory is why do we have the firms we have, and why, over time, have they changed as they have? From an empirical perspective these are major questions to answer. In the first instance there are issues of how individual enterprises start, evolve, and change. But in the background are three much larger and interrelated issues concerning time,

Evolution of Gun-Making in Birmingham

place, and populations of firms: how have cohorts of firms in places emerged and changed as the market pressures and the pressures of their commercial environments have changed?

This is the question addressed in this chapter in the specific context of gun-making in Birmingham in the English Midlands. Along with jewellery making, the manufacture of metal 'toys', and brass founding, gun-making was one of the principal trades on which the industrialization of Birmingham was based, and it has an organizational history that illustrates the dynamic interplay of firms, markets, governance, and technology relevant to a dynamic theory of the firm.

The chapter is organized in seven sections. Following the introduction and Section 3.2, Section 3.3 and reviews current ideas on the boundaries of the firm and the dynamic interface between firms and markets, contrasting incomplete contracts views of transaction cost theory with more recent relational views that emphasize the social dimensions of inter-firm relationships. Section 3.4 explores the nature and form of the group contracting system of gun-making in Birmingham at the beginning of the nineteenth century while Section 3.5 addresses the question of whether this system was contractually or relationally based—whether it was market or non-market driven. Section 3.6 examines the dynamics of the system from an historical perspective and the roles of market-makers, the pressures brought by advocates of factory-based mass production, and the internal contradictions of group contracting. Section 3.7 outlines the evolution of the military section of gun-making to create the Birmingham Small Arms Company (BSA), and the partial shift of the Birmingham gun industry to a form of Fordist mass production. Finally, Section 3.8 outlines the implications of the case study for the interpretation current forms of flexible production and flexible specialization. In particular, it is suggested that non-market, relational interpretations which see firms as having multiple, fuzzy, and essentially indeterminate boundaries are in danger of significantly underplaying the role of hard-nosed contracting in these systems, and the exercise of power by the powerful, and especially by the market-makers outside the local place-based production systems.

3.3 Boundaries and Contracts

The theory of the firm offers two quite distinct and contrasting perspectives on the boundaries of the firm; the incomplete contract view which recognize the importance of transaction costs (the governance, property rights, and evolutionary theories—see Maskell 2001), and the RBV centred on firms' knowledge, competencies, and capabilities. The first is an undersocialized, economistic perspective, focused on legalistic views of contracts and the costs of using market mechanism, which reduces the boundary definition issue to one of 'make or buy'. The second is an oversocialized perspective focused on embedded networks, institutions, and close social interaction in the commercial sphere, which focuses on the permeability of firms' boundaries.

In the transaction cost view of the firm the focus is on allocative efficiency and the coordination within the firm of all kinds of assets, including knowledge. Of necessity, there are costs involved in the internal management of the firm as there are external costs involved in using the market mechanism, including the costs associated with the hazards of opportunistic behaviour in communities of businesses. On any particular activity, the question for the firm is whether to make or to buy; whether to make what it needs itself or whether to write a contract with an external supplier. Logically, firms should internalize activities up to the point where the costs of internalization equal the costs of transacting in the market for the outputs of those same activities. In a dynamic context, these transaction costs become either the real time costs of persuading, negotiating, and teaching external suppliers, or the costs incurred when a firm does not have the capabilities it needs when it needs them (Langlois and Robertson 1995; Araujo, Dubois, and Gadde 2003). Following Casson and Wadeson (1998), the boundary of the firm in this dynamic context becomes the point where information can be most easily and readily codified, because this is where an enforceable contract can be most easily written. Over time, these boundaries of firms will shift. According to Langlois and Robertson (1995), capabilities become increasingly replicated, readily available, and ubiquitous (see Maskell et al. 1998). As such, it becomes easier for firms to write contacts in the market for the supply of goods and services, with a consequent shrinking of the core of the firm that serves to protect the proprietary knowledge that is the essence of the enterprise.

What this stream of transaction cost reasoning produces is a rational landscape of production and exchange, delineated by contracts and populated by firms that are legal entities and owners of assets. Whether those contracts are formal or informal is unclear, but both are enforceable either through the conventions of law or through social-cum-moral pressure (also see Hodgson 2002: 45).

In contrast to the tightly defined boundaries of the firm of the transaction costs formulation based on allocative efficiency, and the firm conceptualized as a production function in neoclassical theory, the more strongly socialized interpretations elaborated in the last three decades have seen the boundaries of the firm as far less distinct. In part, this has arisen from the many conceptualizations of the firm that have been recognized in this literature, and amongst this array the firm has been seen as:

- An organization;
- A decision-making system;
- A collection of assets and liabilities;
- A juridicial person;
- A business unit under a single management;
- An administrative entity;
- A pool of learned skills, physical facilities, and liquid capital;
- A bundle of potential services; and
- A nexus of relationships

(Penrose 1959; Machlup 1967; Chandler 1992; Hodgson 2002).

Given this range of conceptualizations it is unsurprising that the boundaries between firms (hierarchies) and markets have been interpreted as complex and blurred: that the mechanisms of the market can move into the firm just as the firm can have multiple boundaries with the market.

Some argue that market processes have moved into the firm (e.g. Klein 1983) in the form of marketized transactions between departments and divisions of the same firm, internal capital markets and internal labour markets. This is a tempting if somewhat simplistic idea for, as Hodgson (2002) has argued, do internal negotiations, transfers of resources, divisional accounting systems, and profit targets constitute internal markets? Indeed, internal labour markets are not determined by a price mechanism at all. They are, as Doeringer and Piore (1971) recognized, only a set of administrative rules and procedures.

There is also a strong body of opinion that suggests that what lies beyond the firm is something more than market mechanisms. In this literature, the boundaries between firms and between firms and markets are seen as blurred, indistinct, and indeterminate.

In the Third Italy, in Scandinavia and in other industrial districts, especially in Europe and North America, stable and long-standing networked relationships have been recognized beyond the firm, between contractors and subcontractors. They have been interpreted as quasi-integration, creating quasi-firms and even firm–market hybrids (Williamson 1999; Hodgson 2002). And it has even been concluded that the distinction between firms and markets is no more than semantic (Langlois 1995). Hodgson (2002), however, rejects this notion of firm–market hybrids. He builds on ideas of Richardson (1972), Goldberg (1980), and Dore (1983) that what lies beyond the firm is 'relational contracting'—'longstanding ties with other contractors ... infused with considerations of mutual understanding, and trust that are not typical of market trading' (p. 45). These long-term contractual relationships are seen as essentially non-market in character with market transactions being seen as, '... generally more impersonal and ... typically short term' (p. 50).

These relational contracting views jibe with the conceptualization of firms' boundaries associated with the resource-based, competencies, and capabilities views of the firm (Moran and Ghoshal 1999; Rugman and Verbeke 2002; Hoopes, Madsen, and Walker 2003). In sections of this literature firms are seen as having multiple boundaries because of their need to establish, monitor, and supervise relational contracts with subcontractors and other suppliers. They invest in information, knowledge, and capabilities that they do not necessarily use themselves but which they need to operate in networks associated with relational contracting, clusters, learning regions, and industrial districts that are said to be the hallmark of the current era of flexible specialization. As it was summarized by Araujo, Dubois, and Gadde (2003), 'The more firms rely on complex interfirm relationships to access complementary capabilities, the more the boundary of the firm will have to expand to incorporate indirect capabilities mutually specialised to relevant partners' (p. 1257). In other words, firms will have multiple boundaries depending on the nature of the relationships it has with individual customers and suppliers.

The question these two theoretical approaches to the boundaries of the firm pose for the historical record of the nineteenth-century era of flexible specialization as it manifest itself in the gun industry of Birmingham in the English Midlands, is whether firms' transaction structures were essentially contractual or essentially relational. Were those transaction structures market-based or non-market-based? The inference of much current theory is that they should be relational; long-term, trust-based, and socially constructed, involving reciprocity and knowledge transfer to foster technological change and to maintain competitive advantage. The record suggests something very different.

3.4 'Group Contracting' and the Birmingham Gun Industry in the Nineteenth Century

The manufacturing history of Birmingham can be traced back to long before the industrial revolution, and the gun or arms trade is one of the oldest established trades in the city. John Leland, a churchman, who travelled throughout the British Isles wrote in 1538 that:

> The beauty of Bermingham, a good market town in the extreme parts of Warwickshire, is one street (Digbeth) going up alonge, almost from the left ripe (bank) of the brooke (Rea), up a meane hill (Deritend) by the length of a quarter of a mile. I saw but one Parrock Church (St Martin's) in the towne. There be many smiths in the towne, that use to make knives and all mannour of cutting tooles, and many lorimers that make bittes, and a great many naylors. Soe that a great part of the towne is maintained by smithes who have their iron and sea-cole out of Staffordshire.

By the time of the Civil War the manufacture of arms had become an established trade in the city. The town's importance as a key centre for the manufacture of arms was highlighted in April 1643 when the Royalists sacked part of the town to prevent the flow of weapons to the Parliamentary forces. One of the most important developments in the city's history of arms making occurred in 1689 when the Crown placed a trial order for muskets with Birmingham smiths. Prior to this order the British army had been equipped with Dutch weapons. William III had been concerned that the army's guns were obtained from overseas at great expense and difficulty. Sir Richard Newdegate, a member of Parliament for Warwickshire heard about the King's complaint and pleaded the case for obtaining weapons from the Birmingham smiths. The trial order was delivered successfully and the Board of Ordnance entered into a contract with five leading Birmingham gunsmiths, who agreed on behalf of themselves and their fellow craftsmen to supply 200 Snaphance muskets every month. This system of 'group contracting' represents a distinctive form of firm organization in which a small 'group' of firms and individuals obtained orders that were fulfilled by orchestrating a complex and often highly localized production system.

The group contracting system continued for over 150 years. The flexibility of this production system arose from the manner in which many small entrepreneurs were integrated into a complex ever evolving gun supply chain that was orchestrated by a small group of key contract holders. The flexibility and responsiveness of the contract system enabled

Birmingham to become the centre of the British gun-making industry. Between 1804 and 1815, to meet the demands of the Napoleonic wars, 1,743,824 military weapons, 3,037,644 military barrels, and 2,879,203 gun locks were completed by Birmingham gunmakers and their Black Country suppliers (Goodman 1866), along with an estimated million guns for the East India Company and 500,000 sporting rifles (Williams 2004: 43). Birmingham produced twice as many guns as London and exceeded the combined output of France's ten government arsenals by over 600,000 (Williams 2004: 43). To support the industry, the Birmingham Proof House was established by an Act of Parliament in 1813 to enable the manufacture of local barrels proof to national standards.

This production system was extremely flexible in the face of unstable and erratic demand. It enabled the Birmingham gun trade to increase the supply of guns to meet exceptional demands in times of war. During the Napoleonic Wars, Birmingham increased production fivefold from an estimated capacity of less than 3,000 guns per week in 1790 to 14,000 per week in the years after 1803. This increase occurred without the aid of machinery, expect for that used in gun barrel manufacture. Such an increase highlights the flexibility of the Birmingham gun industry; flexibility founded upon the elasticity of small producers with limited capital.

The group contracting system involved the interplay of four distinct groups in the Birmingham gun trade: contractors, small masters, artisan-workmen, and apprentices (Behagg 1998). At the apex of the system was the contractor (sometimes referred to as a 'factor') who negotiated the price for a formal contract with a merchant or the British government's Board of Ordnance to supply guns to a given specification. Though these contractors called themselves gunmakers, they made nothing. They held the contract which was only paid on completion, operated warehouses for materials or to store finished products, and they also supplied capital to the lower tiers of the system. In this respect, the contractors and factors in the system assumed a great deal of risk. In fact, a number of Birmingham's banks in the early nineteenth century were set up by factors working in the gun trade and in other branches of the district's metal trades (see Moss 1982).

The contractors negotiated with a tier of makers referred to as 'small masters' or sometimes (and somewhat misleadingly) as 'middlemen', for the price and supply of components or for the price of 'setting up'—the assembly and adjustment of components into finished guns. They too called themselves gunmakers and operated one and sometimes several workshops in the converted houses of Birmingham's gun quarter centred on the St Mary's district close to the present day city centre. These small masters not infrequently held substantial capital assets, usually in the form of real property.

In their turn, the small masters negotiated price and supply with artisan-workmen, or 'undermen' as they were sometimes called, for the performance of specific skilled tasks. Most frequently, these artisan-workmen worked in the shops of the small masters, but not always. Also, as in the other Midlands metal trades, they supplied their own tools and paid for bench space and power. In this respect, these artisan-workmen were significantly independent and were, at least in part, owners of the means of production. They were jealous and assertive of their independence. They controlled their working and leisure hours and, in a system without factory discipline, frequently observed 'St Monday' and took Thursdays as a break from work.

At the lowest tier of the system, the artisan-workmen coordinated and paid teams of apprentices in the workplace. At the beginning of the nineteenth century these apprenticeships were regulated by statute. They operated as a mechanism for learning and the transfer of knowledge and skills, and as a mechanism for the socialization of new people into the process of the group contract system.

3.5 'Group Contracting' as 'Relational Contracting'

A key question to be asked of this system of gun-making is whether nineteenth-century Birmingham's group contracting system was a precursor of, and an equivalent to, the relational contracting between networked small firms that is now seen as operating in the flexibly specialized clusters and industrial districts of late twentieth- and early twenty-first-century economies. Subsidiary to this question is a series of others. Were the separate tiers of the Birmingham system operated by firms as we currently understand them, or by something lesser? Was the system capable of innovation and technological change, that is, was it a learning system? Were the ties between these separate micro-operations relational or more formal? In other words, did the separate operations in the system have clear cut or more diffuse, multiple boundaries? Here some preliminary answers to these questions can be offered which suggest that greater care needs to be taken not to romanticize present day relational contracting by subsuming its darker capitalist dimensions.

On the first question, concerning the nature of the micro-operations of the nineteenth-century gun-making system, Williams (2004) has labelled them as proto-firms—as something less than a firm but on what basis this distinction is made is unclear. Instead, a starting point from which to approach this issue might be taken as Chesterman's definition of a firm (1977: 46–7). This definition has six criteria. To be a 'firm', an organization must have: (1) a line of business; (2) the repetition and continuity of activity; (3) the employment of assets; (4) the involvement of two or more people as owners, managers, and workers; (5) a degree of autonomy; and (6) entitlement to surplus profits. Table 3.1 matches these criteria against the four tiers of the Birmingham group contracting system.

The separate operations of the *contractor/factor* tier clearly meet Chesterman's six criteria, operating in the commercial rather than the production sphere. These are the system's links with the market-makers in the gun trade—principally the British government or merchants working on behalf of other clients. The *small masters/middlemen* also meet the criteria, but as makers and producers. Indeed, this neglected group (Berg 1993) sometimes operated from multiple sites, controlled substantial capital resources and owned shares in Birmingham's barrel rolling mill in the first decades of the nineteenth century. The artisan-workmen/undermen certainly meet five of the criteria but not necessarily the sixth. The payments they received were generated as negotiated piece rates, and whether those rates generated any surplus profit is difficult to know. They certainly did profit from the work of their apprentices, and in a classic Marxist sense they did extract surplus value from that group of tied workers. As was to be

Table 3.1. Birmingham's group contracting matched against Chesterman's criteria for a firm

Chesterman's criteria for a firm	Tier 1 contractors/ factors	Tier 2 small masters	Tier 3 artisans/ undermen	Tier 4 apprentices
1. Having a line of business	Holds contract, credit trading, warehousing	Making, setting	Making, setting	Making
2. Continuity of activity	Yes	Yes	Yes	Yes
3. Employment of assets	Finance, materials, property	Workshop(s), tools, power, shares	Tools, power	Tools
4. Two or more people involved	Yes	Yes	Yes	No
5. A degree of autonomy	Yes	Yes	Yes	Yes
6. Entitlement to surplus profits	Yes	Yes	Yes, via negotiated piece rate	No

expected, the apprentices did not meet Chesterman's criteria. But, at this level of the group contracting system it can be suggested that strong communities of practice existed that socialized and encouraged younger men to join the independently-minded artisan-workmen/undermen tier of production.

It is possible, therefore, to interpret the group contract system for gun-making in Birmingham in the early decades of the nineteenth century as one of networked, co-located small firms—Florence's classic (1948) 'locational integration' and 'industrial swarming'. It is a system that might also be characterized as one of *fragmented entrepreneurship* in which large numbers of individuals, from the top to the bottom of the system, were exposed at close quarters to elements of the entrepreneurial process. Under these circumstances it was unexceptional and even expected that independently-minded individuals would begin work on their own account (Berg 1993).

On the second question, concerning technological change, there has been a longstanding debate on whether craft-based group contracting was innovative. The nineteenth century advocates of the factory-based mass production of standardized products implied that it was the antithesis of innovative, technologically based production, though that reaction was as much a reaction to the competitive strength of its flexibility and the moral laxity ascribed to work practices outside the constraints of factory discipline. This prejudice was redoubled in the Birmingham context because, '... the vast diversity of small firms and its multitude of inconspicuous businessmen led to the rise of stereotypes which depicted them as "greasy workshop masters", in all respects inferior to the splendour of Lancashire "cotton lords"' (Berghoff 1995: 77). On the evidence she was able to assemble, Berg (1993) concluded, in contrast, that the group contracting system resulted in, '... production processes closely attuned to technical improvement and product development, and firms which could avoid both the costs of high overheads and high inventories' (p. 25).

Indeed, there was significant technological innovation in Birmingham gun-making in the early nineteenth century. In gun barrel making, for example, six patents were granted in the years between 1806 and 1812, during the period of peak production occasioned by the Napoleonic wars (Behagg 1998). But, in a more general way, highly erratic and irregular demand made gunmakers in particular sensitive to customer demands. That capacity meant, in the long run, that it was the gunmakers rather than those who placed contracts with them that suffered, for example, the scorn poured on the Birmingham 'African musket' that powered British colonial expansion. Equally, it was the makers who shouldered the criticism of guns produced to meet one particular British Board of Ordnance contract that specified such a reduction in quality that the guns' barrels and locks rusted and their stocks rotted during use (Behagg 1998: 9).

On the third question, concerning the ties that bound together the elements of the group contracting system, there is evidence for both contract-driven and more relational forms of working. As explained by Behagg (1998: 6) the process of negotiation between contractors, small masters, and artisan-workmen involved the notion of standard or 'fair prices', a convention that ran through more than the gun-making industry. The roots of the system lay in custom and there was a workplace culture shared by small masters, artisan-workmen, and apprentices involving irregular working and closeness. In short, there were at least some superficial elements of relational contracting in Birmingham's gun-making subcontract at the beginning of the nineteenth century. But, drawing on Behagg's evidence (1998), it is too simplistic to see this local production system as entirely relational for at least two reasons. First, negotiating prices against an order within the system was very slow and could take a number of weeks. Small masters did not commit themselves exclusively to one contractor but played one off against another to achieve at least some cushioning against irregular and erratic demand. Second, contracts were enforced, and the example provided by Behagg (1998) illustrates the point:

A number of finishers were summoned [in 1838] under Master and Servant legislation by the gun contractor, William Sargent, for not having completed an order. The finishers were small masters, described in court as 'middlemen'. These had, in turn, given out work to 'undermen', since, as was explained, 'it was perfectly understood that these men would not themselves with their own hands do all that was necessary to finish the work, but that during certain stages of the process they must necessarily put the guns in the hands of other workmen'. In this case, however, the 'undermen' had gone on strike against the small masters. Despite this, the contractors prosecuted the small masters since their contract lay with them and not with the workforce that was striking. (p. 7)

The inference to be drawn from these examples of negotiation and enforcement is that the group contracting system for the making of guns in Birmingham in the early nineteenth century was tightly defined by the real regulation of law, in the form of enforceable contracts, as well as the social regulation of custom and a convention of 'fair price'. When work was short, as it was in 1838, the relational veneer was stripped away to leave the unemotional brutality of contractual obligation. But, it is impossible to know how many disputes never made it to court or how many of the different types of businesses failed because they were excluded through a tarnished reputation from not meeting expected obligations. We would argue that, in essence, the heart of Birmingham group contracting was sharply defined contracts that limited and tightly defined the scope of the separate firms involved.

3.6 The Sustainability of Group Contracting: Market-Makers, Institutionalization, and Internal Contradiction

However, the system of group contracting that proved so flexible and productive in the supply of military arms during the Napoleonic wars was eroded and died out in the later nineteenth century, though the system persisted for the production of sporting guns. Because of the size and complexity of group contracting in gun-making in Birmingham, involving hundreds and possibly thousands of small competing individual producers, it is easy to see it as a self-perpetuating system built on external economies of scale, as in the argument advanced by Florence (1948, 1961) and Wise (1951). This, however, would be to underestimate the power and the potency of the market-makers who operated independently of the system but without whom the system could not exist. In gun-making, the market-makers were clear: merchants and arms dealers working for public and private clients; the British government's Board of Ordnance buying arms for the military; and foreign governments seeking the same materials. The market made by these buyers was based primarily on one-off contracts and is generally agreed to have been extremely unstable. The contracts for guns placed during the Napoleonic wars, for example, encouraged the Birmingham gun industry to expand massively to meet the demand, but, as Saul (1970) has shown, the British government did little in the forty years after Waterloo to suggest that orders would be regular.

During the Napoleonic wars the British government also tried to break Birmingham's monopoly in the gun trade. In 1806, the government established a lock and barrel making unit at Lewisham. This unit was relocated close to Enfield in 1818. The Royal Manufactory at Enfield was established as a barrel making and inspection site that would address variations in demand. Enfield developed a capacity to produce 26,000 barrels a year in comparison to Birmingham's 300,000 (between 1804 and 1815) (Williams 2004: 84). Progressively, however, Enfield began to compete with Birmingham especially after the implementation of the recommendations of the 1854 Report of the Select Committee on Small Arms. This report was heavily critical of the Birmingham system of hand working gun manufacturers compared to the American mechanized system constructed on the principles of interchangeable parts. The report recommended that the system of contracting should continue but that a manufactory of Small Arms under the Board of Ordnance should be created. The manufactory would act as an experiment to demonstrate the advantages of using machinery. It would act as a price check on contractors and respond to exceptional demand for guns. It was decided to invest in the Enfield site. American companies tendered to provide machinery for the making of the Enfield rifle and between 1854 and 1858, £353,583 was spent on the site (Williams 2004: 83). By 1859, Enfield was making 1,200 rifles per week and employed 1,250.

Quite obviously, no gunmaker was willing, under these circumstances of unstable demand and government hostility, to venture capital and to invest in the necessary machine technology to produce guns with the standardized and interchangeable parts that were increasingly seen as essential for the production of military guns. The advocates of standardized mass production saw craft-based group contracting as the very antithesis of technological advancement, and the British government used these views as an excuse for the obsolescence of its arms in the decades following the Napoleonic wars, conveniently forgetting its own purchasing strategies. However, there was in addition a social as well as an economic argument against Birmingham's craft-based production system. Sections of puritanical Victorian Britain saw the system as immoral and promoting a life devoid of discipline and sobriety.

In the face of these pressures what the Birmingham gunmakers did was to 'institutionalize' and create 'institutional thickness' in an attempt to protect their position within the market. A first move was to establish a contractor's cartel, the 'Committee of the Manufacturers of Arms and Materials for Arms' in or about 1807 (Williams 2004: 46). This Committee of self-interested parties handled all negotiations with the Board of Ordnance and represented the collective interests of previously competing firms at the apex of the group contracting system. It was, in addition, a structure of great usefulness to the chief market-maker, the Board of Ordnance, because through this channel it could threaten and cajole the Birmingham system.

A second move was to remove bottlenecks in the Birmingham gun-making system, and identifying and remedying these bottlenecks became a responsibility of the Committee. An important bottleneck that emerged about the time the Committee was established was for the supply of gun locks, and without any subtlety whatsoever, the Board of Ordnance asked if the Birmingham manufacturers, '... were desirous to keep their trade in their own country' (cited in Behagg 1998: 11). To overcome this problem, the Committee renegotiated the apprentice contracts of twenty-seven lock-making firms so that the Committee would pay anyone acquiring the trade two guineas and their teacher three guineas. Applications were made to the Committee at its base at the Stork Tavern in Birmingham. In 1814, this change in apprenticeships went further when the Birmingham Chamber of Commerce supported the repeal of the apprenticeship clauses from the Statute of Artificers, arguing that war production would never have been achieved if these clauses had been observed.

A third move was to tie the system's artisan-workmen to the small masters from whom they contracted work. They were independently-minded skilled workers who controlled their own working and leisure hours, an arrangement that introduced uncertainty and delay into a production system whose capacity was stretched to the limits by the demands of war. Therefore, to tie these artisan-workmen to their masters, the Committee introduced a bounty system. This was a premium payment, set at a maximum of £50 per year, provided in return for a skilled worker binding himself to a small master for a set period of time, and with a requirement to deliver a set volume of guns in that period. It was, fundamentally, an attempt to convert the lengthy process of continuous negotiation that accompanied the placement of every order into one that revolved around negotiation by time and quantity independently of when orders were placed.

The outcome of these pressures and changes within the Birmingham gun-making system was to erode the intensely competitive flexibility that had sustained its viability up to and beyond the Napoleonic wars. It was a competitive flexibility that continued to sustain the city's jewellery industry into the late nineteenth century (Wright 1866; Allen 1929; Wise 1951). The pressures of the market-makers brought a reaction of institutionalization and a reconfiguration of the system that turned the lower levels of the system into waged labour tied to particular small firms (those of the small masters), with, it can be argued, a consequent loss of entrepreneurial vigour.

3.7 BSA, Enfield, and Factory-Based Mass Productions

Effectively from 1855, two different production systems began to compete against each other in the gun industry in Britain: the Birmingham handmade, 'post-Fordist' system and the Enfield machine-based Fordist system. Birmingham began to suffer. By 1861, gun orders to the city had dwindled to such an extent that the contractors at the apex of the group contracting system were forced to consider acquiring machinery or going out of business. The upshot was the foundation on 7 June 1861 of the BSA when eleven of Birmingham's best known gunmakers gathered at the Stork Hotel to consider the manufacture of guns by machinery. The sixteen shareholders of the BSA company all maintained separate manufacturing facilities during the entire history of BSA until it went into voluntary liquidation in 1873. This event was the result of a Prussian government's order for 40,000,000 cartridge cases that resulted in an internal reorganization and the establishment of a new company, The Birmingham Small Arms and Metal Company (BSAM). In 1897, the ammunition business was sold to Nobel Interests (latterly ICI) and the company reverted to its original title.

BSA was established with an initial capital of £24,500 on a 25 acre site located at Small Heath. A factory was built at a cost of £17,050. During the first two years of the company it was run by a committee consisting of all its shareholders. This was not a successful form of governance and, on 30 September 1863, a board was elected under the chairmanship of Mr John D. Goodman. Goodman was to remain Chair of the BSA/BSAM until his death in 1900 at the age of 83. From the 1830s, he was a Birmingham factor and whilst Chair of BSA he continued as a partner in the firm of Cooper & Goodman. By the end of 1863, the company began work on its first large order—20,000 Enfield rifles for the Turkish government that was part of a 50,000 contract given to the Birmingham gunmakers.

Enfield became the British government's primary source of arms and enjoyed the stability of demand that the Birmingham manufacturers had always been denied. Birmingham's system was still used during times of peak demand, and this instability was to continue to plague BSA through to the turn of the century. It is significant that in the 1860s BSA still linked into the vestiges of the group contracting system that persisted for arms production in Birmingham. As it was explained by Goodman (1866: 404):

At Enfield, every part of the gun, from the earliest stage, is produced in the factory. This has not been found necessary in Birmingham; advantage has been taken of having the source of supply so near at hand, to obtain certain parts in unfinished stage from the manufacturers of the town. By this means great saving has been effected in the outlay for machinery ... [at the BSA factory] ... which would otherwise have been required, without prejudice to the quality of the work, as it all passes through the finishing processes of the factory.

Flexibility was still central to gun-making in Birmingham even as factory-based mass production replaced group contracted, high volume craft-based production. What is less clear, however, is whether strong contract provisions persisted or whether more relational arrangements were created as the shareholders in BSA made sure their own separate businesses benefited as subcontractors. This issue must remain open.

The British government's pivotal role in the gun industry's market instability remains only too clear in the two decades following the Crimean War and the American Civil War. In 1866, BSA received its first British government contract. This was to convert 100,000 muzzle-loaders into breech-loading weapons. It was an urgent order related to the Austro-Prussian war, and BSA responded to the demand by introducing a night shift. At this time, BSA was the largest private arms company in Europe (Ward 1946: 15). The outbreak of the Franco-Prussian War brought a request from the British government regarding the number of Snider rifles the company could produce. BSA was in a difficult position as all its machines had been adapted to fulfil a Russian contract for rifles. Work had not yet begun on production due to a last minute design alteration. BSA wrote off the £30,000 it had invested in the Russian contract to manufacture 20,000 rifles for the British War Office.

In 1878, the company was told that no government orders were to be made during the next financial year. To complicate matters the British government decided to auction 100,000 firearms. Foreign purchasers, who would normally have purchased new equipment from BSA, attended and purchased weapons. The Treasury made £15,000 from the sale, but the resulting public outcry surrounding the sale of British arms to foreign armies resulted in a decision to scrap 'obsolete' weapons in the future. The auction had a major impact on BSA. In the same month as the auction (April), BSA had to shut the entire plant. This difficulty led to the, '... directors, finally realizing the precarious nature of Whitehall patronage, [to turn] their attention to other fields of engineering' (Ward 1946: 19). In August 1879, BSA reopened to fulfil a War Office order for 6,000 rifles. This order was too late to prevent the implementation of the BSA diversification strategy. The directors were searching for precision engineered products that could be manufactured at the Small Heath site and the obvious product was the bicycle.

Early in 1880, Mr E. Otto was invited to a board meeting to demonstrate a new cycle he had invented, a machine with a wheel either side of the rider. Otto rode his machine up and down the board room table and at the end of the demonstration he rode down the stairs and into the road in the direction of Birmingham. BSA decided to manufacture 200 of the new Otto cycles. The Small Heath factory began to produce cycles and tricycles to its own designs as well as parts and complete cycles for other companies. However, cycle manufacture remained ancillary to the company's primary interest in arms production. In 1888, the British government placed an order for 1,200 Lee-Metford guns and, in consequence, the directors decided to abandon the manufacture of cycles. The concentration on arms only lasted five years, and in November 1893, BSA had to return to manufacturing cycles, but this time only the production of parts. Along with developments in cycle technology the directors also followed developments in the car industry. In April 1899 they obtained a contract to manufacture a batch of internal combustion engines.

Therefore, by 1900, Birmingham's group contracting system for the production of military guns had all but gone. Flexibility had given way to standardized mass production. The market-makers, particularly the British government, abused and were abusive of the system, and readily blamed it for their own failings. It was only logical that the contractors/factors of the old system should try to consolidate their position by setting up the BSA company, should use the vestiges of the old system for as long as possible to limit their own risk, and should eventually diversify into other engineering products—bicycles and cars.

3.8 Conclusions

The purpose of this chapter has been to explore the nature of the boundaries of the firm under conditions of flexible production and flexible specialization in nineteenth-century Birmingham's gun-making industry. The theory of the firm suggests two polar views of the boundaries of the firm in these circumstances. At one pole, the transaction cost view recognizes a strong contract-based divide between firms and markets—systems of transactions distinguished by prescribed and enforced contracts. At the other pole, relational views see inter-firm transactions based on non-market trust and reciprocity, involving repeat business, and the codependency of firms. As such firms' boundaries are permeable, fuzzy, multiple, and evenindeterminate. Price, profit, and rate of return, as key components of a capitalist economy, are removed from the transactional structures of firms, making capitalism no longer capitalist.

On the evidence available, Birmingham's early nineteenth century group contracting system for gun-making was interpreted as extremely flexible, involving very large numbers of small and micro firms, with tightly prescribed boundaries based on skills, but tied together by strong and enforced contracts. The whole was overlain by a veneer of relational ties. When demand was buoyant that veneer was strong, but as demand fell it weakened. A lesson to be drawn from this analysis is that non-market relations and fuzzy boundaries between firms are not a prerequisite for flexible production. A requirement for high levels of skill coupled with a labour shortage and unstable demand would appear to have been enough to promote the system. However, as other evidence from Birmingham and the Black Country shows, when no great skill was needed, as in handmade nail and chain making, a sweated labour system was more likely to emerge.

The group contracting system examined here was certainly flexible. But, fragmented, de-centred, and with no representative voice, it was open to manipulation and abuse by the market-makers who dominated it. The system's fragmentation was used as a scapegoat for the consequences of contracts drawn to make down to a price rather than up to a quality. It was unfairly portrayed as a system that was non-innovative and as having been bypassed by the industrial revolution. The unstable demand that called the system into existence also contributed to its demise. The producers in the system rather than the market-makers outside it strove for certainty and stability. This led to the creation of institutions, the conversion of the lower tiers of the system into waged labour and, ultimately to the creation of the BSA company. The standardized mass production of guns had finally replaced group contracting. But BSA too was eventually forced out of gun production by the same market-makers.

A key question is: what does this experience of group contracting in nineteenth-century Birmingham add to the theory of the firm and the understanding of the nature of firms' boundaries? In a dynamic context, the issue is what mechanisms led to a system of small and micro firms (using Chesterman's criteria (1977)), tied together by strong contracting arrangements, being replaced by a more concentrated and integrated form of factory production within, ultimately, a single combine—BSA? The powerful players were the market-makers, but they did not control the technology of production. The micro firms in the lower tiers of the group contracting system had effective control of that technology. So, why were they willing to relinquish their traditional independence to become waged labour? Perhaps the beginnings of an answer are to be found in the contractual nature of the firm as this has been elaborated by Cheung (1983).

Cheung (1983) builds on Coase's views (1937) on transaction costs and the problem of establishing the price for a commodity when it involves a number of separate contributions from a number of input owners—a situation directly analogous to the group contracting arrangement in nineteenth-century gun-making in Birmingham in which the 'factor' was a coordinator. According to Cheung (1983);

> In principle, all contributions of input owners as well as the services of the coordinator can be separately priced and sold to customers by measuring directly various attributes related to each contribution. In this case product and factor markets coincide. (p. 9)

This direct measurement of contributions finds resonance in the protracted negotiations between factors, small men, and artisan craftsmen in Birmingham's group contracting system before a single gun was made to fulfil an order. Put, somewhat differently, the costs of 'discovering' the price in this system were very high.

For Cheung (p. 9), '[o]ne effective way to reduce the costs of discovering prices is to substitute some other device other than the direct and separate pricing of activities'. Such a measure is a proxy, '... that entails the delegation of use rights from *private* input owners, to the extent that the contribution or activity of each is not directly priced. ... An *"entrepreneur" therefore emerges*' (p. 9, emphasis added). In other words, without the costs of measuring and pricing there would be no firm. As Cheung concluded, however, '[i]t is *not* quite correct to say that a "firm" supersedes "the market". Rather, one type of contract supersedes another type' (p. 10).

The decline of group contracting in Birmingham gun-making, the creation of BSA, and its eventual demise can clearly be interpreted in terms of one type of contract superseding another. In the first half of the nineteenth century that change led to a major redefinition of firms' boundaries and the emergence of the factory system in gun-making and in the other metal trades of Birmingham and the Black Country. Changes to apprenticeships and the introduction of a bounty system had the effect of creating proxy prices converting owners of micro firms into wage labour. This change squared with Victorian moral values and the social benefits that were seen in the discipline of factory work. At the same time, the self-interested made a grab for power and set themselves up to negotiate contracts with government—in effect institutional thickness created for self-promotion.

For studies of the firm in economic geography there is a clear conclusion to be drawn from the analysis of this chapter. There is a need to more fully unpack relational views of inter-firm ties, to move beyond the caricature of 'fuzzy' boundaries and multiple boundaries to consider both the hard edge and the subtleties of contractual ties.

References

Allen, G. C. (1929). 'Industrial Organisation in the West Midlands, 1860–1927', *Economic History (Economic Journal Supplement)* January. Reprinted in G. C. Allen (1970). *British Industry and Economic Policy*. London: Macmillan, pp. 20–38.

Araujo, L., Dubois, A., and Gadde, L.-E. (2003). 'The Multiple Boundaries of the Firm', *Journal of Management Studies*, 40(5): 1255–77.

Asheim, B. T. (2001). 'Learning Regions as Development Coalitions: Partnership as Governance in European Workfare States?', in *Concepts and Transformation. International Journal of Action Research and Organizational Renewal*, 6(1): 73–101.

Behagg, C. (1998). 'Mass Production Without the Factory: Craft Producers, Guns and Small Firm Innovation, 1790–1815', *Business History*, 40(3): 1–15.

Berg, M. (1993). 'Small Producer Capitalism in Eighteenth-Century England', *Business History*, 35(1): 17–39.

Berghoff, H. (1995). 'Regional Variations in Provincial Business Biography, the Case of Birmingham, Bristol and Manchester', *Business History*, 37(1): 64–85.

Brusoni, S., Prencipe, A., and Pavitt, K. (2001). 'Knowledge Specialization, Organizational Coupling, and the Boundaries of the Firm: Why Do Firms Know More Than They Make?', *Administrative Science Quarterly*, 46: 597–621.

Casson, M. and Wadeson, N. (1998). 'Communication Costs and the Boundaries of the Firm', *International Journal of the Economics of Business*, 5(1): 5–27.

Chandler, A. (1992). 'What Is a Firm—a Historical Perspective?', *European Economic Review*, 36(2–3): 483–92.

Cheung, S. N. S. (1983). 'The Contractual Nature of the Firm', *Journal of Law and Economics*, 26(1): 1–21.

Coase, R. H. (1937). 'The Nature of the Firm', *Economica*, 4: 386–405.

Chesterman, M. (1977). *Small Businesses*. London: Sweet and Maxwell.

Doeringer, P. and Piore, M. (1971). *Internal Labor Markets and Manpower Analysis*. Lexington, MA: Heath.

Dore, R. (1983). 'Goodwill and the Spirit of Market Capitalism', *British Journal of Sociology*, 34(4): 459–82.

Florence, P. (1948). *Investment, Location and Size of Plant*. Cambridge: Cambridge University Press.

—— (1961). *The Logic of British and American Industry*. London: Routledge and Keegan Paul.

Goldberg, V. (1980). 'Relational Exchange: Economics and Complex Contracts', *American Behavioral Scientist*, 23(3): 337–52.

Goodman, J. (1866). 'The Birmingham Gun Trade', in S. Timmins, (ed.), *Birmingham and the Midland Hardware District*. London: Robert Harwicke, pp. 381–431.

Hodgson, G. (2002). 'The Legal Nature of the Firm and the Myth of the Firm-Market-Hybrid', *International Journal of the Economics of Business*, 9(1): 37–60.

Hoopes, D., Madsen, T., and Walker, G. (2003). 'Guest Editors' Introduction to the Special Issue: Why Is There a Resource-Based View? Towards a Theory of Competitive Heterogeneity', *Strategic Management Journal*, 24: 889–902.

Klein, B. (1983). 'Contracting Costs and Residual Claims: the Separation of Ownership and Control', *Journal of Law and Economics*, 26: 357–74.

Langlois, R. (1995). Capabilities and Coherence in Firms and Markets', in C. Montgomery (ed.), *Resource-Based and Evolutionary Theories of the Firm: Towards a Synthesis*. Boston, MA: Kluwer, pp. 71–100.

—— and Robertson, P. (1995). *Firms, Markets and Economic Change: A Dynamic Theory of British Institutions*. London: Routledge.

Lundvall, B.-Å. and Borras, S. (1999). *The Globalising Learning Economy: Implications for Innovation Policy*. Luxembourg: Office for Official Publications of the European Communities.

Machlup, F. (1967). 'Theories of the Firm: Marginalist, Behavioural, Managerial', *American Economic Review*, 57(1): 1–33.

Maskell, P. (2001). 'The Firm in Economic Geography', *Economic Geography*, 77(4): 29–43.

—— Eskilinen, H., Hannibalsson, I., Malmberg, A., and Vatne, E. (1998). *Competitiveness, Localized Learning and Regional Development—Specialization and Prosperity in Small Open Economies*. London: Routledge.

Moss, D. (1982). 'The Private Banks of Birmingham: 1800–1827', *Business History*, 24(1): 79–94.

Moran, P. and Ghoshal, S. (1999). 'Markets, Firms and the Process of Economic Development', *Academy of Management Journal*, 24(3): 390–412.

Penrose, E. (1959). *The Theory of the Growth of the Firm*. New York: Wiley.

Rathe, K. and Witt, U. (2001). 'The Nature of the Firm—Static Versus Developmental Interpretations', *Journal of Management and Governance*, 5: 331–51.

Richardson, G. (1972). 'The Organization of Industry', *Economic Journal*, 82: 883–96.

Rugman, A. and Verbeke, A. (2002). 'Edith Penrose's Contribution to the Resource-Based View of Strategic Management', *Strategic Management Journal*, 23: 769–80.

Sabel, C. and Zeitlin, J. (1985). 'Historical Alternatives to Mass Production: Politics, Markets and Technology in Nineteenth-Century Industrialization', *Past and Present*, 108: 133–76.

Saul, S. (ed.) (1970). *Technological Change: The United States and Britain in the 19th Century*. London: Methuen.

Soskice, D. (1999). 'Divergent Production Regimes: Uncoordinated and Coordinated Market Economies in the 1980's and 1990's', in Kitchelt et al. (eds.), *Continuity and Change in Contemporary Capitalism*. Cambridge: Cambridge University Press, 101–34.

Ward, D. M. (1946). *The Other Battle: Being a History of the Birmingham Small Arms Co. Ltd, With Special Reference to the War Achievements of B.S.A. Guns Ltd, B.S.A. Cycles Ltd, and Other Subsidiary Companies Directly Administered from the Head Office of the Parent Company at Small Heath Birmingham*. York: Ben Johnson & Co.

Williams, D. (2004). *The Birmingham Gun Trade*, Stroud, OK: Tempus.

Williamson, O. (1999). 'Strategy Research: Governance and Competence Perspectives', *Strategic Management Journal*, 20: 1087–108.

Wise, M. J. (1951). 'On the Evolution of the Jewellery and Gun Quarters in Birmingham', *Transactions of the Institute of British Geographers*, 15: 59–72.

Wright, J. S. (1866). 'The Jewellery and Gilt Toy Trades', in S. Timmins (ed.), *Birmingham and the Midland Hardware District*. London: Robert Harwicke, pp. 452–62.

Yeung, H. W.-C. (2004). 'Rethinking Relational Economic Geography', *Transactions of the Institute of British Geographers, New Series*, 29.

Zeitlin, J. (1997). 'Between Flexibility and Mass Production: Strategic Ambiguity and Selective Adaptation in the British Engineering Industry, 1830–1914', in C. Sabel and J. Zeitlin (eds), *World of Possibilities*, Cambridge: Cambridge University Press, pp. 241–72.

Part III
Collective Agency and Narratives on Performance

4

The Firm: Coalitions, Communities, and Collective Agency

Michael Taylor

4.1 Introduction

Research on local and regional economic growth and regeneration has always had the firm at the centre of its deliberations. In this literature, the firm is seen as a key driver of economic change, innovation, and knowledge transfer. It is the site of enterprise and entrepreneurial endeavour. It is the locus of job creation and wealth creation. It is the source of competitive advantage.

But, how much do we know about how the firm functions: what creates it, what drives it, what shapes it, what destroys it? There is a range of theories that attempts to come to grips with these processes and issues that are built on different ontological and epistemological foundations. These theories range from the market rationality of the neoclassical 'black box', to the calculus of markets versus hierarchies in transaction cost reasoning, to the bounded rationality of behaviouralism, and the single category, 'capital', of structuralism. More recent institutionalist theories have added layers of socio-economic understanding to the austerity of economism, adding processes of networking, embedding, competencies, learning, and performativity (Taylor and Asheim 2001). As Taylor (2004) has argued, the firm is always context, never process. The social sciences are preoccupied with defining the boundaries of the firm. How do we mark it out, delimit it, and stylize it? Are its boundaries clear cut or diffuse and 'fuzzy' (see, e.g. the debate in Hodgson 2002)?

It is argued here that in most of the social science literature on the firm it is not conceptualized in terms of processes of enterprise and of people being enterprising. Instead, two polar issues have been marked out. The first is entrepreneurship—the actions of an individual, an entrepreneur, in initiating a new enterprise or innovation. The second is governance—the problems and issues of control, especially within large organizations, centring on the separation of ownership from managerial control, and the problems of control within managerial hierarchies. Between these two issues is a gulf; the gulf between individual action and inter-group conflict. To some extent this gulf is bridged by ideas on communities of practice (Amin and Cohendet 2000) with firms viewed as communities of communities. But, the notion of communities of practice cannot be applied unproblematically to firms because they centre principally on collaboration, socialization, and learning and push issues of dissonance, conflict, and rejection into the background. It is contended here, however, that what has been unappreciated to the point of neglect in understandings on the dynamics of enterprise and firms are:

- The key role played by the coalitions of people who establish, run, strategize, and control those firms and enterprises—the principal community in a community of communities; and
- The nature of the collective agency these strategic coalitions create, exercise, and dissolve which is more than the individual agency they each contribute.

The focus of this chapter is, therefore, the collective agency of the strategic coalitions who run firms. They are the coalitions of decision-makers—the risk-takers, the organizational innovators, controllers, visionaries, strategists together with the risk averse, blinkered, unimaginative, and the outdated—who, through the power they wield, shape, reshape, drive, misdirect, retard, and destroy firms and businesses.

The argument of the chapter is developed in six sections. Following the introduction, Section 4.2 presents very briefly the principal elements of a range of theories that stylize the firm. Section 4.3 outlines in detail the limitations and shortcomings of these theories whilst Section 4.4 offers an alternative conceptualization based on an interpretation of the notion of collective agency twinned with the concept of temporary coalitions and their connectivity. Respectively, Sections 4.5 and 4.6 explore these ideas in the context of SMEs and large corporations. As a conclusion, in Section 4.7 the ideas of coalitions and collective agency are matched against the emerging literature on communities of practice.

4.2 Stylizing the Firm

In recent literature, eight separate but complementary perspectives on the nature of the firm have been identified that fall into two groups, 'rationalist' pespectives, concerned with efficiency, and 'socio-economic' perspectives, concerned with the social construction of economies (see the fuller discussion in Taylor and Asheim 2001). Separately, these theories explore processes of maximizing, transaction costs, uncertainty, social relations, networking, embeddedness, institutionalization, governance, and learning as they impact on the definition and operations of firms. Each contributes a quite distinctive layer of meaning to what constitutes a firm, stylizing the firm in a different way.

The *neoclassical* theory of the firm treats the firm as completely defined by its production function and as a decision-making black box that responds rationally to external pressures (Archibald 1971). *Transaction cost* theory defines the firm in terms of the costs of using the price mechanism coupled with rational decision-making (Coase 1937; Williamson 1991). *Structuralist* theory shares this rationalism but relegates the firm to the status of an irrelevant analytical category, subsuming it within the category 'capital' (Walker 1989). *Behaviouralist* theory adds ideas on bounded rationality to the equation, and considers the role of information flows and knowledge in the shaping of firm–environment interactions (McDermott and Taylor 1982). The firm in this theoretical tradition is a site of decision-making in the face of conflict and uncertainty, which uses problem-stimulated search, learning, and adaptation to cope (Cyert and March 1963).

Socio-economic perspectives on the workings of economies have created new conceptualizations of the firm. The *institutionalist* perspective sees the firm as a refuge from market pressures within which rules and routines can be used to fashion strategies to counter competitive uncertainty (Hodgson 1988). The *embedded enterprise* perspective envisages the firm as enmeshed in socially constructed networks of reciprocity and interdependence involving untraded interdependencies (Grabher 1993, 2001; Storper 1997). The RBV of the firm emphasizes competencies and 'learning', with firms being bundles of activity-specific resources combined into firm-specific competencies (Maskell et al. 1998: 4). Finally, the *discursive* view of the firm uses actor-network theory to interpret the firm as a discourse of managerialism centred on information, knowledge, and 'talk', involving unequal power geometries and contestation (Thrift 1998*a*, 1998*b*; Yeung 2000).

A layering and deepening of the conceptualization of the firm is implicit in these theories (Taylor 2004: 5). Neoclassical theory recognized the firm as a production function. Transaction cost approaches deepened this view by conceptualizing the firm as enmeshed in a network of incomplete contracts but still focused on products and profits. Behaviouralism added further layers of meaning, including conflict, uncertainty, and the problems of decision-making, though still, at base, driven by the need to make products and profits. More recent institutionalist, embedded networks, and RBVs of the firm have gone beyond the framework of firms' commercial ties in an effort to deepen understanding of causality by emphasizing social processes within, between, and surrounding firms. Firms, by this interpretation, are bundles of unique competencies that are the emergent products of social interaction that involves more than the calculus of costs. In the discursive-performative view, human relations have causal primacy in firms in a ritualistic 'dance' that is not wholly driven by profit.

4.3 The Limitations of Conceptualizing the 'Firm' as a Phenotype

Current approaches to theorizing the firm certainly add increasing layers of depth to the notions of causality in firms' actions and activities. However, they all share one pivotal assumption—that the firm is a *phenotype*, a formative element of the capitalist system (Nooteboom 1999; Foss, Lando, and Thomsen 2002; Taylor 2004). It is the smallest unit of collective agency, a crystallization of commercial endeavour (Taylor 1984). The forces that meet and are played out in the firm are, in effect, the separate mechanisms and conditions rehearsed in the current range of theories of the firm: costs, social relations, resources, complexity, uncertainty, search, technology, knowledge, learning, innovation, and institutions. The firm is reduced to a stylized fact, always at the heart of theoretical propositions, but always just beyond the action. It reacts to economic forces, is socially constructed and a product of processes of institutionalization, and it is performative. It is rarely seen as collective agency, as Clegg (1989) has contended, that is purposive, goal-centred, and a driver of society in its own right.

Indeed, it must be questioned whether current theorizing of the firm is realistic and appropriate, especially as organizational structures and forms have become increasingly complex (a thesis of which Chandler (1962) is perhaps one of the best known exponents) and globalization has heightened awareness of patterns and structures of commercial control, powerfulness, powerlessness, and subordination (also see Chandler, Amatori, and Hikino 1997). But, is this an adequate or appropriate assumption about the role of the firm-based processes within an economy? The argument presented here suggests that it is not. To treat the firm as a phenotype and a stylized fact, ignores the processes within and around firms that create enterprise, prescribe and proscribe directions of change, mould perceptions of opportunity, engender a willingness to bear risk, and create the ability to learn and the desire to innovate (Taylor 2004). Indeed, to treat the firm naively as a phenotype creates a compound of problems of which six are particularly debilitating.

First, in most current theories of the firm, as indeed in most empirical research on firms, the firm is almost invariably theorized as a *legal unit*. The legal container of enterprise is equated unproblematically with the process of enterprise. As Taylor (2004) has pointed out, this tends to obscure and deflect attention away from more organic, social processes of *people being enterprising*. Legal frameworks have profound impacts on the workings of economic systems. They define 'stylized shells' to contain economic activity so that it can be regulated, controlled, and made socially responsible (Taylor 1999). Coase (1994: 11) has argued that, in an environment of positive transaction costs (denied only in general equilibrium theory in economics), law determines the rights, duties, and privileges of actors in an economic system that would otherwise have to be renegotiated and established for each and every transaction. It codifies social regulation and, recursively, impacts on that social regulation to shape the rules of meaning and membership of economic activity at a particular time and place (Clegg 1989; Taylor 1995). In other words, the legally defined firm is an institutional construct, but only to the extent that it embraces those aspects of capitalist behaviour that it is possible to regulate. Regulation maintains and enforces a set of rules over parts but not all of the capitalist game played by entrepreneurs (Taylor 1996, 2004). For example, contract law creates a set of circumstances that allow the provisions of commercial contracts to be enforced, but it does nothing to modify or ameliorate the unequal power relations between firms that can influence the negotiations that establish those contracts in the first place. Such system-forming regulation sets the stage on which the commercial play of firms is performed and system-guiding regulation attempts to add stage direction. Unlike theatre, however, the actors in a sort of perpetual improvisation script the play.

To achieve even an imperfect degree of regulation, the firm itself must necessarily be defined. In other words, the institutional products and patterned outcomes of people 'being enterprising' need to be contained, codified, and solidified in some way. Such a definition, according to Chesterman (1977: 46–7), might comprise a line of business to generate gain, repetition and continuity of activity, the employment of assets, the involvement of two or more people as owners, managers, and/or workers, together with a degree of autonomy, and an entitlement to surplus profits.

Defined in this way, the firm can be regulated through competition law, tax law, financial regulation, labour regulation, and environmental controls, for example. What is important here is not the detail of regulation but that the means (regulation) have become the reality (the firm). All those elements of capitalist behaviour and 'entrepreneurship' that can not be regulated—especially the exercise of power, control, and coercion—are to all intents and purposes dropped from the calculus, leaving the 'firm' as the smallest unit of capitalist endeavour. This mutation of the object *to be regulated* into an object that *can be regulated* is only too evident in the seemingly endless academic discussion about what is a small firm (Taylor 2004; see also Bolton Committee 1971).

The point being made here is simple. Research and theory-building on the 'firm' tends to be concerned principally with the stylized shells of legal form (including transactions as enforceable contracts), rather than with the more organic processes of enterprise and being enterprising that lie behind them. Only the more recently developed 'discursive' view of the firm in economic geography, with its broaching of issues of relational power geometries within firms, has begun to unpack this issue.

Second, current conceptualizations of the firm are significantly constrained because they are all essentially *static*. They treat the firm as the site of timeless processes. Cyert and March (1963) were, in fact, quite aware that their behavioural theory of the firm was, to all intents and purposes, static and that this imposed limitations on their work. By their own admission, only limited attention was paid in their theory, 'to processes by which the coalition [of interacting groups] is changed'. They recognized that this limitation involved 'clear risks when [the models are] generalised to long-run dynamics' (p. 27). This static timelessness inherent in most conceptualizations of the firm, also involves an element of what might be termed 'truncation', since the functioning of the firm tends to be considered only after it has somehow been set up. In essence, theories of the firm are concerned principally with firm growth, effectively divorcing those processes from the equally important processes of firm formation. In the behavioural, institutional, and embeddedness conceptualizations in particular, firms, without ever having been 'born', apparently progress along a biological, evolutionary trajectory, so that timeless processes are configured into a historical time-dependent sequence. Such a conceptual leap is fraught with dangers. Most importantly, it makes the implicit inference that all processes of enterprise operate at all times and all the time, despite what might be thought of as countervailing processes of factor ubiquification, for example, that clearly make them time-specific. Any of those processes of enterprise are also available to be mobilized by government policies at any time and in any place—be it a lagging region or developing country. In other words, most conceptualizations of the firm make the heroic assumption that 'enterprise' as a process is timeless and placeless, and waiting in the ether to be mobilized.

However, this apparently truncated dynamic implicit in static conceptualizations of the firm can also be viewed entirely differently, as a specific representation of *timeless processes* (Massey 1999). Massey's work in this area of timelessness and historical time is particularly important in considering the conceptualization of the 'firm' in economic geography. Most detailed research in economic geography in the past thirty years, as in economic sociology and management science, has been concerned with detailed, microscale, immanent processes. This focus is particularly evident in work on clustering, regional innovation systems, and process of learning and knowledge transfer, with its concern for trust-based relationships, information flows, decision-making, flexibility, transaction costs, untraded interdependencies, managerialism, and especially learning and innovation. To breathe a dynamic into these theoretical propositions, short-term and timeless microprocesses have been bulked-up to create descriptions of economic landscapes at odds with time-bound descriptions involving path-dependence and open futures. In this way, it is perhaps understandable how Silicon Valley could be typified as a site of reciprocal, socially based learning by Saxenian (1994) while also being underpinned by growth stimulated by heavy government defence spending and the US industrial-military complex and large corporations (see the discussion in Markusen 1999). It also goes some way to explaining how the branch plant economy of South Wales, dominated by plants of multinationals (Phelps 1997), can also be interpreted (or misinterpreted (Lovering 1999)) as a 'learning region' (Morgan 1997).

Third, in adding successive layers of understanding to the processes operating within firms, there has been a tendency in attempts to conceptualize the firm to push into the background the reasons for the expenditure of entrepreneurial effort. Increasingly, innovation, learning, embedding, institutionalization, the attainment of trust, and performance are being treated as ends in themselves. These are the implicit goals of individuals and firms in institutionalist and relational interpretations of local growth. The managerial literature on 'clusters' would put a harder edge on these goals, seeing them as significant only if they contribute to enhanced productivity and the competitive edge this is said to bring to the firm. However, it can be suggested that even the goal of improved productivity is secondary to the more powerful, individualistic goal of *personal wealth creation*. As Starbuck (1971) pointed out over thirty years ago, the strongest correlate with corporate growth was not rising profitability or increased turnover, but increase in executive salaries. Current corporate scandals in the USA and Europe would hardly suggest that this motivation has diminished. Indeed, are international software entrepreneurs driven by the altruism of being innovators, or by the commercial leverage innovation gives them to make money, principally for themselves, but colaterally and incidentally for others?

To achieve personal wealth creation requires a particular entrepreneurial talent, the ability to commercialize knowledge. Without doubt, knowledge and learning are important for creating business opportunities. However, while it is one thing to learn, it is another to put learning into practice to achieve a hard commercial outcome in terms of personal wealth creation. Knowledge on its own is of little or no use until it is transformed into commercial action and returns. Indeed, between a *bright idea* and running a *business* is an important, intermediate, entrepreneurial step of *translation* and knowledge transformation. That translation is the application of commercial knowledge. Knowledge and competencies must certainly be performed, as the adherents of the 'discursive' view of the firm would argue. But, they have to be performed not just for the sake of performing, though that may appear to be the case at any single instant in time. Knowledge and competencies have to be performed to achieve a hard commercial outcome. Thus, market knowledge plus commercial knowledge can create new firms as vehicles for personal wealth creation, and scientific knowledge plus market knowledge plus commercial knowledge can create new high-tech firms. This is the skill of the entrepreneur, who brings 'the knowledge of the practical circumstances of time and place' to bear on a commercial opportunity to achieve personal wealth creation. Profits have to be made because owners and shareholders demand returns on their investments, as do other investors and bankers, but this is all part of the process of personal wealth creation. That is, in essence, capitalism's inescapable bottom line. Unfortunately, in the socio-economic interpretations of the firm, this imperative has been all but swamped, buried, and obscured by researchers' zealous embroidering of the purely social dimensions of doing business rather than the individualistic goal of personal wealth creation.

Fourth, as a phenotype, the firm is treated as the site of entrepreneurship and entrepreneurial endeavour. Unfortunately, however, there is significant *ambiguity in the way entrepreneurship is interpreted* in much of this literature in management science, economic, sociology, economics and economic geography (see Swedberg 2000). In much of this literature the skills of the entrepreneur are vested, almost universally in just one person—a single individual, the 'entrepreneur'.

Jointly, the theories of entrepreneurship portray these people as leviathans (see, e.g. Nooteboom 2003). From an economic perspective they must cope with or initiate creative destruction through the combination of resources they deploy. They must, simultaneously, be alert to the gains available through arbitrage and matching supply with demand. They must provide and garner capital, create and enter new markets, configure and efficiently manage an array of factors of production, and achieve and appropriate balance between markets and organization. And, all this must be achieved within a competitive environment in which they, as new entrants, are relatively powerless. At a personal level, these people must be commercially alert and perceptive, imaginative, independent, open-minded, and able to take the initiative. They must be decisive and at the same time realistic in the decisions they make, have sound judgement and yet be willing and able to take risks. Equally, they must be ambitious, tenacious, and persistent. At the same time they must exude charisma, leadership, and managerial capabilities.

But, there is no particular reason why all these skills, capacities, and abilities need to be vested in one person. Already there is empirical evidence that the more successful small firms, for example, are run by coalitions of people who bring different skills, competencies, and experience to commercial ventures (Taylor 1999). There is in fact no reason why appropriate competencies and skills should not be bought in by a firm to supplement the skills of an owning and managing coalition. Indeed, one of the skills of that coalition might be the ability to recognize that they are deficient in some skills and need to buy them in. Nooteboom (2003) has extended this argument further by arguing that there is no particular reason why all the skills and capacities that have been ascribed to successful entrepreneurship have to be available to ensure the commercial success of firms in every context and at all times. Put differently, it would seem reasonable to suggest that the coalition of owners and managers that run firms will change and be changed as the context and circumstances within which those firms operate also change. Nooteboom (1999, 2003) has gone so far as to propose this evolving need for appropriate skills and competencies as a 'cycle of discovery'.

Building on this notion of the suite of entrepreneurial skills and competencies needed by a firm to succeed in a shifting commercial environment is a fifth aspect of oversimplification in theorizing on the firm—an underappreciation of *the complexity of the environment within which firms operate*. Reduced to a phenotype, firms are seen implicitly in theory as operating in a uniform environment in which, at the outset at least, they all have the same potential and prospects. Nowhere is this assumption more clear than in governments' current policies on business and enterprise. These policies raise the knowledge economy to the status of a Holy Grail with economic growth coming from innovation, learning, knowledge exchange, and new firm formation. All new firms are potential winners, and through these mechanisms, new industries are created, a springboard is developed for the launch of new corporate ventures, and international competitiveness is assured. In the UK, for example, this policy approach has been central to government thinking since at least the Bolton Inquiry into small firms in the early 1970s and persists to the present (Bolton 1971; Armstrong 2001).

This assumption of uniform enterprise prospects runs through much current theory in the institutionalist, resource-based competencies, and embeddedness views of the firm. In these literatures, issues of domination and control within and between business organizations are pushed into the background, flying in the face of longstanding empirical research (see, e.g. the work of the Aston Group). However, a significant body of research in management science and related disciplines has long recognized the differential impact of the commercial environment on the operations of firms. That research has highlighted the fact that *different types of firm wield unequal power* in the environments within which they operate (Taylor and Thrift 1983; Taylor 1987, 2001). Those inequalities give firms 'statuses' within networks (Taylor 2000)—degrees of centrality and peripherality, levels of powerfulness and powerlessness. This positionality has been particularly well summarized by Powell and Smith-Doerr (1994). It is the cornerstone of Taylor and Thrift's enterprise segmentation framework (1983) and it lies at the heart of Dicken and Thrift's network ideas (1992).

But, sixth, the failure to incorporate notions of inter-organizational inequalities and power differentials into theories of the firm is further compounded by the failure of theory adequately to consider the impact of *power differentials and inequalities within firms* themselves. When the firm is no more than a phenotype it has, in effect, no internal organizational dimensions—in effect, it has no Coasian hierarchy. As such, an essential aspect of the capitalist firm is ignored—the use of multi-site and legally fragmented and differentiated operations to maintain profitability and to extend the channels through which profits can be made and surplus value can be extracted. The differences and distinctions between the powerful and the powerless operations within firms go unrecognized. In theory, the headquarters is conflated with the branch plant even though the former may drive while the latter is driven. Such intra-organizational differentiation would seem obvious. It has certainly long been recognized in management science in the work of the Aston Group, for example (Hickson et al. 1971; Pugh and Hickson 1976; Pugh and Hickson 1989). It has also long been an essential aspect of economic geography in the notions of corporate control and enterprise segmentation (McDermott and Taylor 1982; Taylor and Thrift 1983; Taylor 1987, 2001, 2004). Yet, it is an aspect of the firm that seems to be all but ignored in regional policy-making where the powerlessness of branch plants goes unrecognized in the scramble to attract corporate-based jobs, while the ephemeralization of jobs that accompanies takeovers and mergers is of no apparent consequence. Indeed, the 'enterprise terrain' recognized by Taylor (1987) as combining the inter- and intra-organizational power inequalities that have shaped and continue to shape network relationships within and between businesses has received little or no recognition in either the theory of the firm or in local economic policy formulation.

4.4 Temporary Coalitions and Collective Agency

The six major limiting assumptions outlined above, that are inherent especially in institutionalist theories of the firm, need at the very least to be rethought if not completely discarded. Only through radical rethinking can we begin to understand more clearly the ways firms in localities, places, and across geographic scales act to create, sustain, and transform local economic growth. The core of the argument of this chapter is that current stylizations of the firm need to be rejected, and that the legally defined firm—the legal 'shell' of an enterprise favoured by Hodgson (2002)—inadequately specifies and articulates the time-specific and place-specific acts of entrepreneurship that drive modern capitalist economies. Thus, '[t]o meet, at least in part, the limitations of current conceptualisations of the firm in the social sciences, it is necessary to disentangle processes of enterprise (of people being enterprising to create personal wealth) from the operations of the enterprise, the firm (as a disconnected, legally defined object)' (Taylor 2004: 10).

Processes of enterprise and of people being enterprising are far broader than the legally defined firm. Firms and business enterprises are more realistically viewed as temporary coalitions of people who identify commercial opportunities to create personal wealth (and also utility), shoulder risk, apply assets to tasks, and trust in theirs' and their partners' competencies to achieve their goals. Their firms are temporary crystallizations of commercial endeavour called into being in time- and place-specific circumstances, and dissolved on whim, by force of circumstance (economic, social, and regulatory), by bad judgement, as a result of disagreement, incompetence, or by the lure of better opportunities. They may be established as partnerships, close companies, or as corporate enterprises. The members of the coalitions that run them may be co-opted, imposed, recommended, tolerated because of the assets and competencies they bring, or be there because of an accident of birth. The coalitions are not necessarily consensual or social. They are purposive, goal-seeking coalitions. And, they are purposive in the sense of existing to create personal wealth rather than for more altruistic motives of creating 'a good society'. Coalition members may sport altruism in private, but the schizophrenia that allows people to do one thing in their private lives and another in their business and professional lives is only too evident in modern capitalist societies. Certainly, socialization among members might be a way to build and strengthen coalitions (and there is a professional industry that attempts to do just that), but it is not a prerequisite. Mistakenly, much institutionalist writing on trust, learning, and economic growth makes precisely that assumption. You do not have to like someone to work with them—though it might help.

It is argued here that, at the heart of the operations of temporary coalitions of strategic decision-makers within economic communities are significant, yet poorly understood processes of collective agency. These are processes that create coalitions and allow their members to combine their skills to a common purpose. Most commonly, these processes have been identified by sociologists in the creation of social movements, for example, and collective agency has been explored as an aspect of actor-network theory. Here, the idea of collective agency is applied to the small group of owner/managers who collectively wield the combination of their technical and positional power to make a firm effective as a vehicle of wealth creation. They wield that combined power internally in an attempt to achieve a cost-effective product or service that can be offered to the market. They wield it externally to secure resources and access markets, through competition, collusion, or whatever mechanism appears most effective at a given time and in a given place.

These ideas build on Clegg's (1989) interpretation of collective agency. In his work on power in organizations, he explained that;

Agency may be vested in non-human entities as diverse as machines, germs, animals and natural disasters. These, and *more especially organizations*, may be agencies under appropriate conditions. ... [O]rganizations may constitute a form of collective agency ... [which] ... is not a second-rate form of agency compared to that of the problematic human subject. (p. 188, emphasis added)

He went on to argue that;

Where organization achieves agency it is an accomplishment, just as it is for an individual but more so, because it involves the stabilization of power relations across an organizational field of action, and thus between subjectivities, rather than within one embodied locus of subjectivities. Once more this is recognized in the ordinary language of organization theory. The common definition of organizations as formal and purposeful goal-oriented entities recognizes the contingent nature of this accomplishment. (pp. 188–9)

In short, the stabilization of power relations is an entrepreneurial-cum-managerial accomplishment of temporary coalitions which is a prerequisite for accumulation and personal wealth creation. Building on the propositions in this section, Sections 4.5 and 4.6 assemble a range of insights into the workings of the temporary coalitions that run both small firms and corporate organizations, before matching these ideas against a 'communities of practice' framework.

4.5 SMEs as Temporary Coalitions

The creation, dissolution, and reformation of coalitions of individuals for the purpose of wealth creation is evident in a myriad company histories as exemplified by the case studies in Schoenberger's work (1997) on corporate organizations. These processes of change are also particularly clear among current businesses in the small firms sector. A systematic view of the nature of the processes is provided in an interview survey of fifty electronics firms, both corporations and SMEs, undertaken in South Hampshire in the UK in 1998 and 1999. The data throw light on the size and composition of coalitions operating businesses at that time. They also enable the reconstruction of the histories of people owning, operating, and working within small electronics companies, and make the centrality of space-time in the processes of 'enterprising' very plain. These histories show a point and counterpoint of activities that work behind or even tangentially to the formally registered companies that were interviewed and their contractually defined transactions—that is, processes working behind the legal landscape that has preoccupied economic theory and analysis for so long.

First and foremost, the South Hampshire data suggest, as shown in Table 4.1, that most small firms are run by coalitions of owners (nearly 70 per cent), and that the majority of those coalitions comprise more than two people. In short, successful businesses come from team start-ups.

The South Hampshire interviews demonstrate very clearly that small firm coalitions are created by people with a desire to work for themselves or as a mechanism to cope with unemployment. In all cases they are set up to exploit perceived commercial opportunities, sometimes not recognized or acted on by entrepreneurs' former employers, though in some cases actually suggested by those employers (Openshaw and Taylor 2002). New coalitions are generated through processes of serial and multiple entrepreneurship, and as Taylor (1999) has shown, up to 40 per cent of SMEs in UK regional economies find their origins in these processes.

The South Hampshire interviews also suggest that, risk minimization lies at the heart of coalition start-ups, and six strategies are used to minimize that risk. First, individuals form coalitions with like-minded people or with those with complementary skills, but the ties are principally commercial and not necessarily social. Second, the founding coalitions of small businesses minimize risk by mobilizing personal financial resources or those of their family networks. Third, coalitions recruit or acquire members (including business angels) through third-party referral—the recommendation and introduction of people by other business

Table 4.1. Ownership structure of South Hampshire electronics firms, 1998–9

Type of coalition	No. of firms
SMEs with coalitions of more than 2 people	21
SMEs with coalitions of 2 people	10
SMEs with a single owner/manager	14
Firms currently operated through corporate boards	5

acquaintances (Uzzi 1996, 1997; Taylor 1999; Search and Taylor 2002). Fourth, they use local solicitors and accountants to get their businesses up and running, and these service providers appear to play a major role in third-party referral networks (Search and Taylor 2002). Fifth, individual entrepreneurs attempt to stabilize personal wealth creation by engaging in portfolio investment. This arrangement offers more opportunities to extract income, either personally or through other family members, and it can act as a hedge against failure. Sixth, the coalitions owning and running SMEs can use the services and facilities offered by central and local governments and by regional development agencies (such as short-rental premises, advice, and other implicit subsidies) to offset the risks of start-up.

Once established, the South Hampshire interviews show that SME coalitions can be expanded to gain access to money, technology, and suppliers, that is to secure inputs and competencies, and people then shift between coalitions through design or through pressure. More specifically, coalitions are reshaped through processes of ageing, retirement, family transition, disagreement, and feud. Less traumatically, but just as radically, coalitions may be reshaped by changes in individuals' goals, or even by boredom. What is important here, however, is that change in coalitions can come for entirely non-commercial and non-economic reasons. Finally, the interviews demonstrate that management buyouts and takeover radically reshape SME coalitions.

However, to categorize processes of coalition formation and risk minimization in this way is to divorce those processes from the time-space context within which they occur. They are the bones of the process stripped of the flesh of lived experience. Four examples of South Hampshire engineering and electronics firms drawn from the database of interviews conducted in the late 1990s place these processes in context.

The first example is of a small electronics firm, here given the pseudonym MITON, that writes and designs software employed in automatic testing equipment which is used to test printed circuit boards. It was born of necessity, in a period of recession that was compounded by major defence cuts and corporate downsizing. The cofounders 'M' and 'T' met in the early 1990s when they worked for a defence contractor, Fergusons, in Gosport. 'M', a local man, had moved there after having been made redundant from Marconi, and 'T' had transferred within Fergusons after their Enfield, London, plant had been closed. In early 1992 they were both made redundant again. But, by their own admission, they received generous redundancy payments, and also assistance from their former employer to buy redundant equipment once they said they were planning to set up their own business. They identified a market niche, to sell their electronics expertise to corporate clients who were fashionably downsizing and outsourcing. They set up as a partnership working first in a friend's garage and living off their reserves for eight months as they established their business. Here, then, was the first coalition, 'M' and 'T' working as a partnership.

To expand business and to achieve sound long-term growth, however, 'M' and 'T' reasoned that they needed additional technical expertise. In their opinion, the only way to secure that expertise was to offer a suitable person a share of the business. So, in 1996, the company was incorporated and a third director, a friend of 'T', was brought in. Here now is a new coalition, and once it was a coalition it was recognized as having significant internal tensions.

A second example demonstrates a different historical dynamic and illustrates coalition shifts from another perspective. The focus of interest here is 'G' an engineer-draftsman. After an apprenticeship in boat-building and National Service in the RAF in the late 1940s, 'G' moves from one job to another in small engineering firms in Eastleigh, outside Southampton. He settles in one, engaged in sheet metalwork and light steel fabrication and, in 1968, is appointed a director. He is now part of his first coalition, a coalition not dissimilar to that of the first Hampshire example. The coalition persists for thirteen years when, in the recession of the early 1980s, business turns sour, internal relations follows suit, and 'G' leaves the company. (In the interview there were veiled hints of dismissal and compensation, and quite intense bitterness.) After a four-week hiatus, a former client, 'C', the owner of another business making compressors and compressed air equipment, suggests establishing a partnership in the same sheet metal and light steel fabrication line of business. A new business, here called INFAB, is formed in 1982 with a new coalition, 'G' and 'C'. 'G' takes care of production and 'C' deals with finance. Indeed, it is 'C', himself now a multiple entrepreneur, who finances the venture. The venture continues for seventeen years with 'G' being part of a single coalition and 'C' with his fingers in two coalitions. Time takes its toll. 'C' dies and his wife becomes a new coalition member. 'G' now 65 wants to retire and pass his directorship to his son who is already working as the General Manager of INFAB. It was age and succession that brought about the most recent transformation of this coalition.

The third example from Hampshire further complicates the picture of shifting coalitions. In 1969 in Southampton, a draftsman 'D', a welder 'W', and a builder 'B', who worked together building Esso's Fawley refinery set up a business, FAB, with Esso's assistance, doing contract pipework maintenance for the refinery. They were in the right place at the right time. A coalition (coalition 1) was created mobilizing three people's competencies. On incorporation in 1971, however, 'B' was bought out for a reason unknown to the person who was interviewed. The adjusted coalition (coalition 2) continued for twenty-two years, until 1993. Two more companies were set up so that other work could be taken on without being tied to the high wages paid at the unionized Fawley refinery site. The FAB coalition now comprised two multiple entrepreneurs with a small network of companies and on-site offices with their main clients. As FAB's business expanded to employ some 120 people, 'D' and 'W' took on managers: 'K' and 'J' in 1985; 'P' and 'M' in the late 1980s; and 'A', who was taken on as a manger in a sister company, in 1990.

In 1993, the owners 'D' and 'W' wanted to retire and the five senior managers agreed to buy them out. In the terms used here, a new coalition (coalition 3) had acquired the assets of FAB and its sister companies, and began to deploy them differently in a bid to generate wealth from them for themselves. They diversified the client base and started taking on new forms of fabrication work for, for example, roller coasters. Quickly, two of the coalition, 'P' and 'M', moved out, taking their gains. The new smaller coalition (coalition 4) grew the companies but also wanted to realize some of their own investment. It was, in the informant's words, 'time to move on'. So, in 1998, the companies were sold to a larger public company engaged in different but complementary work. The wealth-creating coalition dissolved and only 'K' remained and moved on to the new owner's main board. Now a new coalition, the fifth in FAB's existence (and with a small element of continuity) were to begin using this particular accumulated set of assets to continue to generate wealth in its own particular way.

The point of this example is not just to demonstrate coalition shifts, succession, and management buyouts. It is to show how the historical sequence of passing the asset baton from one coalition to another in an era of shifting management fashions can see the assets of a partnership become the assets of a corporation. The bundle of assets had been passed from one coalition to another to create private wealth. It was the five coalitions that had been enterprising, mobilizing, and remobilizing a particular bundle of assets. The firm did not evolve in any organic sense, it was just a name demarcating a legally owned collection of assets that different combinations of people, not all of whom would be classic entrepreneurs, used.

A fourth example further elaborates the links between the corporate sector and SME coalitions, and demonstrates the international dimensions of small firm, shifting coalitions. The company in question, GI, makes electronic data displays, and was set up in 1984. The company had a complex early history being passed from one coalition of private owners to another, as in the previous examples. By the late 1980s, it was part of a conglomerate of small, privately held companies. In 1989, it was bought by its managers, and was financed by a Middle East investment company that, in effect, syndicated the ownership of small businesses. At the time, the investment company had a portfolio of sixty-two businesses. GI was left to manage itself. For six years it made very little for its owners and, in 1996, they put it into receivership.

Downsized, GI was bought from the receivers by another family owned conglomerate, DD, working in a complementary line of business. DD had itself been set up by an engineer with executive experience in the corporate sector. He had worked in the Netherlands for a subsidiary of the corporation before executing a management buyout during the expansionary years of the mid-1980s. DD used the purchase of GI to establish a manufacturing base in the UK in 1996. At the same time, it bought a similar manufacturing base in Ireland, and began to conduct business through offices in France and the USA. This example shows only too clearly that a firm, in this case GI, is of a collection of assets passed between small firm coalitions and a corporate investment operation to become part of the asset base of a small firm multinational.

These four case studies demonstrate the small firm as a temporary coalition, with successive groups of people using the same or modified asset bases to generate personal wealth. The firm itself, as an enterprise, was just a bundle of legally defined assets that could be regulated and taxed. It was animated by its coalition of owners 'being enterprising', and they could be enterprising individually or collectively in a host of other firms. The commercial strengths and weaknesses of those coalitions were in part a reflection of the adequacy of the coalitions themselves. However, just as the formation of new coalitions was time and place dependent, the historically specific conditions of time and place also affected commercial performance.

4.6 Corporate Coalitions

Small- and medium-sized enterprises are however only one of the forms of temporary coalition engaged in enterprise and entrepreneurship. Very similar patterns of coalition formation, dissolution, reconstruction, and transformation can be identified in the strategic management groups of large corporate organizations. Indeed, the mechanisms that can be identified in the creation and construction of boards of directors throw additional light on coalition processes, both social and economic, employed in the pursuit of personal wealth creation.

The Fosters Brewing Group Ltd in Australia offers a striking example of the workings of the temporal and temporary coalitions of the corporate sector in the last twenty-five years. It is a reconfigured corporation constructed in the recession of the early 1990s from the demise and selling down of the entrepreneurially driven Elders IXL Ltd (see the detailed accounts in Fagan 1990 and Taylor 2004).

As globalization forced the Australian government in the 1980s to deregulate the economy and abandon import replacement industrialization policies, local companies were faced with rising costs, falling profits, declining market growth, and intensifying competition (Fagan 1990). The reactions in the Australian business community created a takeover and merger boom, fuelled by debt financing, and the emergence of a group of aggressive entrepreneurs. The manoeuvrings of three of these entrepreneurs, challenging Melbourne-based 'old money', led to the merging of three companies: Elders Ltd, a pastoral and trading company; Carlton and United Breweries Ltd, a brewer; and Henry Jones IXL Ltd, a food processor. This merger set in train a sequence of actions and reactions that illustrate the temporary coalitions interpretation of corporate organizations.

The merger created Elders IXL Ltd, with a new coalition of directors led by John Elliott who began to deploy their newly acquired assets as part of an aggressive new strategy based on acquisition, control of Australia's export trade, rationalization of manufacturing capacity, internationalization of brewing and food processing, entry into the mineral sector, and growing their fiscal strength (Fagan 1990: 658–61). However, debt financing in the 1980s bred short-termist financial manipulation rather than a concern for longer-term profits, and power plays developed between corporate coalitions in which share swaps came to be used as a defensive mechanism. In the late 1980s, just such a power play among Australia's entrepreneurs developed over the control of the Australian mining giant, BHP Ltd. Elliott and Elders IXL were thoroughly embroiled. A key event in these manoeuvrings occurred when BHP Ltd sold its 20 per cent of Elders IXL to '... an investment company "friendly" to Elders, or more particularly to its Board of Directors' (Fagan 1990: 663). The Elders board split, the coalition was fractured. Nine board members retired or resigned within eighteen months, and representatives of a major Japanese shareholder,

Asahi Breweries Ltd, were appointed to the board. A new strategic coalition had been formed to secure resources (see the mechanisms discussed in Pfeffer 1981).

Debt became unmanageable, complicated by the onset of recession in 1989. Radical restructuring was attempted to turn the corporation into an international brewing operation and in 1990 its name was changed to the Fosters Brewing Group Ltd. Now, a boardroom faction, centred on John Elliott, made an abortive attempt to secure control of the company using BHP's shareholding. The company nearly failed in 1992 (FBG 1998). Elliot went, and there was a fresh spate of boardroom resignations and appointments through 1992. BHP people took three seats on the board which they kept until 1997. In effect, between 1992 and 1997, a new coalition of strategists had been fashioned to run Fosters, overseen by the directors nominated by BHP and Asahi, but including significant new people, who fashioned a new vehicle of wealth creation by reshaping the assets they had inherited. With the new coalition came a new corporate philosophy (FBG 1997: 6; 1998): to be a 'lead enterprise' in terms of markets and innovation; to be a global player with a strong base in Australia; and be a premium brand beer and wine company. They sold off non-core assets, focused on the Foster's brand, shifted into wine production and sales internationally, expanded brewing operations into the Asia Pacific region, and moved into the leisure and hospitality sector in Australia. By 1999, the new coalition's deployment of assets was beginning to reap commercial rewards (FBG 1999: 5; FGL 2003).

This example shows how, in the corporate as in the small firms sector, shifting, temporary coalitions of strategic decision-makers configure and reconfigure organizations' assets in fashionable ways to create wealth. Their actions and opportunities are time-specific, and they can fail just as easily as they can succeed. Fundamentally, however, strategic change and coalition change appear to be recursively interrelated in the path-dependent dynamics of corporate organizations.

The strategic role of boards of directors in shaping the futures of firms is a topic that has been extensively examined in the management science literature, much of it building on Hambrick and Mason's upper echelons theory (1984). The theory causally links the values and experiences of upper-level managers and boards of directors to organizational outcomes—innovation strategies, strategic change, and performance (Finkelstein and Hambrick 1990; Smith et al. 1994). Now, the strategic decision-making role of boards of directors is seen as being increasingly important to enable firms to cope with modern, volatile commercial environments (McNulty and Pettigrew 1999). The actions of boards of directors, their composition, skills, knowledge, and abilities send signals to the market that are reflected positively and negatively in share values (Daily and Dalton 1993; Brickley, Coles, and Terry 1994; Westphal and Zajac 1998).

An important question remains, however, concerning the manner in which boards of directors, as corporate sector coalitions, are formed. The inference to be drawn from the SME examples is that often coalitions are formed through mutual acquaintance—sometimes social, sometimes through previous business contacts. Taylor (1999) has suggested from a City of London case study that the mechanism is one of third-party referral. Upper echelons theory, backed by a range of empirical attempts to test its validity, suggests a similar but more complex set of processes behind the formation of corporate sector coalitions as boards of directors.

A significant strand of this research suggests that, strategic as the role of a board of directors might be in framing the commercial future of a firm or corporation, becoming a board member is principally a sociological process which is distinctively class-based and self-reinforcing. The somewhat sanitized, 'scientific' literature from US management science suggests that because people derive self-esteem and self-identity from board membership, CEOs and existing board members select as new board members people from similar demographic and social backgrounds to themselves. These similarities have been recognized in terms of:

- Shared philosphies on strategy and administration;
- Compatible leadership styles;
- A shared language born of common experiences and similar choices;
- Similar functional backgrounds bringing commonality in approaches to strategic decision-making; and
- Shared educational backgrounds (especially through business schools in the USA) which inculcate common beliefs (Bantel and Jackson 1989; Westphal and Zajac 1995; Zajac and Westphal 1996).

Under these circumstances, it is only to be expected that the directors on one board will borrow and imitate models of action, for acquisitions for example, from the other boards on which they sit (Haunschild 1993).

Recruitment to boardroom coalitions in the UK has been explored in detail by Hill (1995) who has put flesh onto these sanitized, scientific bones. His study suggests that 'getting the right people in place seems to account for more than structures, systems and procedures, particularly in the boardroom itself' (p. 251). Patronage is central to the process with the faces of new directors 'having to fit'. That 'fit' is virtually assured because over half of British company chairmen have previously served as executives in the same firm. The selection of new members is achieved through informal soundings of board members, in the first instance, with formal proposals coming only after there is perceived to be broad agreement. Especially significant, according to Hill (1995) are networks of personal recommendation—of being known by the 'right' people with influence on the board (p. 248). These are precisely the third-party referral networks identified by Taylor (1999). In this interpretation of the formation of boards of directors, the world of boardroom elites in the UK is one where reputation and influence count high. 'It is a small world that is bounded by the space of its networks, by the number of people who know each other directly or second hand' (Hill 1995: 273). The pool of potential directors available for appointment is, in fact, heavily populated with ex-CEOs. It is only to be expected then that 'boards ... reproduce themselves in their own image, selecting people like themselves' (p. 276).

This is not to suggest that within their strategic coalitions board members do not perform different roles. They do, but discretely. At the heart of the board, with most influence, is most frequently the Chairman, the CEO, and the finance director (Hill 1995). Non-executive and part-time directors shape ideas and methodologies on strategy, but are less important in collective decision-making (Finkelstein and Hambrick 1996; McNulty and Pettigrew 1999). Their role is particularly important during periods of crisis (Lorsch and MacIver 1989) and in periods of strategic transition (Zald 1969), such as that experienced by Fosters Brewing Group Ltd. They are necessarily there as acceptable faces to outside interests, especially in places like the City of London. 'Outside' directors, as opposed to those appointed from 'inside' the firm, are seen to be more concerned with the discretionary component of corporate responsibilities and less with economic performance (Ibrahim and Angelidis 1995). 'Insiders', in contrast, have firm-specific knowledge (Westphal and Zajac 1995). Nevertheless, as Hill (1995) remarked from his UK evidence, collegiality is highly valued in new board members. Sectional interests can threaten the board's teamwork. Disagreements, at least on UK boards, are kept internal. A common front is maintained through the socialization and incorporation of members into a boardroom culture that tends to weaken individual independence.

This view of corporate culture is reinforced in *The Times* (2004) analysis of the UK power elite, *The Power 100*. This report described the interlocks between the country's most influential corporate boards and 'significant ties' to prominent colleagues. In 2004, each of this group of 100 held, on average, 2.6 directorships of FTSE companies. Nearly a half held two, a third held three, and one held eight. On average, these same people had held 2.03 previous directorships, with one having sat on eleven boards other than those on which he currently sits. The same incestuous arrangement ran through the pattern of significant ties. The report also provided information on the elites' significant ties to other prominent colleagues (but only when there were at least two points of contact). One-third of the members of the *Power 100* had no obvious ties by this definition, but half had between one and four ties, leading *The Times* to remark that appointment to corporate boards in the UK is a function of not what you know but who you know, particularly if your specialism is finance. Indeed, UK corporations appear to have self-perpetuating boards, based on personal connections and their colleague's recommendations. Recruits may be well qualified and talented, or they may simply be the 'right' kind of person. As *The Times* commented;

At their best, such informal selection techniques are based on vital experience and yield inspirational working relationships. At their worst they encourage a 'you sit on my remuneration committee and I'll sit on yours' reciprocity.' (*The Times*, 2 November 2004)

The implication is, therefore, that there is a strong class component to the formation and reproduction of the strategic coalitions of corporate boards of directors, especially in the UK. That class dimension is built on and reinforced by conformity: conformity of social background, professional background, ideas, and action. Here is one fraction of the class system creating and appropriating wealth through the mechanisms of corporate managerialism. It is also possible to extend this argument to the small firms sector, exemplified in the analysis of small South Hampshire electrical engineering firms (Taylor, 2005). These small firms, too, are a particular class fraction (the petty bourgeoisie) creating personal wealth but with a more limited resource base and with far less well-developed networks, support mechanisms, and norms of conformity. In other words, it can be argued that there is a class-based foundation to the process and scope of being enterprising. Different classes have different vehicles available to them to produce and reproduce their wealth.

4.7 Conclusions: Coalitions and Communities of Practice

This chapter suggests that current conceptualizations of the firm in economic geography are concerned principally with the stylized shell of the legally defined enterprise—the codified outcome of regulation—with the result that the object to be theorized has, in many respects, been transformed into the object that it is possible to regulate. This preoccupation is at the very heart of Hodgson's recent outspoken argument (2002) in which he urges that the only consistent view of the firm that can be employed in theory is this legally defined entity.

This chapter has argued that behind the stylized shells of firms are coalitions of people who in very particular circumstances of time and place deploy bundles of assets to generate personal wealth to the best of their collective ability. And, the process is essentially the same in small firms as in large corporations though, on UK evidence, it is also significantly class based. The empirical examples explored in the chapter offer some limited, initial insights into the processes that create, destroy, and reform these temporary coalitions of people 'being enterprising'. However, what is abundantly clear is that currently we have a very partial and imprecise understanding of the processes operating in and on temporary coalitions of strategic decision-makers working in commercial enterprises, just as we have only limited insights into processes of collective agency.

At first sight, small firms and corporate temporary coalitions might simply be thought of as variants of Lave and Wenger's 'communities of practice' (1998) cast in networks of organizations (Fox 2000). Moreover, it might be asked whether these strategic decision-making coalitions are simply the peak communities of practice in firms that are themselves defined as a 'communities of communities of practice' (Fox 2000). Building on the seminal work of Lave and Wenger (1991), a community of practice is a group of people (professionals) informally bound together (i.e. bound together by choice) who face a common set of problems, engage in a common pursuit of solutions and, as a consequence, learn and build a common store of knowledge. Those communities might be exclusive to a firm or organization or they might cross organizational boundaries in the form of professional associations, for example. In these terms they are, essentially, collaborative and internally cooperative groups. It is also recognized that within them not all members are equal. Established, core members hold the current store of knowledge and newer peripheral recruits perform peripheral legitimated tasks to gain centrality and core status. A community of practice is, therefore, by this line of reasoning, a locus of situated learning. And by extension, in an essentially instrumentalist fashion, this learning is currently seen as a source of competitive advantage in a globalizing knowledge economy (Malmberg and Maskell 2002).

The temporary coalitions of strategic decision-makers explored in this chapter heading SMEs and corporate organizations certainly match, in part, these notions of communities of practice. Corporate boards most definitely have core and peripheral members. At the core are the Chairman/CEO and finance directors. Recruits to boards are socialized into accepted practices and through conformity assume the mantle of board solidarity. SME coalitions have initiators, patriarchs, principal investors, and co-investors at their cores, while peripheral members might be the next generation of the family or even salaried managers who may buy into or even buy out the business.

However, though superficially similar to communities of practice, do strategic temporary coalitions function in the same way? It is argued here that they do not. Instead, dynamic inequality created by goal-seeking collective agency in the pursuit of personal wealth, constantly generates latent tension that is typical of commercial temporary coalitions in both the small firms and corporate sectors. The evidence in this chapter suggests that, not infrequently, managing coalitions in SMEs and corporations have strong internal tensions as members jostle for power that lead to their being constantly formed and re-form. Disaffection and peripherality, not to mention dismissal, in both corporate as well as small firm coalitions, may cause individuals to leave and join another coalition, or to establish their own business. The clearest evidence of this destructive potential is evident in Asian family businesses (Taylor 2002) where family friction can lead to the fracturing and even the collapse of substantial business groups. At the same time, the ageing of coalition members, boredom, and new opportunities add to this dynamic of coalition churn.

Dynamic inequality is also evident in larger firms and corporations which have been labelled by Fox (2000) as communities of communities. From the South Hampshire case studies and The Fosters Brewing Ltd example, it would appear that not all the communities comprising firms are equal, just as members within those communities are not equal. This is somewhat at odds with the ideas of some proponents of communities of practice theory. Amin and Cohendet (2000), for example, maintain that the functioning of decentred organizations relies on effective communication between self-governing units; that is, implied equality between communities within communities. This, however, does not square with Handy's views (1999) on managerial control in large corporations in which he sees the head office of an organization—the peak community, its managing coalition—as wielding a set of hefty reserve powers: the right to provide finance, control information, appoint key personnel, and to invade. In other words, current managerial practice, especially in large organizations, is to centralize control and decentralize responsibility. The peak communities have power and delegate significant responsibility, while subordinate communities have responsibility with only proscribed power.

From the discussion in this chapter it is evident that to better understand and theorize the firm it is important to unpack more fully the processes of control and collective agency that operate within the dynamic contexts of temporary coalitions and communities of practice. In this way it should be possible to more fully grasp the processes of enterprise and people being enterprising.

References

Amin, A. and Cohendet, P. (2000). 'Organisational Learning and Governance Through Embedded Practice', *Journal of Management and Governance*, 4: 93–116.

Armstrong, P. (2001). 'Science, Enterprise and Profit: Ideology in the Knowledge-Driven Economy', *Economy and Society*, 30(4): 524–52.

Archibald, G. C. (ed.) (1971). *The Theory of the Firm*. London: Penguin.

Bantel, K. and Jackson, S. (1989). 'Top Management and Innovations in Banking: Does the Composition of the Top Team Make a Difference?' *Strategic Management Journal*, 10: 107–24.

Bolton Committee (1971). *Committee of Inquiry on Small Firms, Report*. Cmnd 4811. London: HMSO.

Brickley, J., Coles, J., and Terry, R. (1994). 'Outside Directors and the Adoption of Poison Pills', *Journal of Financial Economics*, 35: 371–90.

Chandler, A. D. (1962). *Structure and Strategy*. Cambridge, MA: Harvard University Press.

—— Amatori, F., and Hikino, T. (eds.) (1997). *Big Business and the Wealth of Nations*. Cambridge: Cambridge Univeristy Press.

Chesterman, M. (1977). *Small Businesses*. London: Sweet and Maxwell.

Clegg, S. (1989). *Frameworks of Power*. London: Sage.

Coase, R. H. (1937). 'On the Nature of the Firm', *Economica*, 4: 386–405.

—— (1994). *Essays on Economics and Economists*. Chicago and London: Chicago University Press.

Cyert, R. M. and March J. G. (1963). *A Behavioral Theory of the Firm*. Englewood Cliffs, NJ: Prentice-Hall.

Daily, C. and Dalton, D. (1993). 'Board Directors Leadership and Structure: Control and Performance Implication', *Entrepreneurship: Theory and Practice*, 17: 65–82.

Dicken, P. and Thrift, N. (1992). 'The Organization of Production and the Production of Organization: Why Business Enterprises Matter in the Study of Geographical

Industrialization', *Transactions of the Institute of British Geographers*, New Series, 17: 279-91.

Fagan, R. H. (1990). 'Elders IXL Ltd: Finance Capital and the Geography of Corporate Restructuring', *Environment and Planning A*, 22: 647-66.

Foss, N., Lando, H., and Thomsen, S. (2002). 'The Theory of the Firm', in B. Bouchert and G. de Geest (eds.), *The Handbook of Law and Economics*. Aldershot, UK: Edward Elgar, pp. 1-27.

Fox, S. (2000). 'Communities of Practice, Foucault and Actor-Network Theory', *Journal of Management Studies*, 37: 853-67.

FBG (Fosters's Brewing Group) (1997). *Annual Report*.

—— (1998). *Annual Report*.

—— (1999). *Annual Report*.

FGL (Fosters's Group Limited) (2003). *Annual Report*.

Finkelstein, S. and Hambrick, D. (1990). 'Top-Management-Team Tenure and Organizational Outcomes: The Moderating Role of Managerial Discretion', *Administrative Science Quarterly*, 35: 484-503.

—— —— (1996). *Strategic Leadership: Top Executives and Their Effects on Organizations*. Minneapolis, MS: West Publishing.

Grabher, G. (1993). *The Embedded Firm. On the Socioeconomics of Industrial Networks*. London: Routledge.

—— (2001). 'Ecologies of Creativity. The Group, the Village and the Heterarchic Organisation of the British Advertising Industry', *Environment and Planning A*, 33: 351-74.

Hambrick, D. and Mason, P. (1984). 'Upper Echelons: The Organization as a Reflection of its Top Managers', *Academy of Management Review*, 9: 193-206.

Handy, C. (1999). *Understanding Organizations*. London: Penguin Books.

Haunschild, P. (1993). 'Interorganizational Imitation: The Impact of Interlocks on Corporate Acquisition Activity', *Administrative Science Quarterly*, 38: 564-92.

Hickson, D., Hinings, C., Lee, C., Schneck, R., and Pennings, J. (1971). 'A Strategic Contingencies Theory of Intraorganizational Power', *Administrative Science Quarterly*, 16: 216-29.

Hodgson, G. (1988). *Economics and Institutions: A Manifesto for a Modern Institutional Economics*. Cambridge: Polity Press.

—— (2002). 'The Legal Nature of the Firm and the Myth of the Firm—Market Hybrid', *International Journal of the Economics of Business*, 9: 37-47.

Hill, S. (1995). 'The Social Organization of Boards of Directors', *British Journal of Sociology*, 46: 245-78.

Ibramin, N. and Angelidis, J. (1995). 'The Corporate Social Responsiveness Orientation of Board Members: Are There Differences Between Inside and Outside Directors?', *Journal of Business Ethics*, 14: 405-10.

Lave, J. and Wenger, E. (1991). *Situated Learning: Legitimate Peripheral Participation*. Cambridge: Cambridge University Press.

Lorsch, J. and MacIver, E. (1989). *Pawns and Potentates*. Boston, MA: Harvard Business School Press.

Lovering, J. (1999). 'Thoery Led by Policy: The Inadequacies of "The New Regionalism" ', *International Journal of Urban and Regional Research*, 23: 379–95.

Malmberg, A. and Maskell, P. (2002). 'The Elusive Concept of Localisation Economies: Towards a Knowledge-based Theory of Spatial Clustering', *Environment and Planning A*, 34: 429–49.

Markusen, A. (1999). 'Fuzzy Concepts, Scanty Evidence, Policy Distance: The Case for Rigour and Policy Relevance in Critical Regional Studies', *Regional Studies*, 9: 869–84.

Maskell, P., Eskilinen, H., Hannibalsson, I., Malmberg, A., and Vatne, E. (1998). *Competitveness, Localized Learning and Regional Development—Specialization and Prosperity in Small Open Economies*. London: Routledge.

Massey, D. (1999). 'Space-time, "science" and the Relationship Between Physical Geography and Human Geography', *Transactions of the Institute of British Geographer*, New Series, 24: 261–76.

McDermott, P. and Taylor, M. (1982). *Industrial Organisation and Location*. Cambridge: Cambridge University Press.

McNulty, T. and Pettrigrew, A. (1999). 'Strategists on the Board', *Organization Studies*, 20: 47–74.

Morgan, K. (1997). 'The Learning Region: Institutions, Innovation and Regional Renewal', *Regional Studies*, 31: 491–503.

Nooteboom, B. (1999). 'Innovation, Learning and Industrial Organisation', *Cambridge Journal of Economics*, 23: 127–50.

—— (2003). Stages of Discovery and Entrepreneurship, ERIM Report Series, ERS-2003-028-ORG, Rotterdam School of Management.

Openshaw, S. and Taylor, M. (2002). 'Weakening Ties: The Embeddedness of Small UK Electronics Firms', in M. Taylor and S. Leonard (eds.), *Embedded Enterprise and Social Capital: International Perspectives*. Aldershot, UK: Ashgate.

Penrose, E. (1959). *The Theory of the Growth of the Firm*. Wiley: New York.

Pfeffer, J. (1981). *Power in Organizations*. Boston, MA: Pitman.

Phelps, N. (1997). *Multinationals and European Integration: Trade Investment and Regional Development*. London: Jessica Kingsley Publishers.

Powell, W. and Smith-Doerr, L. (1994). 'Networks and Economic Life', in N. Smelser and R. Swedberg (eds.), *The Handbook of Economic Sociology*. Princeton, NJ: Princeton University Press, pp. 368–402.

Pugh, D. and Hickson, D. (1976). *Organizational Structure in its Context: The Aston Programme I*. Aldershot, UK: Gower.

—— —— (1989). *Writers on Organizations*, 4th edn. London: Penguin Books.

Saxenian, A. (1994). *Regional Advantage: Culture and Competition in Silicon Valley and Route 128*. Cambridge, MA: Harvard University Press.

Schoenberger, E. (1997). *The Cultural Crisis of the Firm*. Cambridge, MA: Blackwell.

Search, P. and Taylor, M. (2002). 'Local Embeddedness and Service Firms: Evidence from Southern England', in M. Taylor and S. Leonard (eds.), *Embedded Enterprise and Social Capital: International Perspectives*. Aldershot, UK: Ashgate.

Smith, K., Smith, K., Olian, J., Sims, H., O'Bannon, D., and Scully, J. (1994). 'Top Management Team Demography and Process: The Role of Social Integration and Communication', *Administrative Science Quarterly*, 39: 412–38.

Starbuck, W. H. (1971). 'Organizational Growth and Development', in W. H. Starbuck (ed.), *Organizational Growth and Development*. London: Penguin Books.

Storper, M. (1997). *The Regional World: Territorial Development in a Global Economy*. New York: Guilford Press.

Swedberg, R. (2000). 'The Social Science View of Entrepreneurship: Introduction and Practical Applications', in R. Swedberg (ed.), *Entrepreneurship: The Social Science View*. Oxford: Oxford University Press, pp. 7–44.

Taylor, M. (1984). 'Industrial Geography and the Business Organisation', in M. Taylor (ed.), *The Geography of Australian Corporate Power*. Sydney: Croom Helm.

—— (1987). 'Technological Change and the Business Organization', in J. Brotchie, P. Hall, and P. Newton (eds.), *The Spatial Impact of Technological Change*. London: Croom Helm, pp. 208–28.

—— (1995). 'The Business Enterprise, Power and Patterns of Geographical Industrialisation', in S. Conti, E. Malecki, and P. Oinas (eds.), *The Industrial Enterprise and Its Environment: Spatial Perspectives*. Aldershot, UK: Avebury.

—— (1996). 'Industrialisation, Enterprise Power and Environmental Change: An Exploration of Concepts', *Environment and Planning A*, 28: 1035–51.

—— (1999). 'The Small Firm as a Temporary Coalition', *Entrepreneurship and Regional Development*, 5: 1–19.

—— (2000). 'Enterprise, Power and Embeddedness: An Empirical Exploration', in E. Vatne and M. Taylor (eds.), *The Networked Firm in a Global World*. Aldershot, UK: Ashgate, pp. 199–234.

—— (2001). 'Enterprise, Embeddedness and Local Growth: Inclusion, Exclusion and Social Capital', in D. Felsenstein and M. Taylor (eds.), *Promoting Local Growth: Process, Practice and Policy*, Aldershot, UK: Ashgate, pp. 11–28.

—— (2002). 'Enterprise, Embeddedness and Exclusion: Business and Development in Fiji', *TESG*, 93: 302–15.

—— (2004). 'The Firm as a Connected, Temporary Coalition', in *Spaces 2004–05*. Philipps-University of Marburg, Germany.

—— (2005). 'Globalization and the Dynamics of Local Embeddedness in the South Hampshire Electronics Industry', in A. Lagendijk and P. Oinas (eds.), *Proximity, Distance and Diversity: Issues on Economic Interaction and Local Development*. Aldershot, UK: Ashgate.

—— and Asheim, B. (2001). 'The Concept of the Firm in Economic Geography', *Economic Geography*, 77: 315–28.

—— and Thrift, N. (1983). 'Business Organisation, Segmentation and Location', *Regional Studies*, 17: 445–65.

The Times (2004). *The Power 100*. 2 November.

Thrift, N. (1998*a*). 'Towards a New Regional Geography', in H. Geghardt, G. Heinritz, A. Mayr, and H. Zepp (eds.), *Berichte zur Deurschen Landeskinde. Leipzig.*

—— (1998*b*). 'The Rise of Soft Capitalism', in A. Herod, G. Ó Tuathail, and S. Roberts (eds.), *An Unruly World? Globalization, Governance and Geography.* London and New York: Routledge.

Uzzi, B. (1996). 'The Sources and Consequences of Embeddedness for the Economic Performance of Organizations: The Network Effect', *American Sociological Review*, 61: 674–98.

—— (1997). 'Social Structure and Competition in Interfirm Networks: The Paradox of Embeddedness', *Administrative Science Quarterly*, 42: 35–67.

Walker, R. (1989). 'A Requiem for Corporate Geography', *Geografiska Annaler*, 71B: 43–68.

Wenger, E. (1998). *Communities of Practice: Learning, Meaning and Identity.* Cambridge: Cambridge University Press.

Westphal, J. and Zajac, E. (1998). 'The Symbolic Management of Stockholders: Corporate Governance Reforms and Shareholder Reactions', *Administrative Science Quarterly*, 43: 127–53.

Williamson, O. E. (1991). 'Comparative Economic Organization: The Analysis of Discrete Structural Alternatives', *Administrative Science Quarterly*, 36: 269–96.

Yeung, H. (2000). Reconceptualising the Firm in New Economic Geographies: An Organisational Perspective, Paper presented to the workshop 'Conceptualising the Firm in Economic Geography', 9–11 March, University of Portsmouth, UK.

Zajac, E. and Westphal, J. (1996). 'Director Reputation, CEO-Board Power and the Dynamics of Board Interlocks', *Administrative Science Quarterly*, 41: 507–529.

Zald, M. (1969). 'The Power and Function of Boards of Directors', *American Journal of Sociology*, 5: 97–111.

5

The Corporation, Shareholder Value Added, and the Power of Financial Management Narratives

Phillip O'Neill

5.1 Introduction

BHP Billiton is the world's largest resources company, although it is a relatively new global corporation having been assembled from the merger of BHP Ltd, a large Australian mining and steel manufacturing company, and Billiton Plc, a UK-listed company with extensive mining histories in southern Africa. Previously, both BHP and Billiton underwent major transformations in structure, assets, and operations during the 1990s. While each of the companies built wealth for its shareholders over many decades, their creation of shareholder wealth was always compromised by other claims on the surplus values they generated including from workers, governments, and local communities; and there have been a variety of means for reconciling these claims. In 2002, BHP Billiton introduced a new yardstick to guide its accumulation ambitions and its distributional flows. The Strategic Framework for the newly merged company announced that BHP Billiton's 'ultimate goal must be to be a core holding for global equity investors' (BHP Billiton Group 2002: 3) thereby positioning the global funds managers as BHP's single most important stakeholder group, a decidedly different relationship to those that historically underpinned both companies.

The history of changes leading to the creation of BHP Billiton provides a valuable case-study opportunity to examine the nature of the modern firm—in particular the way that financial management narratives of the firm, including the calculus of shareholder value added (SVA), are driving contemporary corporate structures, organizational performance, regulatory and performance standards, and the nature and use of management devices.

The first part of this chapter discusses the reasons why defining the firm and its nature is a difficult task. The second part recognizes that the same definitional problem confronting the academic commentator confronts the manager of the firm, who is forever concerned with the production, organizational, financial, and legal domains of what it is to be managed. The third part examines the financial domains as one example of the way that firms are comprised and the issues managers face. The operation of the financial domain is demonstrated by a case study of changing financial management at BHP Billiton and the chapter concludes with implications for alternate accumulation and distributional pathways.

5.2 The Fuzziness of the Firm

Given the dynamic nature of companies as they grow and change, it is not surprising that the *idea* of the firm is a fuzzy thing which defies attempts at clear, enduring definition. Attempts at theoretical definition have been halting.[1] It would be generally agreed that the firm is a vehicle for maintaining relationships between a collection of stakeholders in the management of economic transactions for a range of purposes especially the acquisition of wealth. Yet since the components and purposes of firms are dynamic through time and space, having knowledge of any firm becomes a difficult task. At the very least a firm's boundaries are difficult to discern. Thereafter, knowing exactly what a firm does and how it does it becomes extremely thorny. Little wonder there are many review essays across the social sciences on approaches that have been taken to define and know the firm.[2]

---

[1] Recent economic geography, for instance, sees the firm as a problematic object, a site of shifting power relations embedded in broader discourses and practices (Thrift and Olds 1996; Schoenberger 1997; Yeung 1998; Taylor 1999; Thrift 1999).

[2] For useful reviews of the firm in economic geography see Dicken and Malmberg (2001), Maskell (2001), Taylor and Asheim (2001), and Yeung (2002). For an excellent review of the problematic status of the firm in economics see Schrader (1993). Norton (1995) adds an expert commentary on the neglect of distributional flows within the firm in economic analysis.

Perhaps the firm is viewed in a variety of ways because of uncertainty over the firm's endeavours to resolve competing demands for accumulation and distributional outcomes. Mainstream economics, for instance, has struggled to acknowledge distributional flows (other than as profit) as a normal to a firm's operations. More specifically, neoclassical economics has largely sidestepped the complexity of the firm as a social institution and its engagement in distributional processes. By assigning to the firm the subjectivity of an individual with pure economic agency, neoclassical economics naturalizes the firm as the key agent of accumulation within capitalism and in so doing ensures the continued relevance of the foundational works of Adam Smith and his focus on the growth/accumulation process. Similarly, George Stigler, Milton Friedman, and others from the Chicago School portray the firm as an unproblematic economic subject, undifferentiated from persons and households as rational economic agents in a world explainable by marginal analysis.

Schrader (1993) nominates John Stuart Mill as first to acknowledge the growing complexity of the firm as an entity engaged in the resolution of social claims over distributional flows, an issue arising chiefly from the separation of business management from business ownership. After John Stuart Mill, there was growing interest in economic theory about what the firm is, how it behaves, and the market conditions it constructs, corrupts, and participates within. The works of Jensen and Meckling (e.g. 1976) are a more recent manifestation of understandings about these questions. On another tangent, Schrader shows how in the work of Marshall, Chamberlin, Robinson, and Baumol, the firm required considerably more differentiation and analysis because of the argument that it is through the interplay between firms with specific structures, powers, and actions that market structure is shaped. In summary, Schrader (1993) demonstrates that each version of the theory of the firm in economics has had its own representation, or normative view, of the firm, a representation linked explicitly to the realm of economic behaviour under examination. My interest here is this: just as economic theory of the firm has built representations of firms according to a chosen message about the firm (and the market); we should acknowledge the importance of representational analysis in building knowledge of the firm.

Beyond theory, it is easy to create fuzzy boundaries around the firm as we know it in a day-to-day sense. Yet the use of language is predominantly a process of conveying meaning, so it is not surprising that we (the community at large) have an agreed set of meanings about what the firm actually is. To be a firm requires the exhibition of agreed commonalities.

A firm cannot be just anything, a limitless domain of networks and flows defined according to convenience. Meaning derives from common understandings among language users. At the very least, owners and managers require explicit definitions or common understandings of the thing that is their firm. These commonalities have four key roles: *first*, they secure the firm's legal rights, especially those rights that have evolved from the firm's designation as an autonomous legal subject; *second*, they enable compatibilities between the need to maximize economic cooperation among a firm's stakeholders and the need to maintain opportunities to pursue self interest; *third*, they secure a firm's property and territorial jurisdictions; and *fourth*, they legitimize the firm's right to exploit labour and appropriate surplus values. Critically, those responsible for the firm—especially its owners and managers (but also other stakeholders like employees, host communities, and government authorities)—must enact these roles continuously so common meanings about the firm persist. The way this is done is through the business of talk (Boden 1994). Narratives about the firm are assembled which construct and reconstruct common understandings about firms' rights, organizational arrangements, and jurisdictions. These narratives take particular forms and may be reduced to just four: production and investment narratives, organizational narratives, financial narratives, and legal narratives. Each narrative carries its own logics, unique vocabularies and dedicated calculus. The focus in this chapter is on the logics, vocabularies and calculus of financial narratives. Some preliminary discussion of the four narratives follows while more detailed treatment can be found in Resnick and Wolff (1987), Norton (1995), Gibson-Graham (1996), O'Neill and Gibson-Graham (1999), Gibson-Graham and O'Neill (2001), and O'Neill (2001).

What is meant by the firm, then, appears and fades according to which narrative of the firm a particular interest intersects with. Sometimes these intersections will be simple and linear. The day-to-day interests of waged workers, for instance, intersect predominantly with production and investment narratives of the firm. Managers often frame their view of the firm through organizational narratives. Funds managers concentrate on financial representations of the firm. And in all sorts of disputations—between firms, governments and firms, suppliers and firms, community activists and firms—it is the legal narrative of the firm which constructs the firm and its legitimate domain (or jurisdiction) of interests, rights, and obligations. Of course, it would be rare for production, investment, organizational, financial, and legal representations of the firm to operate as independent representations. Each form of the firm is historically derived and mutually constituted by each other form. The production narrative of the firm, for instance, is a long history of negotiated work arrangements alongside shifts in a firm's productive capital investments, in circumstances overdetermined by legal, financial, and organizational necessities and options. Importantly, what the firm becomes—the common understanding—is the set of performances that are undertaken in the firm's name.

Yet while emphasizing the performative nature of the firm, too much can be made of how deliberative each and every performative act is, a tendency which seems to accompany a number of what have been labelled relational views of the firm especially those concerned with the role of networks of firms in the creation of learning regions and the role of social and cultural networks (such as ethnic and familial connections) in the operation of business. In fact, most performances which create the production, organizational, financial, and legal structures of firms are mundane, repeated acts taken without reference to higher supervision, management, external authority or innate knowledge systems, or without the use of horizontally worked contacts and networks. Much of what happens in firms, and what is encouraged by management, is performance that just happens, generally because that is the way it has happened successfully in the past; the act of repetition freeing a lot of people (be they factory or office worker, supervisor, manager, whatever) from having to become involved in the action. Rather than wanting performances to be innovative, management (mostly with workforce agreement) simply wants the overwhelmingly number of performances within a firm, its norms,[3] to be ones that are anticipated and reproducible *without* need for decision-making input. And this expectation seems to me to apply as much to firms engaged in producing knowledge-intensive goods and services as those which are not.

Tensions arise within firms, however, not over whether stability is a good thing but over the type of circumstances to be stabilized. The choice of circumstances to be patterned results from particular managers' narratives becoming hegemonic. For there are good reasons for managers to

---

[3] Narratives of the enterprise provide a portrait of corporate structure and behaviour *and*, simultaneously, a set of norms to drive a pathway of corporate stability and progress (Fligstein and Freeland 1995). Schoenberger (1997), for example, who sees the firm as 'both a collection of individuals and a self-reproducing institution whose identity is linked with, but not the same as, those of the people who work in it' (pp. 115–16), notes that the management literature often locates the origin of corporate culture in top management and sees the function of culture as integrative, producing stability and consistency in the firm (p. 117).

build hegemonic narratives of performance within a firm since these drive a firm's accumulation and, probably more importantly, its distributional outcomes, including those which advantage managers in particular ways such as through direct remuneration, the allocation of investment funds to particular projects, the maintenance of employment levels in certain divisions, and control over corporate succession arrangements. Hence, because each management narrative produces both an accumulation and a distributional outcome, there will always be a struggle over a narrative's formulation and enactment. Other managers will seek to displace a dominant narrative with another. Employees will contest it in order to claw back a greater proportion of surplus value in all sorts of monetary and non-monetary forms. On the edges of the firm, other stakeholders (shareholders, communities, host environments, state agencies) will want a say in the narratives that drive the firm's operations, and they will focus also on the form and balance of accumulation and distribution options. At any point in time, then, the firm can be shown to be composed of a very deeply institutionalized set of structures, though at every other point in time these will change, driven by a contest of talk over accumulation and distributional outcomes.

5.3 Financial Narratives of the Firm

Financial narratives script and stage the modern corporation and its investment patterns, just like production, investment, organizational, and legal narratives. This part of the chapter briefly explores the shifting *financial* narratives of the firm within the critical accountancy literature.[4] While this literature speaks mainly about accountancy, it serves as an excellent guide to the financial management narrative, with accountancy at its heart. Financial narratives—the package of logics, vocabularies and calculus—produce three outcomes: *first*, they create organizational structures; *second*, they create management devices; and, *third*, they create

---

[4] While a critical approach to accounting practices and financial strategies was developed in the 1950s (e.g. Argyris 1952; Simon, Guetzkow, and Tyndall 1954; Whyte 1955; March and Simon 1958; Wildavsky 1964; a very early insight is Scott 1931; for overview see Birnberg, Turopolec, and Young 1983), its progress seemed to have stalled until the rise of Anthony Hopwood's *Accounting, Organizations and Society* group in the 1970s. Hopwood published his ideas in a major collection of four research books, four edited collections, and over seventy articles over three decades, his portrayal of the discursive effects of accounting languages occupying a radical position in the generally highly conservative publishing field of accounting.

regulatory and performance standards, some of which are internal to the financial community and others which are governance measures imposed on it. The latter are often state-sponsored. These three outcomes of financial management narratives are dealt with in turn.

5.3.1 The Role of Financial Narratives in Creating Organizational Structures

Ever since the headline-capturing takeovers, mergers, and asset stripping ventures of the 1980s, there has been considerable public awareness that financial management, including accounting, plays a powerful role in building the structures and strategies of firms (Hopwood 1987a). Yet the finance story of a firm has always played a key role in constituting the firm. Poovey (1998), for instance, shows how double-entry bookkeeping was devised in the fifteenth century in Italy as a device to create public legitimacy for commercial trading in the face of church-led disquiet, thereby cementing the firm as a legitimate social entity.

Accounting and finance departments have always been integral to firms' structures historically rivalling, in manufacturing firms for instance, production, engineering, and sales departments for their influence on firm behaviours. The introduction of Taylorism to workplaces in the early twentieth century, though, led to the dramatic insertion of accounting practitioners and their instruments into the management of production processes in a way that saw the nature of production redesigned to take account of what financial, especially accounting, narratives dictated. What the firm looked like changed radically. So too, the discovery that idle cash flows internal to a firm gave the firm much potential as a debt-raising and payment device saw profound changes to the structure of firms in the 1980s. These changes not so much shifted individual modes of production—though these modes were certainly changing for technological reasons and in response to rising international market competition—as brought a consciousness to the production manager of the need to capture and steer value creation as quickly and as efficiently as possible. Once again, new ways of doing financial business changed firms' organizational structures, the internal structures of firms being reorganized to mimic financial rather than production representations of the firm.

Meyer writes about the role of accounting in these processes at once foretelling the accounting scandals of the early twenty-first century yet, on a more general level, noting the timeless role of accountants as key architects of firm structures:

> Well why can't they tell the truth (a question often asked about accountants)? Because accounting structures are myths, and important ones, subject to requirements of their own. As myths, they describe the organization as bounded and unified, as rational in technology, as well-controlled and as attaining clear purposes. The myths are important; they help hold the organization together with their justifications...; and they legitimate the organization with the controlling external environment by locating it clearly in environmentally-established categories. (Meyer 1983: 235)

Also in 1983, Hopwood drew attention to the role of accounting in creating hierarchical organizations and confining management attention to economic rationales.[5] Rather than simply measuring firm performance, Hopwood noted the powerfully discursive role of financial and accounting systems in producing organizations and their histories, and coercing firms to take new forms. Through highly technical languages and ostensibly transparent reporting procedures, accounting stories generate organizational power, advance particular stakeholder interests over others, and thereby reconstitute organizational order (Hopwood 1983: 295). Hopwood emphasized the performative nature of this interplay,

> At the individual level, all organizational participants construct their own maps of the organizational terrain, delineating the significant, the problematic and the possible, accounting in their own terms for significant organizational boundaries, what they see to be the centres of power and influence, and those rationales which they think do and ought to influence choices and actions. Even in the sphere of rationalized systems of information and management, a multitude of accounts pervade organizational life. (Hopwood 1983: 298)

---

[5] Certainly accounting is now unchallenged as the base for management of both economic *and* social arrangements in both public and private organizations (Burchell, Chubb, and Hopwood 1980; Miller 1994; see also Poovey 1998). Hopwood (1979, 1987a) gives a detailed account of the development of the accounting profession, its institutionalization and the accompanying rise of a state-sponsored regulatory environment around the supervision of the enterprise. Accounting creates independent measurable concepts quite separate from the problematic economic notions from which concepts such as profit and productivity were originally drawn (Hopwood 1986). By distilling the operations of the organization into accounting categories, accounting plays a major role in elevating certain economic outcomes over others while devaluing many social activities. At the core of this process is the role of the financial narrative in constituting what is held to be economic. Miller (1994: 4) shows how the economic domain is constituted by the changing calculative practices that provide a knowledge of it. By transforming the physical flows of organizations into financial flows, an economic calculus is created through which judgements can be made, strategies devised and justified, and disputes adjudicated.

Financial narratives, built on accounting systems, thus frame modern organizations and dictate their nature and direction. Moreover, they give managers a language to depict disruptive changes as rational and purposeful (Meyer 1983: 235). They create particular social and political ways of governing individuals, activities, and organizations (Hopwood 1992: 125). They aid the development of coercive controls over labour practices and they strive to eliminate otherwise useful behaviours and structures measured as inefficient, even uneconomic (Hopwood 1987a; Burawoy 1979, 1986).

5.3.2 The Role of Financial Narratives in Creating Management Devices

In the delivery of a narrative system that frames and constitutes the enterprise, financial management involves operationalizing a normative core which removes managers from the burden of making each and every decision (Power and Laughlin 1996: 461). A system of financial management focuses managers' attention on a wide range of performance measures (asset values, gearing levels, cash flows, labour costs, and so on) which thereby demand particular behaviours. At the same time, the favoured system de-powers competing narratives that provide other measurement, management, and operational options.

The role of financial management, therefore, is to create a logic, a direction, and a process of change. Each management model constructs a new language, replete with its own formation, representations, vocabulary, and calculus. Financial management, then, is a process of scripting the operations of an organization and the behaviours of its members. The discursive authority of a financial management methodology draws from the ways that it is constructed by sets of micro-politics (Hopwood 1988: p. xxiii). Measuring for SVA, for instance, does much more than simply report economic 'facts'. It translates complex social processes into assayable quantities eliminating the need for further external auditing (Miller 1994: 2). At the same time, it reminds a firm's divisional and line managers of the existence of a wider set of expectations and demands contained within a dominant management model. Of course, these expectations are realized and transmitted through all sorts of business talk conducted across the organization.

As noted, financial narratives play a major role in the constitution of the organization; by reducing complex social events to measurable entities they create possibilities for their reconstitution enabling new organizational arrangements to emerge. In this normative guise, the processes of financial management channel information flows, periodize time, change understandings of the past and reshape options for the future, thereby propelling new organizational behaviours (Hopwood 1987b: 229). Calculative practices permeate and shape organizational concerns, and influence conceptions of the problematic, the desirable, and the possible (Meyer 1983: 235; Hopwood 1988: pp. xxx–xxxi).

5.3.3 Management Narratives Based on Shareholder Value Added

Since the 1980s, financial management narratives have become increasingly dominated by powerful performance scripts seeking the maximization of SVA. Fligstein (2001) traces the emergence of SVA-driven management practices as devices to secure control of a firm in the context of rising numbers of hostile corporate takeovers during the last two decades as corporate raiders sought access to shareholder value locked up within underutilized cash flows, minimally leveraged assets or excess expenditure payments, especially to labour. By the 1990s major accountancy and consultancy firms had devised a range of procedures for measuring the worth of companies via SVA calculation and reporting.[6] The use of SVA calculus became widespread both as internal management devices and as indicators of comparative firm performance to external parties especially funds managers and general audiences via the major financial media. Management remuneration packages were devised which linked SVA maximization to executive incomes. In some instances, these packages, especially where they included share options schemes, became directly linked to an obsession with SVA maximization in the short run including by deliberate manipulation of corporate balance sheets.[7] So

---

[6] Most SVA methodologies have evolved from Rappaport (1986) and include Stern Stewart and Co.'s popular economic value added (EVA) model (Stewart 1991) and the Boston Consulting Group's (1995a, 1995b, 1995c) more complex total shareholder return (TSR) model. The popular feature of Stewart's (1991) EVA methodology is its inclusion of the cost of capital employed in creating free cash flows. Hence, EVA = (rate of return − cost of capital) × capital employed. The Boston Consulting Group's TSR methodology is a more sophisticated attempt at measuring SV because of its use of market valuations of the cost of debt rather than book valuations, its attempt to incorporate an estimate of the residual or closing value of the business at the end of the forecasting period and, importantly, its incorporation of the 'cash flow fade concept' involving the probability that high rates of return will recede to market norms due to erosion by new firm entries and other competitive pressures.

[7] Inquiries into the collapse of trading house Enron in the USA and insurer HIH in Australia have revealed extensive manipulations of accounts including booking recurrent expenditures as capital investment items in order to artificially reduce costs and booking forward sales into current accounts in order to artificially inflate revenues. Paradoxically, what were devised, or at least explained, as means to align the interests of managers and shareholders led directly in some cases, such as Enron and HIH, to the financial collapse of the enterprise and the annihilation of shareholder value.

the practice of managing for SVA has borne considerable criticism recently. Yet the need for firms to be vigilant about maximizing returns to shareholders continues: managers and directors continue SVA maximization as a protection against takeover; and, as is explained below, funds managers demand competitive SVA returns as a prerequisite for the continued place of a stock in a fund's portfolio.

Beyond threats of corporate raiding in the 1980s, concern with shareholder value can be traced to the popularity of a view of the modern corporation as a collection of stakeholders each with various contributions to and claims on value added, a view which evolved from long-standing concern that the operations of the public corporation had been hijacked by management self-interest (e.g. Jensen and Meckling 1976). As Goold, Campbell, and Alexander (1994) note, the stakeholder model of the firm customarily elevates shareholders as the group with primary claim on the corporation. Not surprisingly, then, financial management based on maximizing SVA is seen as the natural accompaniment to the stakeholder model of the firm.

The adoption of maximizing shareholder value[8] as the goal of financial management requires new accounting methodologies. Traditional (accrual) accounting measures were designed to aggregate a firm's financial operations in order to calculate net change in total value. In accrual accounting, a firm's key performance indicators are earnings, some measure of profitability, and earnings per share, showing the relationship between firm performance and market valuation. In short, accrual accounting methodologies measure a firm's historical performance; and (like all histories) they provide management with opportunities to smooth the historical record through the discretionary use of depreciation rates, asset valuations, and write downs.

By contrast, SVA methodologies are used to guide current actions and future pathways. They are designed to determine the contribution to corporate value made by existing and potential investments within a portfolio of investments. SVA methodologies are *assessment* measures rather than reporting measures. They concentrate on determining the extent of a firm's available (or free) cash flows as the means to pay dividends, meet debt obligations, and access capital for new investment opportunities. SVA methodologies also enable the evaluation of new projects by

---

[8] Sometimes called economic value added.

comparing expected net cash flow returns discounted by the cost of the capital needed to generate them. In these ways, SVA methodologies are seen to construct a direct link between the behaviour of corporations and the expectations of shareholders (Barbera and Coyte 1999: 45). Of course, SVA methodologies drive certain norms: managers are compelled to use the model's financial criteria in strategy formation and decision-making, to the exclusion of other criteria; resources are shifted to areas where returns can be maximized, making other investments redundant; and efforts are focused on the sustenance of dividends and the accrual of sharemarket-based capital gains to shareholders rather than on returns to other stakeholder groups. In short, SVA methodologies construct a powerful accounting and management language which prioritizes the aspirations of shareholders, ensures the collaboration of managers, and acts both as a motivational and a disciplining device throughout the enterprise.

At the core of SVA methodologies are an acknowledgement that there are varying levels of uncertainty (or risk) in predicting future earnings and that the value of money changes through time. The calculation of free cash flow is the key to SVA models. An increase in shareholder value takes place when there is an increase in cash flow generated from operations over and above the drain on cash flow due to debt repayments, taxation, and the cost of working capital. Free cash flows are then available for shareholder return through dividends or for the payment of capital costs in reinvestments which increase the future capacity of the enterprise to produce shareholder value.

In conjunction with portfolio management, SVA models construct a view of the firm as a set of separable investments within a portfolio rather than as a set of integrated, complementary value-adding tasks and processes. Increasing SVA involves one of three strategies: improving free cash flow returns from an existing capital base; employing more capital to secure higher rates of free cash flow generation; and discarding poorly performing investments, where the loss of earnings produces higher savings than the cost of capital employed. In other words, SVA methodologies require the division of large post-war industrial conglomerates (like BHP Billiton) into separate accounting entities for measurement and evaluation purposes. Deciding what to sell, reform, or close down proceeds thereafter. Not surprisingly, then, SVA financial management strategies often lead to the break-up of vertically and horizontally integrated firms.

5.3.4 *The Role of Financial Narratives in Creating Regulatory and Performance Standards Within the Financial Community*[9]

Financial models of the enterprise are thus part of an external field of financial discourses and of wider societal discourses of social and economic transformation. Hopwood (1983: 302) notes that financial discourses of the firm are heavily influenced by sociological and political events, themselves heavily implicated in organization-building processes. The legitimacy and survival prospects of a firm, for instance, are enhanced by adopting key financial management practices and procedures consistent with wider political directions and institutional processes. Successful financial management depends on the societal network of practices and discourses in which it is set. Yet, simultaneously, financial management constructs and transforms social institutions, and the (largely economic) truths that are associated with them (Hopwood 1992: 125).[10]

Four major trends in financial markets need to be considered here. *First*, mutual funds, especially pension and superannuation funds own an ever increasing proportion of equity in the world's corporations (Clark 2000). One consequence is that a firm's share price, which determines the conditions for its access to finance, is directly related to the propensity of funds managers to hold that firm's stock in their investment portfolios. *Second*, there is a growing concentration of financial transactions in the world's largest financial centres especially London, New York, and Tokyo, which are also the location of the largest funds management offices (Clark 2002). If a stock is not listed on exchanges in these centres, or if it traded in small volumes to the extent that it is difficult to acquire or discard large share quantities, then it is likely the stock will underperform in share price terms. *Third*, in order to secure sufficient volumes of trading to become prominent in the leading financial centres, thereby securing a place in the funds investment portfolios, there have been rising numbers of mergers and takeovers especially among leading firms. This activity—termed *sector consolidation*—has largely taken place within discrete industrial sectors,

---

[9] The interaction between a corporation's internal financial narrative and wider financial narratives is the subject of more detailed examination elsewhere (O'Neill 2000).

[10] Of course, the intersection of financial narratives and societal talk is enhanced by the status of finance professionals in the wider community, in the political process (Covaleski and Dirsmith 1988), and in the control of large corporations (Fligstein 1990). Accounting, as a technology and an agent of financial management, has become part of the 'institutionalized and rationalized myth structure of society' (Miller 1994: 11) with increasing capacity to overpower other managerial practices and stories within and outside the enterprise. Accounting stories (and their normative hearts) are the intersection of a field of powered-up narratives internal and external to the firm (Power and Laughlin 1996: 460).

Power of Financial Management Narratives

again in response to the way information is collected and portfolios arranged within the major funds and investment houses. *Fourth*, growth in the number of new financial *instruments* has continued, especially in interest rate and currency products, as has the competence of traders in trading in them. Markets in these newer financial instruments compete with share markets for investments forcing the more rapid demise of firms with relatively poorer performing stocks.

In this context, the financial management of a firm will be closely supervised by the wider financial community. The common calculus and vocabularies of the SVA narrative have been major forces in its establishment as the common device used by funds and other trading houses to compare the financial performance of firms especially their ongoing prospects for the delivery of dividends and, especially, capital gains via share price increases.

5.3.5 The Role of Financial Narratives in Creating State-Sponsored Regulatory and Performance Standards

Of course, a key historical role of accounting has been to describe the operations of a firm using fixed, measurable categories in order to meet a firm's public obligations. The payment of a fair rate of taxation, for instance, requires agreed-on categories and procedures for nominating revenues, expenditures, levels of depreciation, and so on; issues of legal ownership and control require monitoring of share sales and transfer; while assessment of a firm's stewardship of natural resources and environmental conditions requires formal public reporting. The financial narratives of a firm, then, intersect with wider public interests and the state has always played a major role here.

5.4 Financial Narratives at BHP and BHP Billiton

BHP Billiton is the world's largest minerals resources company with an annual turnover in 2001–2 exceeding US$17 billion. The company was formed in 2001 following the merger of BHP Ltd, an Australian resources company, and Billiton Plc, a UK resources company with a strong South African heritage. Table 5.1 describes the shifts in financial narratives at BHP and BHP Billiton and is the focus of discussion that follows. Table 5.2 shows the extent of BHP Billiton's global spread by commodity type, source, market, and shareholder base.

Table 5.1. The shift in BHP and BHP Billiton's financial management strategy

Characteristics and instruments	The financial management models	
	The Big Australian model (post war)	The Portfolio Business model (from late 1990s)
Mission	Construction of market power	Creation of shareholder value
Measure	Size (especially assets and earnings)	SVA
Enacting device	Rate of investment and acquisition	Level of free cash flow
Operating horizon	Infinite	Fixed
Internal structure	Integrated production and management systems	Competitive, stand alone projects
External relations	Oligopolistic	Coalitional
Key stakeholder group	National fractions of capital	Global funds

5.4.1 Reform of the Big Australian

BHP Ltd (named from the original Broken Hill Proprietary Company) was a large Australian resources and steel manufacturing company. In 1996, BHP was Australia's largest and most globalized corporation, with operations and offices in fifty-nine countries employing more than 65,000 people. At the time it ranked in the top 200 of the Fortune Global 500 list with over 40 per cent of its cash flow generated outside Australia. From the mid-1990s, however, the corporation suffered disarray and its share price began to fall (see O'Neill 1997, 2000). Stockbroker analysts, backed

Table 5.2. Diversification in BHP Billiton: the world's largest resources company

By commodity	%	By shareholder	%
Petroleum	35	Australia	37
Carbon steel materials	22	UK and Europe	30
Aluminium	13	North America	17
Base metals	12	South Africa	8
Energy coal	9	Asia	6
Steel	7	Other	2
Stainless steel materials	2		
By market	%	By geography	%
Asia/Oceania	47	Australia	37
Europe	24	South America	35
North America	18	Southern Africa	20
Rest of the world	11	Europe	3
		Rest of the world	5

Note: Data for financial year 2001 or at 30 June 2001; shareholder data for 31 December 2001.
Source: Gilbertson (2002).

by financial journalists, demanded improved financial performance. A succession of senior managers and key board members departed the company ending a long tradition of senior management being dominated by engineers and other production-based BHP lifers, invariably Australian. The two new senior appointments, American imports, Chief Executive Officer, Paul Anderson and Chief Financial Officer Charles (Chip) Goodyear,[11] were charged with refocusing BHP away from its historical interest in growth and security towards the maximization of SVA. Anderson and Goodyear quickly overturned BHP's production configurations, asset portfolio, financial returns and share register.

Paradoxically, since the mid-1980s Anderson's and Goodyear's predecessors had devoted considerable management resources to resisting moves by corporate raiders to unlock value circulations within the Big Australian, as BHP became known colloquially, chiefly by a succession of international debt-funded acquisitions (Haigh 1987; Fagan 1990; O'Neill 2001). By the early 1990s, BHP suffered severe debt-overhang which stymied the company's capacity to raise further finance. Meanwhile, many of its offshore acquisitions performed poorly. International accountants KPMG were commissioned to advise on investment options for BHP's capital-starved steel division and oppressive financial stories were inserted. Steel management was forced to adopt new systems of accounting measurement designed to drastically cut unit production costs chiefly through labour intensification practices. New projects were assessed against high rates of returns obtainable in petroleum and minerals investments in a period of buoyant world commodity prices. Only one of BHP's three steel sites, Port Kembla (50 kms south of Sydney in New South Wales), secured substantial capital upgrade funds while old steel assets at Newcastle (100 kms north of Sydney) and Whyalla (in South Australia) were managed by intensification and exhaustion exit strategies (O'Neill 1994; O'Neill 1997; O'Neill and Green 2000). Irrespective of financial improvements in the Steel Division, the financial community attacked the Big Australian and its lifer managers with a viciousness unparalleled in Australian corporate history (O'Neill 2000) leading directly to the replacement of the senior management team.

---

[11] Mr Paul Anderson, from Duke Energy Corporation Inc. in the USA, was appointed Chief Executive Officer (CEO) in November 1998 and Mr Charles (Chip) Goodyear, formerly from Freeport-McMoRan Inc., also in the USA, was appointed chief financial officer (CFO) in March 1999. A third key appointment was Mr Brad Mills, formerly Executive Vice-President Magma Copper Company (USA), who became BHP's Chief Strategic Officer (CSO) in 1999. The CSO position was created to oversee the assessment of new ventures as part of BHP's portfolio management model.

With BHP's new American managers and their focus on SVA came new financial management and accounting systems. The package, labelled by Anderson as a 'portfolio management model', coincided with intense pressure from analysts, financial journalists, and institutional shareholders for the generation of higher levels of free cash flow and for better share price performance:

The company's objective is to deliver superior shareholder value. We have strengthened our focus on earnings per share and cash flow per share growth. At a portfolio level, we have two performance measures. The first is to achieve at least an average 12 per cent return on capital over the five-year period to June 2004. We also intend managing the portfolio to generate a net positive cash flow before dividends and funding every year. The main strategic components by which we seek to deliver our shareholder value objectives are:

1. the implementation of new business models and a major cultural change process
2. the delivery of operational excellence
3. active portfolio management
4. the delivery of significant value creating growth. (Anderson 2000)

BHP in the future is going to be depending on people and relationships that are focused on one single thing, and that thing has got to be value. It is not tonnes, it is not pounds, it is not barrels, it is nothing other than that value, and value as we define it is going to be creating a return that is net in excess of the cost of the capital that it takes to get that return ... The old model of saying we find it, we operate it and we close it isn't necessarily the best model for the BHP of the future. (Goodyear 1999)

The portfolio management model sees the firm as based around a core of decision-makers with the task of building and operating a set (or portfolio) of discrete investments with performances judged against common criteria (Goold, Campbell, and Alexander 1994). The introduction of a portfolio management model at BHP resulted in broad ranging reforms to management and financial practices. On appointment, Anderson and Goodyear moved quickly to focus on shareholder value creation through the extraction of returns from BHP's existing balance sheet, rather than from new ventures. Notable were substantial write downs of BHP assets (A$5.5 billion during 1999), asset sales (A$4 billion for the three years to June 2001), the booking of negative profit results,[12] restructured debt

---

[12] Under accrual accounting, write downs are funded from a diversion of earnings away from profits. Large write downs, then, have a major negative impact on reported profit levels.

arrangements, and cash flow management (BHP Ltd 2000); all devices recognized by financial analysts as moves to enhance SVA.

The jobs impact of the strategy was severe: BHP's global employment fell from 61,000 people to under 35,000 between 1998 and 2001 chiefly through the closure of the Newcastle steelworks and the San Manuel copper facilities in Arizona, USA, business sales and general downsizing and intensification. A restructured balance sheet produced lower gearing levels and access to new sources of debt-finance for new ventures.

The dramatic changes were driven by Anderson's three-phase strategy for creating shareholder value at BHP (Anderson 1999; Stevens 2000). The first phase involved closures and sales of assets that failed to meet criteria for inclusion in the company's portfolio. The second phase involved the institution of strategies to improve returns available from retained assets. The third phase, seeking investment in new high performing assets, was superseded by BHP's merger with Billiton. In any event, Anderson and Goodyear demanded the replacement of pre-existing management behaviours within BHP with financial management strategies designed explicitly to improve shareholder value.

The advancement of shareholder value, then, became BHP's mission statement under the portfolio management model, displacing the drive for market power (through earnings and asset growth) which previously dominated management of the Big Australian. Of course, like any financial management strategy, SVA methodologies within BHP involved a very small number of indicators of economic performance and focused on only a small portion of the possible domains of management action. So while Anderson's and Goodyear's statements were very explicit guides to BHP managers for making decisions about write downs, closures, sell offs, and shifts in debt arrangements, they required the company's divisional and operational managers to second guess follow-on decisions about such things as cost cutting programmes, mining and processing technologies, workplace relations, competitive behaviours in localized markets, maintenance of mature investments, the length of investment life cycles, access to state-controlled mining and drilling leases and so on. The attraction of the variables measured directly by SVA methodologies, of course, is that they are indicators which respond readily to balance sheet clean-outs, leading quickly to improvements in a corporation's share price to appease an antagonistic investment community. And the adoption of SVA calculus ensured that management action in all other domains proceeded in step, obedient to the Anderson–Goodyear management narrative.

Yet institutional investors remained wary. After a short-term rally associated with the balance sheet clean-out, share prices performed below the expectations of new management. During the year 2000, BHP's market capitalization slumped as traders provided glib assessments of the company's prospects and of the prospects of resources stock in general (Kohler 2000: 56). Despite concentrated efforts to propel BHP's new financial story to analysts and institutional investors, Anderson and Goodyear could not counter the market's disinterest in an old economy stock.

5.4.2 The Insertion of BHP into the Orbit of the Global Funds Managers

BHP Ltd and Billiton Plc agreed to merge their operations in March 2001 and received all regulatory approvals to enable dual listings on the London and Sydney stock exchanges on 29 June 2001. Financial commentators commonly drew attention to the merger as another instance of accelerating consolidation within the world mining industry (Figure 5.1). In 1990 the world's top five minerals companies accounted for 24 per cent of total equity in the resources segments of the world's leading markets but by 2002 the share of the top five companies rose to 47 per cent of the resources aggregate, a growth produced by takeovers and mergers (Goodyear 2002).

There are two prime reasons for this sector consolidation. *First*, there is the need by minerals companies to gain portfolio recognition by large institutional investors. To be seen by funds managers as an essential part of an investment portfolio is to be guaranteed consistent demand for shareholding thereby ensuring a steady, perhaps rising, share price. Firms which have sufficient market capitalization and high volumes of daily trading to warrant inclusion in share market indices (especially the FTSE All-Share Index) will be more likely to be held by funds managers who commonly 'track' a sharemarket index as a guide to portfolio makeup. *Second*, as a consequence of having substantial market capitalization, of having stock that is seen as highly liquid (because it is readily tradeable) and of having a presence in a key financial centre like London, a company substantially improves its access to competitively priced global finance markets.

Once operational as a single company, BHP Billiton was astonishingly open about its desire to forge a close financial relationship with the world's key funds managers in order to secure the share price and financial access advantages flowing from such a relationship. The group's new vision statement contains the usual lofty aspirations,

BHP Billiton aspires to be one of the world's premier companies. This will be accomplished by delivering upon our vision to earn superior returns for our

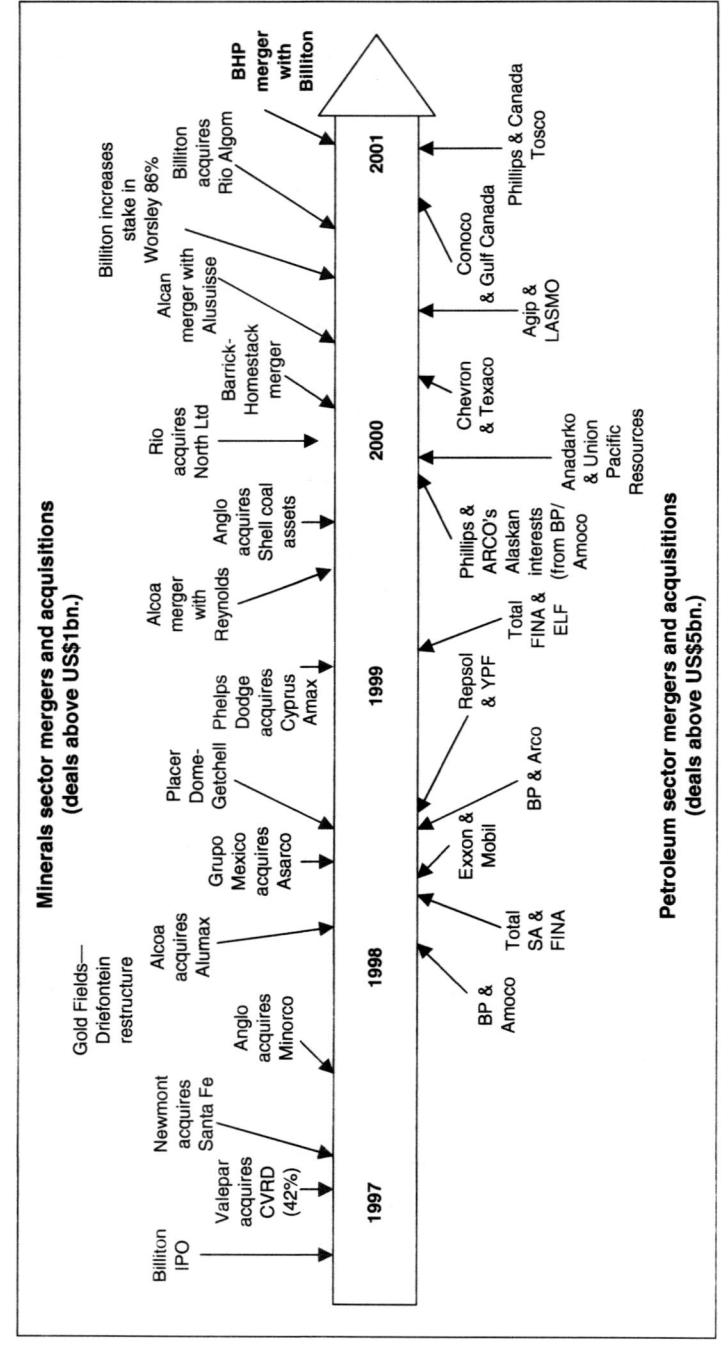

Figure 5.1: Industry consolidation in the world's minerals and petroleum industries 1997–2001.
Source: Goodyear (2002).

shareholders as the world's premier supplier of natural resources and related products and services. (BHP Billiton Group 2002)

The group then reveals its prime objective for realizing this vision being,

The delivery of superior total shareholder returns through a focus on Net Present Value (NPV) enhancement, sustainable returns above the costs of capital and free cash flow generation. This is associated with a recognition that *the Group's ultimate goal must be to be a core holding for global equity investors*. (BHP Billiton Group 2002, emphasis added)

Thereafter in order to impress 'global equity investors' the document outlines the key strategies the group is pursuing in its attempt to strive for SVA maximization across a complex resources portfolio, viz, clear intelligible financial performance measures for assessment of productive assets, inventories, marketing, and innovation activity; a derived organizational structure; and disciplines for capital management including for management of financial risk. What is apparent, then, is the continuity in the group's emphasis on financial outcomes from the portfolio management strategies, with their focus on maximizing shareholder value, commenced by Anderson and Goodyear at BHP. What has been added, though, is a redefinition of what is seen as the target shareholding group, a redefinition now centred on the global equity investors.

A dual listing of the group's stock in London, as well as Sydney, was a logical first step. London is host to the most international of the world's financial markets and the most powerful of the world's stock markets. The London stock exchange lists nearly 500 non-UK company stocks and conducts more than twice the volume of trading in international equities than the NASDAQ, NYSE, Deutsche Bourse, and Euronext exchanges combined. The London Metals Exchange is the world's leading non-ferrous metals markets and attracts its own pool of research companies specializing in minerals analysis. London's International Petroleum Exchange is Europe's leading energy futures and options exchange (petroleum is also a key asset in the BHP Billiton portfolio). In terms of foreign exchange management, including hedging in a volatile minerals pricing market, London hosts the largest number of foreign banks (481 in 2000) for any city in the world and is the site for over one third of the global total of forex trades per day (about US$637 billion).[13]

---

[13] Data on London's financial role are extracted from websites for the London Stock Exchange, the UK Parliament, the Corporation of London, the UK Department of Trade and Industry, and the London Metals Exchange.

Importantly, a London base and stock exchange listing provides BHP Billiton with access to the world's biggest store of investment funds through the city's funds management institutions. The world's largest financial houses, irrespective of national base, manage their global securities operations from London. These include UBS Warburg, Deutsche Bank, CSFB, Morgan Stanley, ABN Amro, and WestLB Panmure. It is estimated that 73.8 per cent of the assets managed by London's international funds managers, including this list of notables, are foreign owned (FMA 2001).

A consequence for BHP Billiton of this commitment to attract the interest of the global funds as key owners and finance providers is that CEO Anderson and his replacement since mid-2002, Brian Gilbertson (former Billiton Plc CEO), have had a continuing set of international engagements as speakers to investment conferences and funds managers meetings. Perhaps more importantly, BHP Billiton's pitch to the funds locks the company into its SVA-based financial management narrative, and the extraordinary level of public data production and revelation and the deep penetration of SVA calculus and practices throughout the organization that ensue. In terms of accumulation strategy, this penetration has brought a set of common benchmarks for investment returns to all BHP Billiton divisions. In terms of distributional outcomes, it has severely diminished arguments for alternate distributional returns including to competing stakeholders: local communities and labour in particular. Two examples are illustrative: BHP Billiton has abandoned its ownership of the Ok Tedi copper and gold mines in Papua New Guinea's Western Province concerned at the drain on earnings due to liabilities for ongoing environmental damage; and BHP Billiton has floated off its Australian steel manufacturing interests where complex distributional issues involving organized labour and historically built political relationships required considerable hands-on management. In short, BHP Billiton is conscious of avoiding analytical difficulties for London-based funds managers who seek to list BHP Billiton unproblematically as a global resources company.

5.5 Discussion and Conclusions

So, new financial and accounting approaches at BHP Billiton have constructed new organizational structures, new management methods, and new investment patterns, alongside rationalizations and closures. Knowing the financial narrative, then, is critical to knowing the geographies of accumulation and distribution pursued by the corporations. BHP Billiton's courtship of the funds and its preparedness to shift the organizational makeup of the group to take on a major London presence can be seen as new expressions of the power of the financial narrative.

There are important consequences to be considered as a result. While the stakeholder model of the firm, with its SVA focus, can be attractive to the investment community seeking control of managers over distributive rights a priori (agency costs), investors (funds managers) are not necessarily attracted to an embracing stakeholder model which might recognize the legitimacy of workers' demands for decent wages and working conditions, management largesse, community petitions for social and environmental benefits, governments' desire for mutually beneficial partnerships, and customers' insistence on quality, service, and value for money. Outcomes from such an embracing view might reasonably include progressive industrial relations practices, enforceable ethics guidelines, effective corporate governance policies, and the satisfaction of community obligations. BHP Billiton's embrace of the London financial community, its languages and aspirations, is a move away from such considerations.

As noted earlier, the portfolio management model confines attention to a small set of measurable outcomes with a reliance on divisional and operational managers to second guess ideal strategies for corporate domains not explicitly defined in the Anderson–Goodyear–Gilbertson master plan. This partiality produces problems. At a general level, the drive to align shareholder and management interests through SVA financial management systems, with an explicit use of the calculus of global funds managers, automatically excludes or marginalizes other stakeholder claims. More specifically, the concentration of SVA analysis on quantifiable categories devalues what Barbera and Coyte (1999: 46) term 'soft assets' such as organizational capabilities, cultures, learning abilities, and creative capacities. Thus a potential consequence of the narrowing of the organization through SVA methodologies might be the generation of instability. On the one hand, shareholders demand the maximization of returns in defiance of nurturing organizational capabilities. On the other hand, as proponents of the learning organization have observed (e.g. Brown and Duguid 1995), the neglect of soft assets may stall the creation of shareholder value, a paradox for the proponents of SVA methodologies to ponder.

The volatility inside and outside corporations that financial narratives seek in vain to temper opens up an analytical possibility. In this chapter they suggest questions such as: what accounting narratives have dominated the BHP Billiton group and its parent firms from time to time; how were they unsettled; what production and investment disruptions resulted; how were financial narratives replaced; what were the tendencies towards instability and abnormality; how were new normalizing/normatizing narratives assembled?

The volatility also shows that there has always been a financial turn in the corporation, a narrative assembled and propagated, guiding management decisions on both day-to-day operations and on new investments, a practical guide and a normative heart. These financial stories are recoverable and can be analysed to show their derivation and effects. At times they co-exist with and build other management stories—engineering, organizational, legal, even social. Sometimes they are brutally obliterating, driving change and silencing protest.

It would be wrong, though, to suppose that the financial narrative of the enterprise is always thus. Like the construction of any discourse, building a financial narrative is a complex and uncertain event. First, it must compete with other narratives of change and stability inside the enterprise. Second, it must concur or mould external stories, those from markets, governments, competitors, even indigenous groups and environmental protestors.

So simultaneously, the accounting and financial narrative is powerful but uncertain. On the one hand, crisis can emerge from the incapacity of an existing accounting framework to accommodate and subsume both internally and externally generated forces; on the other, a replacement financial narrative can be empowered by crisis and alternative corporate change models suppressed or deferred for more certain times.

Still, there is no guarantee of enduring success for any financial narrative just because it successfully replaces pre-existing management stories. The narrative must drive an organizational form as well as guide management decision-making within the enterprise (i.e. get the 'micro-politics' right) and find a place within the current of externally generated financial stories. Hegemonic status for any financial narrative is never guaranteed. Certainly Anderson and Goodyear produced SVA from their balance sheet clean-out at BHP. And, with Gilbertson, the BHP Billiton merger has immediately placed the group firmly on the 'buy' lists of the leading funds. But the narrative will eventually be tested by the way it creates new accumulation and distributional outcomes acceptable to its investment community (now largely the funds) involving the selection of new investment alternatives from an infinite and ultimately unknowable set of investment futures; and a vigilant internal and external audience will be on hand to pass judgement, an audience alerted increasingly by BHP Billiton's own desires to have its financial narratives judged publicly.

The reflexive nature of the development of the enterprise's financial narrative also raises the broader question about realizing the corporation's potential as a 'public sphere' (Deetz 1992; Power and Laughlin 1996), a potential enlivened by debates about corporate governance, rights of access to information, mutual and social obligations, philanthropy, and so on. In such complex issues, it is clear that an understanding of the dynamics of the financial narrative is critical to opening the enterprise to broader and more socially responsible agendas. Thus the examination of the BHP Billiton experiences in this chapter draws attention to the potential of financial stories as practices 'for realizing new organizational realities, latent but not yet active' (Power and Laughlin 1996: 461). Of course, the antisocial application of new financial management principles into public sector organization and management has disenchanted the wider public with such exercises. Economic rationalist arguments and measures are not popular. Yet, BHP Billiton's productive and financial history demonstrates that the enterprise, and its accumulation and distributional functions, are founded on broader, often unstated, social contracts. Power and Laughlin articulate an agenda here,

... the creation of new facts around the organization which challenge and disturb the factual universe of strategic decision making may provide the basis for realizing counter-factual elements of organizational life. New accountings ... could provide the possibility for new domains of intra-organizational communicative action, new forms of linkage between formal and lifeworld organizational structures and new conceptions of the boundaries between organizations and their natural and social environments. (Power and Laughlin 1996: 461)

It is an ambitious agenda. The point to be made here is that is underpinned by understanding the ways that we construct financial accounts of enterprises and managers and their behaviours.

Acknowledgements

Funding for this research has been provided by Australian Research Council Large Grant A79802359. Research assistance was provided by Natalie Moore and helpful comments were provided by participants at the Workshop on the Firm in Economic Geography, University of Portsmouth, 9–11 March 2000. All are much appreciated.

References

Anderson, P. (1999). *Interim Results Announcement, Briefing to Media*, 25 June, transcript provided by BHP Ltd, Melbourne.

—— (2000). *Address to the Securities Institute of Australia*, Melbourne, 28 February, transcript provided by BHP Ltd, Melbourne.

Argyris, C. (1952). *The Impacts of Budgets on People*, School of Business and Public Administration, Cornell University, New York.

Barbera, M. and Coyte, R. (1999). *Shareholder Value Demystified: An Explanation of Methodologies and Use*. Sydney: University of NSW Press.

BHP Billiton Group (2002). *Strategic Framework Briefing Paper*, April, mimeo available from BHP Billiton, 600 Bourke St, Melbourne, Vic., 3001.

BHP Ltd (2000). *Briefing Paper: BHP Strategic Framework & Performance Measures*. Melbourne: BHP Investor Relations.

Birnberg, J. G., Turopolec, L., and Young, M. S. (1983). 'The Organizational Context of Accounting', *Accounting, Organizations and Society*, 8: 111–29.

Boden, D. (1994). *The Business of Talk: Organizations in Action*. Cambridge: Polity Press.

Boston Consulting Group (1995a). *Financial Benchmarking*. Managing for Value Series, 1 (BCG1). Boston, MA: Boston Consulting Group.

—— (1995b). *Shareholder Value Metrics*, Managing for Value Series, 2 (BCG2). Boston, MA: Boston Consulting Group.

—— (1995c). *Estimating the Cost of Capital*, Managing for Value Series, 3 (BCG3). Boston, MA: Boston Consulting Group.

Brown, J. S. and Duguid, P. (1995). 'Organizational Learning and "Communities-of-Practice"', in M. D. Cohen and L. S. Sproull (eds.), *Organizational Learning*, London: Sage, pp. 76–92.

Burawoy, M. (1979). *Manufacturing Consent: Changes in the Labor Process Under Monopoly Capitalism*. Chicago, IL: University of Chicago Press.

—— (1986). *The Politics of Production*. London: Verso.

Burchell, S., Chubb, C., and Hopwood, A. G. (1980). 'Accounting in its Social Context: Towards a History of Value Added in the United Kingdom', *Accounting, Organizations and Society*, 10: 381–413.

Clark, G. L. (2000). *Pension Fund Capitalism*. Oxford: Oxford University Press.

—— (2002). 'London in the European Financial Services Industry: Locational Advantage and Product Complementarities', *Journal of Economic Geography*, 2: 433–53.

Covaleski, M. A. and Dirsmith, M. W. (1988). 'An Institutional Perspective on the Rise, Social Transformation and Fall of a University Budget Category', *Administrative Science Quarterly*, 33: 562–87.

Deetz, S. (1992). *Democracy in an Age of Corporate Colonization*. New York: SUNY Press.

Dicken, P. and Malmberg, A. (2001). 'Firms in Territories: A Relational Perspective', *Economic Geography*, 77: 345–63.

Fagan, R. H. (1990). 'Elders IXL Ltd: Finance Capital and the Geography of Corporate Restructuring', *Environment and Planning A*, 22: 647–66.

Fligstein, N. (1990). *The Transformation of Corporate Control*. Cambridge, MA: Harvard University Press.

—— (2001). *The Architecture of Markets: An Economic Sociology of Twenty-First-Century Capitalist Societies*. Princeton, NJ: Princeton University Press.

—— and Freeland, R. (1995). 'Theoretical and Comparative Perspectives on Corporate Organization', *Annual Review of Sociology*, 21: 21–43.

Fund Managers' Association (FMA) (2001). *Fund Management Survey 2000*, February 2001, mimeo available from Investment Management Association, 65 Kingsway, London, WC2B 6TD, UK.

Gibson-Graham, J. K. (1996). *The End of Capitalism (As We Knew It): A Feminist critique of Political Economy*. Oxford: Blackwell.

—— and O'Neill, P. M. (2001). 'Exploring a New Class Politics of Enterprise', in J. K Gibson-Graham, S. Resnick, and R. Wolff (eds.), *Re/Presenting Class: Essays in Postmodern Marxism*, Durham, NC: Duke University Press, pp. 56–80.

Gilbertson, B. (BHP Billiton CEO) (2002). *Fairy Tales for Investors: Presentation to J. P. Morgan CEO Conference*, Lake Como, Italy, April 2002, mimeo available from BHP Billiton, 600 Bourke St, Melbourne, Vic., 3001.

Goodyear, C. W. (BHP Chief Financial Officer) (1999). *Financial Strategies and Statistics: Business Briefings*, August, transcript provided by BHP Ltd, Melbourne.

—— (BHP Billiton Chief Development Officer) (2002). *Industry Trends: Consolidation and Diversification, A Presentation to the Morgan Stanley Basic Materials Conference*, London, September 2002, mimeo available from BHP Billiton, 600 Bourke St, Melbourne, Vic., 3001.

Goold, M., Campbell, A., and Alexander, M. (1994). *Corporate Level Strategy: Creating Value in the Multi-business Company*. New York: John Wiley & Sons.

Haigh, G. (1987). *The Battle for BHP*. Melbourne: Allen & Unwin.

Hopwood, A. G. (1979). 'Criteria of Corporate Effectiveness', in M. Brodie and M. Bennett (eds.), *Managerial Effectiveness*. London: Thames Valley Regional Management Centre, pp. 81–96.

—— (1983). 'On Trying to Study Accounting in the Contexts in Which it Operates', *Accounting, Organizations and Society*, 8: 287–305.

—— (1986). 'Economics and the Regime of the Calculative', in S. Bodington, M. George, and J. Michaelson (eds.), *Developing the Social Useful Economy*. London: Macmillan pp. 69–77.

—— (1987*a*). 'Accounting and Organizational Action', in B. E. Cushing (ed.), *Accounting and Culture*. New York: American Accounting Association, pp. 50–63.

—— (1987*b*). 'The Archaeology of Accounting Systems', *Accounting, Organizations and Society*, 12: 207–34.

Hopwood, A. G. (1988). 'Observing the Accounting Craft: An Introduction', in A. G. Hopwood (ed.), *Accounting from the Outside: The Collected Papers of Anthony G. Hopwood*. Garland, New York, London: pp. xv–xxxiii.

—— (1992). 'Accounting Calculation and the Shifting Sphere of the Economic', *European Accounting Review*, 17: 125–43.

Jensen, M. C. and Meckling, W. H. (1976). 'Theory of the Firm: Managerial Behaviour, Agency Costs and Ownership Structure', *Journal of Financial Economics*, 3: 305–60.

Kohler, A. (2000). 'Divided, Resources Won't Rule', *Australian Financial Review*, 26 February, 56.

March, J. G. and Simon, H. A. with the collaboration of Guetzkow, H. (1958). *Organizations*. Wiley: New York.

Maskell, P. (2001). 'The Firm in Economic Geography', *Economic Geography*, 77: 329–44.

Meyer, J. W. (1983). 'On the Celebration of Rationality: Some Comments on Boland and Pondy', *Accounting, Organizations and Society*, 8: 235–40.

Miller, P. (1994). 'Accounting as Social and Institutional Practice: An Introduction', in A. G. Hopwood and P. Miller (eds.), *Accounting as Social and Institutional Practice*. Cambridge: Cambridge University Press, pp. 1–39.

Norton, B. (1995). 'The Theory of Monopoly Capitalism and Classical Economics', *History of Political Economy*, 27: 737–53.

O'Neill, P. M. (1994). *Capital, Regulation and Region: Restructuring and Internationalisation in the Hunter Valley, NSW*, unpublished PhD thesis, School of Earth Sciences, Macquarie University, NSW.

—— (1997). 'So What Is Internationalisation? Lessons from Restructuring at Australia's "Mother Plant"', in M. Taylor and S. Conti (eds.), *Interdependent and Uneven Development: Global-Local Perspectives*. Aldershot, UK: Ashgate, pp. 283–308.

—— (2000). 'On the Corporate Drip: Analysts, Journalists, Managers and Stories of Shareholder Value', Paper presented to the Global Conference on Economic Geography, 5–9 December, University of Singapore, mimeo available from the author, School of Geosciences, The University of Newcastle, NSW.

—— (2001). 'Financial Narratives of the Modern Corporation', *Journal of Economic Geography*, 1: 111–29.

—— and Gibson-Graham J. K. (1999). 'Enterprise Discourse and Executive Talk: Stories that Destabilize the Company', *Transactions of the Institute of British Geographers*, New Series, 24: 11–22.

—— and Green, R. (2000). 'Global Economy, Local Jobs', in P. McManus, P. M. O'Neill, and R. Loughran (eds.), *Journeys: The Making of the Hunter Region*. Sydney: Allen & Unwin.

Poovey, M. (1998). *A History of the Modern Fact: Problems of Knowledge in the Sciences of Wealth and Society*. Chicago and London: University of Chicago Press.

Power, M. and Laughlin, R. (1996). 'Habermas, Law and Accounting', *Accounting, Organisations and Society*, 21: 441–65.

Rappaport, A. (1986). *Creating Shareholder Value: The New Standard for Business Performance*. New York: Free Press.

Resnick, S. A. and Wolff, R. D. (1987). *Knowledge and Class: A Marxian Critique of Political Economy*. Chicago, IL: University of Chicago Press.

Schoenberger, E. (1997). *The Cultural Crisis of the Firm*. Oxford: Blackwell.

Schrader, D. E. (1993). *The Corporation as Anomaly*. Cambridge: Cambridge University Press.

Scott, D. R. (1931). *The Cultural Significance of Accounts*. H. Holt, New York, reprinted Scholars Book Co., Houston, 1973.

Simon, H. A., Guetzkow, G. K., and Tyndall, G. (1954). *Centralization vs Decentralization in Organizing the Controller's Department*. New York: American Books & Stratford Press.

Stevens, M. (2000). 'The Big American', *The Australian Magazine*, 19: 19–20 February: 18–23.

Stewart, G. B. (1991). *The Quest for Value: A Guide for Senior Managers*. New York: Harper Business.

Taylor, M. (1999). 'The Small Firm as a Temporary Coalition', *Entrepreneurship and Regional Development*, 11: 1–19.

—— and Asheim, B. (2001). 'The Concept of the Firm in Economic Geography', *Economic Geography*, 77: 315–28.

Thrift, N. and Olds, K. (1996). 'Refiguring the Economic in Economic Geography', *Progress in Human Geography*, 3: 311–37.

—— (1999). 'The Place of Complexity', *Theory, Culture & Society*, 16: 31–69.

Whyte, W. F. (1955). *Money and Motivation*. New York: Harper & Row.

Wildavsky, A. (1964). *The Politics of the Budgetary Process*. Boston, MA: Little & Brown.

Yeung, H. W. (1998). 'The Social-Spatial Constitution of Business Organizations: A Geographical Perspective', *Organization*, 5: 101–28.

—— (2002). 'Producing "the Firm" in Industrial Geography III: Industrial Restructuring and Labour Markets', *Progress in Human Geography*, 26: 366–78.

Part IV
The 'Political' Firm and the State

6
Distortions in Industrial Geography: Triangulating Among Industrial Firms, Financial Firms, and the State

Ann Markusen

6.1 Introduction

Using variants of location theory, economic geographers have long focused on industrial (both goods and service) firm behaviour as a major force in spatial patterns of industry across regions and nations. Employing cost and profit maximization theories on the one hand, and working with agglomeration theory on the other, they offer a fairly coherent version of firm logic in deciding where to place production and related activities spatially. In this chapter, I explore two other significant actors in the contemporary economy: financial firms and the nation state. I argue that these latter two sets of actors play powerful roles in shaping industrial firm strategy, with marked effects on locational outcomes. I suggest that triangulation among the three sets of actors occurs in many spheres of activity and that although it is difficult to theorize satisfactorily about the spatial priorities of the latter two sets of actors, they nonetheless weigh in and may seriously distort the distribution of economic activity over space.

The central argument of this chapter is that financial firms, seeking short-term returns, may induce economic and geographical restructuring which would not have otherwise taken place. They may, as well, be more successful in pressing for favourable government policies than industrial firms, and the latter may be brought on board in a unified strategy. The

Distortions in Industrial Geography

financial firms in question may not explicitly take up spatial concerns, leaving these to industrial firms, but their priorities and actions may trump the locational preferences of industrial managers. Governmental actors and agencies have a more complicated impact on this process. They also undertake initiatives with spatial consequences. Furthermore, some of them exhibit explicit spatial concerns: members of legislatures and parliaments, in particular, care about territorial consequences of different state policies where politicians' bases are fundamentally territorial.

To probe these relationships, I have chosen to focus on the aerospace industry in the USA, a large, mature industrial sector with government and commercial customers, an income-elastic product line, and ongoing innovation of major proportions. Dramatic redistribution of aerospace production capacity has taken place within and outside of the USA in the past two decades, and these changes cannot be adequately explained on the basis of industrial location theory. Any adequate account, I argue, must admit the financial and state sectors into the analysis, which means probing internal hierarchies and struggles between and among top-level industrial managers with conflicting missions and between and among actors in the financial and state sectors, levels of analyses rarely attempted in economic geography. (Exceptions include Schoenberger's intriguing study (1997) of Lockheed's northern and southern California operations in the early post-Second World War period and Clark's probe (1989) of conflicts among national and local union leaders over plant closings in places like Allenstown and Kenosha.) I focus particularly on the dominant role of finance capital in fashioning contemporary mega-mergers and the resulting distortionary impact on economic geographical outcomes. I believe my analysis is relevant to other sectors undergoing consolidation and monopolization.

6.2 Financial Versus Industrial Firms

The distinction between capital invested in production and that invested in circulation activities was well made by Marx. Unfortunately, the normative priority Marx placed on industrial capital influenced a generation of economic geographers to focus chiefly on firms that directly produce goods and services, rather than those which finance the processes of investment and distribution. Scholarly comparisons of competitive performance of Japanese, European, and American firms in the 1980s and early 1990s began to focus on a fundamental institutional difference between the three continents—that American firms were subjected to higher profit expectations than their counterparts abroad (Poterba and Summers 1991; Porter 1992; Harrison 1994). Yet even in these accounts, financial firms tended to get short shrift. Consider this summary of the Poterba and Summers' findings by Harrison:

> They found that U.S. investors tend to demand considerably higher minimum acceptable rates of return for their capital—so-called hurdle rates—than do their foreign competitors. This behavior on the part of American investors is way out of whack... (1994: 184)

This statement assumes that all investors in American firms are Americans, and it reads as if there are no firms occupying the space between atomistic investors and firms who borrow money capital.

In reality, there are a large number of firms operating in the market for money capital. Industrial, construction, or service firms who wish to borrow money to innovate, expand, acquire existing firms, build a new plant or office tower, or cover inventory turn to financial firms for the cash to do so, which can be procured through diverse means: initial or new stock offerings, bonds, and loans of various sorts. They also use financial firms' services to invest retained earnings in anticipation of future investments or for short-term asset management. At the peak of this hierarchy, '... are the "bulge bracket" underwriting and trading monsters like Morgan Stanley and Goldman Sachs. They bring forth new securities issues to their customers, and trade them for their own and their customers' accounts' (Henwood 1997: 82).

Simply put, the fundamental difference between the two types of firms is that financial firms make money on the turnover of money capital and assets, while industrial and service firms make money by successfully creating and selling products and services which more than cover the costs of doing so. The short-termism so heavily criticized in the competitiveness literature is ascribable to the separation, or externalization, of finance from management in the American industrial firm, and its placement in a separate tier of firms. In Europe and Asia, at least to date, finance and management functions have been more heavily intertwined institutionally. This is changing, which is why it is particularly important for scholars of regional development to understand the distinction. The huge mega-mergers unfolding in Europe are the handiwork of investment banking practices, much like those that have dominated in the USA for over a decade.

The size of the financial sector is significant and has been increasing over the past two decades. In 1991, the finance, insurance, and real estate sector (FIRE) surpassed manufacturing's share of American GDP, and by 1993, accounted for $1.2 trillion in output, compared with manufacturing's $1.1 trillion.[1] In 1992, FIRE accounted for 16 per cent of corporate revenue but 37 per cent of US profits, a share which rose steadily from 14 per cent in 1980 and 25 per cent in 1985. Manufacturing profit shares fell concomitantly, from 53 per cent in 1980 to 36 per cent in 1992 (Henwood 1997: 79–80). These figures suggest the ascendancy of financial capital over industrial capital in this period. A financial crisis might again alter these shares, but for the period in question, one of dramatic geographical industrial restructuring, this shift cannot be ignored.

This shift is the product of institutional changes associated with the well-documented 'shareholder revolt' that has accelerated the trend towards the externalization of capital over internal corporate redeployment of retained earnings, reinforced via the transformation of managers into owners by tying executive compensation to stock performance (Dymski, Epstein, and Pollin 1993). This shift in managerial affinity has had a corrosive effect on longer-term investment strategies, because current managers are tempted to side with stockholders in cashing out, taking their compensation today and reinvesting it elsewhere. In an example from the aerospace industry, CEO William Anders did just this in downsizing General Dynamics and was rewarded with compensation in excess of $200 million for a single year, catapulting him onto the front cover of *Business Week* as one of the nation's top ten in executive compensation. Whether or not industrial firms are actually better or worse allocators of financial capital than are external markets is a hotly debated issue in the finance literature, with inconclusive evidence (for a review, see Markusen 1999*a*).

6.3 Fads and Fashion in the Financial Sector

Finance capital would not be so significant if it operated according to neoclassical economists' and business school financial theorists' models. Then it would simply be quickening the pace of regional restructuring that would occur anyway. But there is ample empirical evidence that it does not. Rather than simply keeping managers in line, so that they maximize profits and forego satisficing and empire-building, financial firms engage in extensive market manipulation, bribery to secure insider information,

---

[1] H. Peter Gray points out to me that these shares may be altered by the after-effects of 'irrational exuberance', through a sharp decline in the stock market indices with an effect similar to a financial crisis.

political influence-peddling to alter tax and regulatory mechanisms, and clever use of the press. 'They view investing as war', Henwood (1997: 105) cites Norm Zadeh, who rates money manager performance, as saying, 'and in war, all is fair'.

Financial industry leaders work to create 'fashions' in investment strategies which attract herding behaviour on the part of others and can dominate for a decade or more. Investment bankers, in particular, populate a highly concentrated industry where lead firms wield considerable market power. Their clustering in major money market centres like Wall Street is tied to the relative absence of full information, free market competition in this segment of the capital market, and the significance of consensus-forming and selectively exclusive face-to-face interactions.

Frequent merger waves over the past century-and-a-half bear witness to this process of financial fashion-making (Brealey and Myers 1991). The buzz words in this most recent era are 'core competency' (a concept many economic development-minded scholars have adopted without reflection) and 'pure play'. Beginning in the mid-1980s, conglomerate firms, whose creation had dominated the 1970s merger wave and generated billions in financial firm profits, were discredited, and a rash of hostile takeovers and divestitures ensued, further enriching investment bankers.

These financial machinations make it difficult to theorize about the spatial consequences of financial firm pressures on industrial firms. Since short-term profits are preferred over longer-term returns (Porter 1992), we can hypothesize that active financial sector pressures on industrial firms will tend to favour the latter's dispersion of activity to lower cost sites over continued presence in more expensive agglomerations where innovation and 'high road' strategies could be pursued. But beyond this, the particular form that new fashions take cannot be anticipated, as I show in the next section.

6.4 Mega-Mergers and 'Pure Play' Prescriptions in Aerospace

To achieve high short-term returns, financial firms may induce economic geographical outcomes which would not have happened in the absence of their machinations. This can be illustrated in the American aerospace industry, where firms in the 1990s were subjected to intense merger pressures of a particular kind from investment banking firms, pressures compounded by a successful Wall Street bid for permissive government policy and significant pro-merger strategies. The aggressive Wall Street initiative overrode incipient diversification and conversion efforts on the part of aerospace industrial managers and led to significant plant closings and relocations that would not otherwise have been undertaken.

Aerospace is a relatively mature industrial sector that is still experiencing growth and considerable innovation, especially in the 'payload', or instrumentation, guidance and communications systems. It consists of an increasingly small number of very large firms, the products of recent mergers, who design, assemble, and market civilian and military aircraft to commercial airlines and governments, and a large number of small- and medium-sized firms within whose ranks there is much ferment. It is somewhat unique in that governments form a major portion of the market—in 1996, military sales account for about 55 per cent currently of the value of American industries' aircraft sales, down from 74 per cent during the Reagan defence build-up but above the trough of 46 per cent in 1992 (Aerospace Industries Association 1997)—and remain major underwriters of research and development. But in many ways, the industry's experience is quite mainstream, while its engagement with government permits a rare public view into the operations in the corporate office suite.

Just at a point when long-term minded aerospace managers awoke with a hangover from the Reagan military spending bubble (an increase in procurement spending of more than 70 per cent in real terms from 1980 to 1989) and were attempting to move engineers, technologies, and high-tech facilities into commercial product lines, from satellites to intelligent highways and smart cars, Wall Street counselled the opposite. Rather than conversion strategies, aerospace firms, they claimed, should cope with the rapid decline of defence spending by divesting themselves of commercial divisions and acquiring other defence firms, transforming themselves into specialized pure play defence giants (Markusen 1999*a*, 1999*b*; Oden 1999*b*).

The Wall Street firms were able to succeed in their campaign through their extensive control of financial research, investor publications, and influence over the financial and trade association press. The latter had written confidently about an era of defence conversion in the early 1990s (Miller 1991; Morrocco 1991; Schine 1991; Velocci 1991) and were taken aback by the pure play offensive. Members of large consulting firms began writing their own articles in the business press and talking to journalists about the futility of defence conversion and uncertain returns to diversification (Lundquist 1992).[2] They pooh-poohed conversion, citing one or

---

[2] Lundquist, a former Air Force officer, White House Fellow and staff assistant to Sam Nunn, was a principal at McKinsey & Company's New York Office at the time he wrote this article.

two anecdotes of failures in the past, and counselled narrowing firm focus to profitable defence activities and spinning off units not closely related to these. Less publicly visible but already active in negotiating takeover deals were Wall Street investment banking houses such as Bear Stearns, CS First Boston, Salomon Brothers, and Merrill Lynch.

Beginning in 1993, both analysts and the business press began to use the language of game theory to characterize the merger dynamic. Two Booz/Allen vice-presidents warned against 'fence sitters' in a 1993 trade press account on defence mergers.[3] 'The notion that management can wait out the coming consolidation is one of the popular myths among many industry executives', they argued, forecasting a rapid surge in activity lasting only a few years, during which 'the most attractive partners are taken out of action early in the process' (Anon., *Aviation Week & Space Technology* 1993). Citing consolidation in other industries like printing and publishing, they went on, 'We expect a similar pattern to evolve in aerospace, with pre-emptive moves by aggressive companies foreclosing opportunities for others'. Such mergers 'could establish world-class leaders and lock out other players from the first tier. We believe the acquisition lull in recent months represents the eye of the hurricane and will precipitate a sharp increase in consolidation activity.' By early 1996, articles were appearing under headlines such as 'Mergers Becoming a Business Imperative' (*Jane's Defence Weekly* 1996).

The Wall Street challenge was replicated in the corporate boardroom, where powerful shareholders pressed for higher short-term returns promised by the investment bank formula, and even in the corporate suite, where Chief Financial Officers, recent products of business schools, and financial firms, fought with Chief Executive Officers who were engineers who had risen through the ranks. The former were successful. Elsewhere, I show the sequence of defence-specialized giant-generating divestitures and mergers chalked up by the investment bankers, beginning with family dominated General Dynamics, furthered through the meteoric success of leveraged buyout expert Bernard Schwartz of Loral and capped by the capitulation of the previously resistant Lockheed Martin top management (Markusen 1999b). By 1999, the numbers of top defence contractors imploded from more than fifteen to four, all of whom were more defence

---

[3] In another press account, one of the same consultants is quoted as citing 'countless reasons why defence businesses should steer clear of conversion. Only the smallest businesses and the most basic technologies can readily move between one and the other. Big defence companies can no more adapt to the commercial world than can the products they churn out' (*The Economist* 16 January 1993: 63–4).

dependent than at the outset of the decade (Markusen 1999b, 1999c). The largest US contractors have remained highly defence dependent, while previously more diversified Boeing and Raytheon, by acquiring large military divisions and entire firms, have become more defence specialized, as have firms like Litton who have spun off their civilian divisions and new firms like Alliant Tech, created when Honeywell spun off its military work (Markusen 1997). As I show below, although these mergers have not achieved the claims made for them, their emergence has dramatically reshaped aerospace industrial and managerial geography.

What is the evidence for the superiority of 'focus' or 'pure play' over conglomerate firm form? Although a number of business school theorists have written compelling theoretical rationales for the advantages of focus (see the review in Denis, Denis, and Sarin 1997), the empirical evidence is quite mixed. A number of studies have been done comparing conglomerate to focused firm performance, and most conclude that the latter have generated greater stockholder returns (Liebeskind and Opler 1994; Comment and Jarrell 1995; Berger and Ofek 1996; Denis, Denis, and Sarin 1997). However, these studies rely on a controversial indicator of performance—stock values. The link between stock market prices and economic efficiency is tenuous, however, and relying on stock market signals may lead to suboptimal investments (Dow and Gorton 1997). The value of a stock is not a measure of return to investment, since it is an evaluation of the entire firm including proprietary intangible capital rather than of a marginal investment. Moreover, stock prices do not necessarily reflect all available information so that managers may under invest relative to the rate indicated by the stock price. Nor do all scholars agree on the inferiority of conglomerates. In a careful historical study, Servaes (1996) shows that in the past, conglomerate mergers did not suffer a diversification discount, suggesting that a changing Wall Street consensus holds sway over stock market responses (see also Matsusaka 1993).

I have gone to some lengths in this section to demonstrate that both in the finance literature and in our own research on the aerospace industry in the 1990s, financial firms with short-term profits in mind have dominated industrial firm choices, suppressing longer-term investment and diversification options. The strategies dictated by the Wall Street analysts and investment bankers were embedded in a consensus about appropriate firm form that was a fashion in its time and with hindsight, unwarranted. The consensus was successfully marketed to the press and to key government decision-makers, many of whom hailed from the investment banking sector themselves. In what follows, I demonstrate both the spatial consequences of this fad-driven restructuring and the ultimate failure of the strategy on its own terms, except for the generation of excessive short-term profits.

6.5 The Spatial Consequences of Financial Firms' Strategies

The American defence industry, within which the aerospace sector forms the largest and growing share, faced prime military contract cuts of 64 per cent in real terms between 1987 and 1996. For reasons which we have documented extensively elsewhere (Markusen 1991; Markusen et al. 1991), defence capacity was heavily concentrated in the 'Gunbelt', a crescent running from New England through the south and west coasts. In the rash of downsizing and plant closings which ensued, two spatial shifts were pronounced.

First, operations in relatively expensive locations such as the north-east and Los Angeles were disproportionately shuttered in favour of relocations and existing operations in the south and mountain states. In Oden's analysis (1999*a*, 1999*b*), he shows that while all regions lost prime contracts, the negative regional shift component was highest for New York, California, and Massachusetts, in that order (Table 6.1). In contrast, the South Atlantic, East South Central, and Mountain states all experienced net positive regional shifts.

Second, several key corporate headquarters and a disproportionate share of new high-tech aerospace and electronics activity relocated to the greater Washington, DC area, the latter principally to northern Virginia. Virginia was the only state to actually increase its prime defence contract receipts in real terms in this period (Table 6.1). General Dynamics moved its headquarters from St Louis to the DC area, and the merged Lockheed Martin shuttered its historic Los Angeles headquarters and consolidated corporate management in Bethesda, Maryland. Several large (more than $1 billion in annual sales) high-tech defence service firms—BDM Corporation and SAIC Corporation—have the bulk of their employment in northern Virginia's 'Pentagon City' and nearby suburbs.

Financial firm pressures do not account for all of this spatial restructuring. Changes in the composition of defence spending protecting military readiness and operations at the expense of new and existing weapons systems favoured regions specializing in troop provisioning, ongoing tactical aircraft programmes, maintenance and engineering, and information services at the expense of advanced weapons research and production

Distortions in Industrial Geography

Table 6.1. Changes in DoD prime contract awards by select states and region (in the billions of real 1994 dollars)

	Average contracts 1986–7	Average contracts 1995–6	Total loss in real contracts	Change due to decline in national contracts	Change due to regional shift
			Change in average from 1986–7 to 1995–6		
Connecticut	6.6	2.6	−4.0	−2.5	−1.5
Massachusetts	11.0	4.6	−6.4	−4.2	−2.3
NEW ENGLAND	20.0	9.0	−10.8	−7.5	−3.3
New Jersey	4.1	2.7	−1.4	−1.5	0.1
New York	12.3	3.4	−9.0	−4.7	−4.3
Pennsylvania	5.1	3.2	−1.8	−1.9	0.1
MIDDLE ATLANTIC	21.5	9.3	−12.2	−8.1	−4.1
Illinois	2.2	1.2	−1.1	−0.8	−0.2
Michigan	2.7	1.2	−1.4	−1.0	−0.4
Ohio	6.1	2.6	−3.6	−2.3	−1.3
EAST NORTH CENTRAL	15.2	6.8	−8.4	−5.7	−2.7
Minnesota	3.0	1.0	−2.0	−1.1	−0.9
Missouri	7.3	6.2	−1.0	−2.7	1.7
WEST NORTH CENTRAL	13.7	8.9	−4.8	−5.2	0.4
District of Columbia	1.4	1.2	−0.2	−0.5	0.4
Florida	7.2	5.8	−1.4	−2.7	1.3
Georgia	4.6	3.6	−1.0	−1.7	0.8
Maryland	5.9	4.2	−1.7	−2.2	0.5
Virginia	8.3	10.5	2.2	−3.1	5.3
SOUTH ATLANTIC	29.9	27.9	−1.9	−11.3	9.4
Alabama	2.0	1.8	−0.2	−0.8	0.5
Mississippi	1.9	1.7	−0.2	−0.7	0.5
EAST SOUTH CENTRAL	5.9	5.2	−0.7	−2.2	1.6
Louisiana	1.9	1.0	−0.8	−0.7	−0.1
Texas	12.3	8.6	−3.7	−4.7	1.0
WEST SOUTH CENTRAL	16.1	10.6	−5.5	−6.1	0.6
Arizona	3.7	2.6	−1.1	−1.4	0.3
Colorado	3.0	2.0	−0.8	−1.1	0.3
MOUNTAIN	9.0	6.3	−2.7	−3.4	0.7
California	33.0	17.6	−15.4	−12.5	−3.0
Washington	3.5	2.3	−1.3	−1.3	0.1
PACIFIC	38.2	21.4	−16.9	−14.4	−2.4
US TOTAL	169.3	105.4	−63.9	−63.9	0.0

Source: Oden 2000: 28, table 1. Prime contract data from *DoD Prime Contract Awards by Region* and State (P 06) Fiscal Years 1985–7 and 1994–6. Price deflators are from the National Defense Budget Estimates for FY 1998, Table 5–8 Procurement Category.

centres (Oden 1999*a*, 1999*b*: 29). However, in our field research on four aerospace regions, managers reported intense financial mandates to cut costs explicitly by moving and consolidating production in lower cost regions. Grumman responded to Navy aircraft contract cuts by transferring remaining aircraft manufacture and upgrade work to lower-cost facilities in Louisiana and Florida in the early 1990s (Oden, Mueller, and Goldberg 1994). From Los Angeles, Hughes moved all its tactical missile work to Arizona, Lockheed relocated aircraft production to Georgia, and McDonnell Douglas transferred roughly 3,800 C-17 aircraft jobs from Los Angeles to lower cost St Louis (Oden et al. 1996). Cost cutting discipline helps to explain why Los Angeles and Long Island suffered deeper defence-related industrial job loss than St Louis (Table 6.2). In the summer of 1998, a business school intern at one of the top investment banking houses reported hearing his boss dictate to Boeing that it would have to lay-off tens of thousands of workers before the firm would reverse its publicly proclaimed negative evaluation of Boeing's stock.

These consolidations often took place in the context of Wall Street-instigated mergers. Cost cutting as a major means of extracting short-term profit is widely acknowledged in the literature on mergers and the ascendancy of financial firms. Higher returns are realized chiefly through selling off undervalued units and real estate, subcontracting out more routine portions of production to lower labour costs at home or abroad and to avoid unions, and cutting back on longer-term, more speculative corporate research (Dymski, Epstein, and Pollin 1993). In a 1980s study of hostile takeovers economy-wide, Bhagat, Shleifer, and Vishny (1990) concluded that lay-offs were an important source of windfall profits, as were tax breaks from increasing indebtedness. Such cost cutting often yields short-term gains which are later less than functional for the firm, as we recount below. But the spatial story is not complete without an appreciation for the powerful role of the state, not so much as an autonomous actor, but as a group of powerful politicians (including the President) and bureaucrats heavily influenced by the money and views of the Wall Street financiers and the lead firms in the aerospace industry.

Table 6.2. Employment in defence-related manufacturing in four US aerospace regions, 1989–94

	Total employment 1989	Total employment 1994	Per cent change	Share of national 1989	Share of national 1994
Los Angeles–Long Beach	262,749	133,067	−49.4	11.2	7.6
Nassau–Suffolk, NY	58,437	34,062	−41.7	2.5	1.9
St Louis	47,678	31,762	−33.4	2.0	1.8
Seattle–Bellevue–Everett	103,887	83,749	−19.4	4.4	4.8
Total four regions	472,751	282,640	−40.2	20.1	16.1
Total US aerospace	2,348,909	1,753,360	−25.4		

Source: Oden 2000: 33, table 3. Based on County Business Patterns data as compiled and estimated by Andrew Isserman, University of West Virginia, Regional Research Institute.

6.6 State Roles in Defence Industry Spatial Restructuring

It is difficult to theorize the role of the state in regional restructuring, which is one reason why many analysts leave it out. Nevertheless, state actions are fundamental to the evolving spatial pattern of economic activity, both intentionally (as in industrial policy or pork-barrelling) and unintentionally. Elected officials often have strong spatial preferences in programme and spending distributions, because they are supported in their campaign bids, via both money and votes, by groups associated with particular regional economies and particular factions within them (Markusen 1994*a*, 1994*b*). The spatial calculus of government agencies is harder to determine generically. Elsewhere, I have shown how the location of military industry capacity in the USA was shaped by Pentagon strategic concerns, by the preference of top military personnel, and by the desire to link industry spatially with government users, in this case military bases (Markusen 1991). But the particulars would of course be different for other industrial segments. What we can say is that to the extent government spending and regulation affect industrial activity; they influence location and are thus targets of spatial designs of both financial and industrial sectors.

The state's encouragement and more importantly, financial underwriting, of the large aerospace mergers is key to understanding their contribution to spatial restructuring in the 1990s.[4] At the outset of the decade, the Bush administration continued a long-standing Pentagon posture of discouraging mergers to ensure competition, innovation, and choice. Like Bush, a major beneficiary of lavish Wall Street and aerospace industry campaign funding (Project on Demilitarization and Democracy 1995; Hartung 1996), President Clinton shifted this strategy as political payoff to the industry, especially since he was proposing additional major military spending cuts. Clinton's first Secretary of Defense, Les Aspin, set up a new Office of Economic Security in the Pentagon under the leadership of a Wall Street investment banker, Josh Gotbaum, who brought with him a 'mergers and acquisitions' perspective. Bill Perry, later Secretary of Defense himself, oversaw procurement issues from the outset of the Aspin period. Perry had most recently been running his own Silicon Valley investment banking/venture capital firm and was considered merger-friendly on joining the Pentagon (Markusen 1998).

---

[4] The following discussion draws upon Markusen 1997, 1998.

The Clinton Pentagon, however, never produced a defence industrial base analysis to evaluate whether its future demand for individual weapons systems could reasonably sustain one, two, three, or more competitors, despite the advice of experts like the Brookings Institution's Ken Flamm, at the time a staffer in the Office of Economic Security, and Rand economists William Kovacic and Dennis Smallwood (Kovacic and Smallwood 1994; Flamm 1999). The Rand team laid out a robust procedure for preserving rivalry among contractors by monitoring proposed mergers and preventing them in cases where demand could sustain greater competition. Instead, Perry openly encouraged consolidation, in a famous 'last supper' speech in 1993, basing his advocacy on the promise of cost savings to the Pentagon.[5] He left the means and particulars to the firms themselves, a decision in which we can see reflected the interests of the financial sector.

Perry embarked on an aggressive programme which included special antitrust rules to permit greater consolidation of the defence industrial base and succeeded in overcoming the antitrust reservations of the Department of Justice and the Federal Trade Commission, a move welcomed by the Wall Street and business consultants. The Defense Science Board, comprised predominantly of defence contractors and consultants, recommended against formal Pentagon scrutiny of the mergers, which facilitated this backdoor approach—the Pentagon was presumably the most knowledgeable about the competitive impacts of the mergers, but this way it did not have to issue formal reports. 'By publicly advocating the need for consolidation of the defence industry, the Defense Department accomplished a number of goals. Perhaps most important is that the government was able to isolate itself from the politically charged task of picking winners and losers by letting the market make those decisions' (Dowdy 1997: 91–2).[6]

At about the same time, the Department of Defense played an active role in creating new financial incentives favouring 'pure play' mergers by subsidizing and aggressively promoting liberalized arms exports and by permitting defence contractors for the first time to include the costs of consummating mergers as charges against current contracts, on the promise that they would generate future savings. Both of these moves provided

---

[5] Perry was explicit, saying he hoped that 'several aircraft firms would disappear through mergers, as well as three of the five satellite firms in business then, and one of three missile companies' (Mintz 1995).
[6] Dowdy's article is the only one which has appeared in a major foreign policy journal on defence mergers—Dowdy is a partner in the Los Angeles office of McKinsey & Company.

billions in new subsidies that helped to tilt the balance for contractors in favour of remaining defence specialized and engaging in the merger spree. These initiatives overwhelmed the significance of other Pentagon's efforts to encourage dual use and civil/military integration.

The change in Pentagon practices permitting companies to charge the costs of making mergers work against their existing contracts was crucial in encouraging the mergers. Boeing at one point said it would not have acquired McDonnell Douglas without these subsidies (Markusen 1999*b*). They, thus, quickened the pace of spatial restructuring. During the mid-1990s, the Pentagon reimbursed the large aerospace firms billions of dollars for closing down lines and laying off people on the promise that such closings would save the military money in the future. These funds were used neither for serious worker retraining nor for moving engineers and technologies into commercial work, but for golden parachutes for top executives, meagre severance pay for workers, and the costs of disposing of or demolishing property. In what bi-partisan critics, including a conservative New Jersey member of the House of Representatives, dubbed 'payoffs for layoffs', Lockheed Martin raked in more than $1 billion in taxpayer dollars to complete its merger, just one of thirty reimbursement requests to the Pentagon. A General Accounting Office study found that actual savings fell far below those promised, but firms were not required to reimburse the government for poor performance (United States General Accounting Office 1995). It is likely that fewer lines would have been closed and fewer relocations undertaken in the absence of these massive subsidies.

Politics and access to state bureaucracies have also contributed to recent aerospace industry spatial restructuring. The targeting of certain southern districts for relocated and consolidated operations—Newt Gingrich's Georgia district, for instance—was acknowledged by managers in interviews we conducted. The south-east, with its preponderance of Republican members of Congress in powerful appropriations and armed forces committees, was especially favoured in the production shift (Oden 1999*a*, 1999*b*: 29–30). The gravitation of aerospace, military electronics, and defence service sector activities around Washington, DC, is a testimony to the increasing significance of government as market and can be considered the belated construction of a state-based agglomeration.[7]

---

[7] See Markusen 1999*a*, for a typology of industrial districts which include the state-anchored agglomeration.

Distortions in Industrial Geography

In this account, it is easier to detect the role of military industrial firms in shaping government policy than it is to uncover the role of Wall Street. My own experience running a study group at the Council on Foreign Relations with ongoing participation of investment firms has convinced me that many of the major innovations of this period, including the change in merger cost reimbursement practices, have been the brainchildren of financial firms, who were also active, if less visible, in promulgating them in Washington. As this case shows, the triangulation among financial and industrial firms and the state is best researched inductively, if the analyst wishes to understand the particular spatial outcomes of a sector and the potential to alter them. It is not that the state's role cannot be theorized but that it must be theorized in context and will differ among sectors.

6.7 The Consequences for American Aerospace

For several years following the mega-mergers, military industrial profits were extraordinarily high while defence workers were left behind (Powers and Markusen 1998). These profits appear to have been associated principally with deep employment cuts, property sell-offs (e.g. many aerospace operations had been sited at what had become prime real estate, just south of the Los Angeles airport), relocations, and of course, the upfront reimbursements for such costs from the Pentagon. But by 1999, despite a reversal in the defence budget, the defence giants' stock plunged, as analysts increasingly reported failures in merging operations and corporate cultures and in finding new markets and product lines. Profits did not recover until after the events of September 2001.

These failures should not have been surprising. Before the Boeing–McDonnell Douglas merger, McDonnell Douglas CEO Harry Stonecipher acknowledged that size had its disadvantages and predicted that the mid-decade defence mega-firms might someday choose to split themselves into smaller, more manageable, and entrepreneurial units (Mintz 1995). Disparate corporate cultures (e.g. at Hughes and Raytheon) posed formidable problems to successful integration (Velocci 1997). Even Boeing appears to have suffered from the diversion of its energies into the absorption of McDonnell Douglas, whose acquisition was widely interpreted as Boeing's effort to be a larger player in the military market (and not, as Europeans feared, to establish an American monopoly in commercial aircraft, which it more or less already enjoyed). In 1999, for the first time, orders for the Airbus outpaced orders for Boeing commercial aircraft.

Distortions in Industrial Geography

More recently, one wing of the Wall Street investment banking community has been vigorously crafting international mergers, but these have so far proved difficult to consummate for political reasons (Markusen 1999c). It is quite possible that if these efforts remain blocked, breaking up the defence giants will become newly fashionable. Such dismemberment would also generate impressive fees for the investment bankers.

Ironically, those aerospace firms which have maintained dual use capabilities, chief among them Boeing and TRW, did much better over the decade of the 1990s than the pure play giants. Even in the early years of the decade, Seattle's aerospace complex was much better positioned to absorb military spending cuts than were the Long Island and Los Angeles agglomerations (Table 6.2). This differential performance suggests that internally-financed corporate diversification rather than dual use—destroying divestiture and defence specialization—building acquisition would have produced a more successful and a more spatially stable industry with fewer permanently displaced engineers and blue-collar workers (Powers and Markusen 1998; Markusen 1999b; Oden 1999a, 1999b, 2000).

6.8 Acknowledging Financial Firms and the State in Regional Development

The prominence of financial firms in remaking the face of the aerospace industry produced long-term negative consequences after the short-term profits from large merger fees and stock appreciation evaporated. It would be facile to argue that this was simply a case of a mature industry, previously protected from the industrial restructuring forced on other sectors by its special role in Reagan's defence build-up and suddenly subjected to Wall Street financial discipline. The aerospace industry still accounts for an impressive share of the high-tech science and engineering market and a disproportionate share of government R&D funds, and it is still a growth market internationally. The particular path chosen by Wall Street investment banks for the industry was not the only one possible: it could have pressed for smaller, defence-specialized firms, or larger, more diversified firms, either of which could form the basis for the next consensus.

The disturbing lesson from this analysis is that not only should financial firms, as suppliers of capital to other firms in the economy, be left out of the analysis, but that even when incorporated, their behaviour is not easily theorized a priori. The case of the aerospace industry in the 1990s underscores the point made eloquently by Lovering (1990) in response to Scott's work (1988): contingency matters.

Although the aerospace industry is a special case in that the government is a major market for its output, it is in many ways similar to other relatively high-tech producer and consumer durable goods industries, such as computers, computer software, and communications equipment which operate in less than fully competitive markets. Because of their special relationship to the Pentagon, aerospace firms are in many ways more transparent than are other firms, and the role of Wall Street in their restructuring is somewhat easier to research. But most other firms in the economy must rely on financial capital and are subject to the same vicissitudes of fads and fashions. Wall Street's stature and influence in Washington, in government at all levels (including international bodies like the World Bank and the IMF) is extraordinarily high and shows up in myriad government postures: tax law, commercial practices, trade policy, securities regulation, property rights, antitrust and so on. All of these may have important consequences for spatial outcomes.

Financial firms' motivation and behaviour are hard to detect. Precisely because they are so shielded from competition because they enjoy discretionary space and are skilled at market manipulation, and because they are so politically powerful, their modus operandi is deliberately kept under wraps. Regional economists and geographers, I believe, understate the role of financial capital because it is just plain hard to research. Even when the researcher obtains access, the sector's operations are not simple or straightforward, as are lean production practices in manufacturing. We understate the clout of financial capital because much of its power lies in its ability to shape national economic policy through its domination of both the national banking system and the most powerful agency, Treasury. In the recent past and on into the foreseeable future, finance capital will play a significant role in how and where business operates at the global and regional scales.

The state is similarly complicated to model in this process, but its significance cannot be ignored. If the state in this case had not been staffed by elected officials (Clinton, in this case) and agency leaders (the Pentagon) who sided with the financial sector on the course of the industry, the spatial outcome would have been quite different: some capacity would have been created and retained through diversification and more would have remained in place than was the case with pure play defence restructuring strategies. To build adequate interpretations of actual industrial spatial distributions, the economic geographic researcher has no choice but to acknowledge this role of the state, interacting with other major actors.

References

Aerospace Industries Association of America (1997). *Aerospace Facts and Figures, 1997/98*, AIA. Washington, DC.

Anon. (1993). 'Consolidation Myths Pose Risks to "Fence-Sitters"', *Aviation Week & Space Technology*, 139(9): 46.

Bhagat, S., Schleifer, A., and Vishny, R. (1990). 'Hostile takovers in the 1980s: The Return to Corporate Specialization', *Brookings Papers on Economic Activity: Microeconomics*, 1–85.

Berger, P. and Ofek, E. (1996). 'Bustup Takeovers of Value-destroying Diversified Firms', *Journal of Finance*, 51: 1175–200.

Brealey, R. and Myers, S. (1991). *Principles of Corporate Finance*, 4th edn. New York: McGraw-Hill.

Clark, G. (1989). *Unions and Communities Under Siege*. Cambridge: Cambridge University Press.

Comment, R. and Jarrell, G. (1995). 'Corporate Focus and Stock Returns', *Journal of Financial Economics*, 37: 67–87.

Denis, D., Denis, D., and Sarin, A. (1997). 'Agency Problems, Equity Ownership and Corporate Diversification', *The Journal of Finance*, 52(2): 135–60.

Dow, J. and Gorton, G. (1997). 'Stock Market Efficiency and Economic Efficiency: Is There a Connection?', *The Journal of Finance*, 52(3): 1087–130.

Dowdy, J. (1997). 'Winners and Losers in the Arms Industry Downturn', *Foreign Policy*, Summer, 88–101.

Dymski, G., Epstein, G., and Pollin, R. (1993). *Transforming the U.S. Financial System: Equity and Efficiency for the Twenty First Century*. New York: M. E. Sharpe.

Flamm, K. (1999). 'Redesigning the Defense Industrial Base', in Ann Markusen and Sean Costigan (eds.), *Arming the Future: A Defense Industry for the 21st Century*. New York: Council on Foreign Relations, pp. 224–46.

Harrison, B. (1994). *Lean and Mean: The Changing Landscape of Corporate Power in the Age of Flexibility*. New York: Basic Books.

Hartung, W. D. (1996). *Welfare for Weapons Dealers: The Hidden Costs of the Arms Trade*. New York: World Policy Institute, June.

Henwood, D. (1997). *Wall Street: How it Works and for Whom?* London: Verso.

Jane's Defence Weekly (1996). 'Mergers Becoming a Business Imperative', 12 January: 23.

Kovacic, W. and Smallwood, D. (1994). 'Competition Policy, Rivalries, and Defense Industry Consolidation', *Journal of Economic Perspectives*, 8(4): 91–110.

Liebeskind, J. and Opler, T. (1994). 'Corporate Diversification and Agency Costs: Evidence from Privately Held Firms', Working Paper, Ohio State University.

Lovering, J. (1990). 'Fordism's Unknown Successor: A Comment on Scott's Theory of Flexible Accumulation and the Re-emergence of Regional Economies', *International Journal of Urban and Regional Research*, 14(1): 159–74.

Lundquist, J. (1992). 'Shrinking Fast and Smart in the Defense Industry', *Harvard Business Review*, November–December.

Markusen, A. (1991). 'Government as Market: Industrial Location in the US Defense Industry', in H. Herzog and A. Schlottmann (eds.), *Industry Location and Public Policy*. Knoxville, TN: University of Tennessee Press.

—— (1994a). 'American Federalism and Regional Policy', *International Regional Science Review*, 16(1 and 2): 3–15.

—— (1994b). 'Studying Regions by Studying Firms', *The Professional Geographer*, 46(4): 477–90.

—— (1997). 'The Economics of Defence Industry Mergers and Divestiture', *Economic Affairs*, 17(4): 28–32.

—— (1998a). 'America's Military Industrial Makeover', in C. Lo and M. Schwartz (eds.), *Social Policy and the Conservative Agenda*. Oxford: Basil Blackwell, pp. 142–50.

—— (1998b). 'The Post Cold War Persistence of Defense Specialized Firms', in G. Susman and S. O'Keefe (eds.), *The Defense Industry in the Post-Cold War Era: Corporate Strategies and Public Policy Perspectives*. Oxford: Elsevier, pp. 121–46.

—— (1999a). 'Fuzzy Concepts, Scanty Evidence, Policy Distance: The Case for Rigor and Policy Relevance in Critical Regional Studies', *Regional Studies*, 33(9): 869–84.

—— (1999b). 'The Rise of World Weapons', *Foreign Policy*, 114: 40–51.

—— Hall, P., Campbell, S., and Deitrick, S. (1991). *The Rise of the Gunbelt*. New York: Oxford University Press.

Matsusaka, J. (1993). 'Takeover Motives During the Conglomerate Merger Wave', *Rand Journal of Economics*, (24): 357–79.

Miller, W. (1991). 'After Desert Storm: What Next for Defense?', *Industry Week*, 240 (July 1): 48–53.

Mintz, J. (1995). 'Going Great Guns', *The Washington Post*, 2 October: H01.

Morrocco, J. (1991). 'Uncertain U.S. Military Needs Hamper Industry Restructuring', *Aviation Week & Space Technology*, 134 (June 17): 62–3.

Oden, M. (1998). 'Defense Mega-mergers and Alternative Strategies: The Hidden Costs of Post-Cold War Defense Restructuring', in G. Susman and S. O'Keefe (eds.) *The Defense Industrys in the Post-Cold War Era: Corporate Strategies and Public Policy Perspectives*. Oxford: Elsevier.

—— (1999a). 'Cashing-in, Cashing-out and Converting: Restructuring of the Defense Industrial Base in the 1990s', in A. Markusen and S. Costigan (eds.), *Arming the Future: A Defense Industry for the 21st Century*. New York: Council on Foreign Relations Press, pp. 74–105.

—— (2000). 'Federal Defense Industrial Policy, Firm Strategy and Regional Conversion Initiatives in four American Aerospace Regions', *International Regional Science Review*, 23(1): 25–47.

—— Mueller, E., and Goldberg, J. (1994). *Life after Defense: Conversion and Economic Adjustment on Long Island*. New Brunswick, NJ: Rutgers University, Project on Regional and Industrial Economics.

Oden, M. Markusen, A., Flaming, D., Feldman, J., Raffel, J., and Hill, C. (1996). *From Managing Growth to Reversing Decline: Aerospace and the Southern California Economy in the Post Cold War Era.* New Brunswick, NJ: Rutgers University, Project on Regional and Industrial Economics, February.

Porter, M. (1992). *Capital Choices: Changing the Way America Invests in Industry.* Washington, DC: Council on Competitiveness.

Poterba, J. and Summers, L. (1991). *Time Horizons of American Firms: New Evidence from a Survey of CEOs.* Washington, DC: Council on Competitiveness and the Harvard Business School, October, unpublished MS.

Powers, L. and Markusen, A. (1998). *A Just Transition? Lessons from Defense Workers' Experience in the 1990s.* Washington, DC: Economic Policy Institute.

Project on Demilitarization and Democracy (1995). *Hostile Takeover.* Washington, DC: PDD, November.

Schine, E. (1991). 'Defenseless Against Cutbacks', *Business Week*, 14 January: 69.

Schoenberger, E. (1997). *The Cultural Crisis of the Firm.* Cambridge: Blackwell.

Scott, A. (1988). 'Flexible Production Systems and Regional Development: The Rise of New Industrial Space in North America and Western Europe', *International Journal of Urban and Regional Research*, 12(2): 171–86.

Servaes, H. (1996). 'The Value of Diversification During the Conglomerate Merger Wave', *The Journal of Finance*, 51(4): 1201–25.

United States General Accounting Office (1995). *Defense Downsizing: Selective Contractors Business Unit Reactions*, GAO/NSIAD-95-144, May. Washington, DC: US Government Printing Office.

Velocci, A. (1991). 'Ill-Defined U.S. Defense Priorities Making Industry a "gambler's paradise"', *Aviation Week & Space Technology*, 17 June: 141–2.

—— (1997). 'Competitive Advantages of Scale Could Elude Aerospace Giants', *Aviation Week & Space Technology*, 10 February: 88–89.

7
Firms as Political Actors in Processes of Capital Accumulation and Regional Development

Ray Hudson

7.1 Introduction

Contrary to the assumptions of mainstream, neoclassical economics, the economy and its institutions, such as firms and markets, are not naturally occurring phenomena. They are, and must be, socially produced and politically regulated. Most fundamentally, this is because the contradictory class structural relationship between capital and labour is at the core of any capitalist economy but, in addition, there are permanent tensions, expressed in varying forms of collaborative and competitive relationships, marked by typically asymmetric power relations, among both firms and groups of workers. As such, a chronically recurring characteristic of capitalist societies is a formal separation of the economic and political spheres. This separation necessarily arises as a consequence of the state mediating competitive relations between capital and labour and because of the impossibility of any single firm ensuring the conditions that make capitalist production possible. As such the state, typically in the form of the national state, emerges and evolves via processes of political and social struggle as a mediating institution. However, a corollary of capital existing in the form of competing firms is that the state cannot simultaneously satisfy the interests of all firms and so of necessity is selective in its priorities and policies. Conversely, a further corollary is that firms seek to influence the

Firms as Political Actors

content, form, and implementation of state policies and as such are necessarily political actors, albeit actors endowed with differing capacities, powers, and resources to try to shape the state policy agenda and the ways in which policies are implemented.

The remainder of this chapter falls into two main sections. In the first, the necessity for firms to act politically is explored theoretically, drawing in particular on the State Derivation debate of the 1970s and subsequent critiques of it, regulationist approaches and Foucauldian approaches to governmentality (see Hudson 2001: ch. 3). In this, I seek to establish both the necessity for and limits to political action by firms—political here denoting power relations between social actors and the exercise of power. However, the existence of the state within a political sphere formally separate from that of the economy requires consideration of a more restricted conception of political action and relations as social actors—not least companies—seek to influence and shape state policies within this defined formal political sphere. In the second, the issue of the firm as a political actor is explored empirically in the context of the creation of new forms of regional policy in north-east England in the 1920s and 1930s as constituent elements of a new governmentality, a new interventionist mode of regulation. This emphasizes the ways in which firms are involved in policy creation and in defining the content, scope, and boundaries of state policies and not simply in the ways in which given policies are implemented (see Carney and Hudson 1978; Hudson 1989). Finally, some conclusions are briefly drawn.

7.2 On the Theoretical Necessity for the Emergence of the State and the Consequent Necessity for the Firm as a Political Actor

Although there may be a variety of collaborative relationship among firms, workers, and other social actors, competition is the driving force of a capitalist economy, the mechanism via which successful companies prosper, unsuccessful ones fail, and the trajectory of the accumulation process is maintained. However, the conditions that make a competitive capitalist economy possible must be socially established and politically regulated and governed in order that competition does not become 'ruinous' and create anarchy in markets, undermining the conditions needed for smooth capital accumulation. In particular, two conditions are necessary for the continued viability of capitalism and the realization of both requires that firms act politically. First, it is necessary to control or eliminate problems of capital accumulation and circulation that are inherent in decentralized processes of production, competition, market exchange, and distribution. Second, it is necessary to ensure the continual biological and social reproduction of a wage labour force that accepts (willingly or unwillingly) existing power structures, relationships of ownership and domination, and the political character of production and exchange relations. However, neither condition is automatically realized within the confines of capitalist social relations; indeed, these are *structured* to lead precisely in the opposite direction. First, because the accumulation process is grounded in competitive relations between social agents, it is inherently crisis prone and does not automatically smoothly reproduce itself. Second, the reproduction of a wage labour force providing labour-power as and when required and on terms defined, if not dictated, by capital, is chronically challenged at both individual and collective levels within workplaces, local communities, and national territories. Thus, the smooth operation of commodity production and exchange is constantly under threat from the contested basis of production and political conflicts within and among the classes of capital and labour over the distribution of social product (of the output produced), and the relative magnitudes of wages, profits, and rents. Two important implications follow. First, firms must act politically in their relations with labour and in relations amongst themselves. Second, the chronically competitive and political (in both the broad and narrow senses) character of social relations between capital and labour, companies, and groups of workers *implies* the need for some systematic 'mediating' regulatory agency that is relatively autonomous from these various class interests. In short, the existence of the state is a necessary (though not sufficient) condition for firms to be able to act politically.

During the 1970s the 'state derivation' debate sought systematically to derive the state as a 'relatively autonomous' political form,[1] existing in a political sphere formally separate from that of the economy, from the character of capitalist relations of production, and the category of capital.[2] As such, the state derivation debate can be seen as an attempt logically to

---

[1] This degree of relative autonomy is periodically reduced by the contradictions of capitalist development.

[2] The state derivation debate was in part a reaction to an earlier debate between structural theorists of the state, such as Poulantzas (1975, 1978), for whom the state acted in the interests of capital because of constraints imposed on its mode and scope of operations by wider structures of social and economic power and Miliband (1969), who argued that the state acted as the instrument of the ruling class in response to class interests located, constituted, and organized outside of the state system, in the economy or civil society.

derive the form of *the* capitalist state while at the same time acknowledging its grounding in relations of mutual dependence between capital and the state. The former requires the latter to guarantee its existence while the latter requires taxes from profits and other forms of income to fund its activities. Furthermore, recognition of the distinction between the economic and political spheres, with the state located in the latter and possessing a degree of autonomy from other social forces, including firms, points to the way in which the latter of necessity will seek to act politically to influence state policies and priorities. In this sense, firms are of necessity constituted as political actors from the outset. Capitalist reproduction requires the separation of the state from capital while that separation in turn requires that firms (as units of capital) act politically to try and secure their interests via shaping the formation and implementation of state policies within the formal political sphere. However, because capital exists as competing units (firms), representing and securing the general interests of capital is a non-trivial task for the state, as individual companies and/or groups of companies compete to promote their specific interests via state policies.[3]

State derivation theorists subsequently came to recognize the need to analyse the evolution of particular state forms historically (see, e.g. von Braunmuhl 1978). Recognizing that the state typically exists as a national state drew attention to the varying historical-geographical forms that the state could take—and to similar variations in the political strategies of firms. It also emphasized variations through time and over space in the ways in which the state sought to secure the conditions for accumulation as it responded to varying pressures from companies, trades unions, and other social groups and forces.

Theorists such as Habermas (1976) and Offe (1975) drew attention to the crisis-prone character of state involvement as crisis tendencies (notably a tendency for the rate of profit to fall) are translated from the economy into the operations of the state itself. The state's response to crises in its repertoire of crisis management tactics in turn helps trigger a search for new forms of state policies and involvement in economy and society. Habermas and Offe drew an important distinction between a liberal and

---

[3] There are several strands to the debate, but these can be condensed to two main approaches: those who sought to derive the necessity of the form of the state from relationships between capitals and those who sought to derive it from relations between capital and labour (see Holloway and Picciotto 1978). For present purposes, however, the differences among these approaches are of less significance than the ground they share in common but it is important to note that they have different implications as to the thrust of the political strategies of firms—in terms of relations with other firms as opposed to relations with labour.

an interventionist mode of state involvement with economy and society. The former mode of involvement emphasizes the role of the state in setting the legal frameworks that make markets possible—for example, in terms of labour and product markets, product standards, health and safety at work regulations and so on. In contrast, an interventionist mode of state involvement sees the state taking responsibility for the provision of goods and services, replacing the market as a resource allocation mechanism. Examples would include nationalizing industries or otherwise taking them into public ownership, or directly providing educational, health, or welfare services via the state. This raises important questions as to the conditions under which the state acquires the authority and legitimacy to contravene the 'normal' private property relationships of a capitalist economy and of the implications of this for the accumulation process and the political strategies that firms adopt.

The issue of the ways in which the state secures the conditions that allow the inherently crisis-prone accumulation process generally to proceed reasonably smoothly within tolerable limits was further addressed by the French regulationist school (see, e.g. Boyer 1990).[4] Initially privileging the national scale, regulationists emphasize the role of the state in bringing about an accommodation between the interests of capital and labour, balancing growing productivity in the economy with rising working-class living standards via an appropriate mix of policies on issues such as taxation and redistributive welfare policies. As models of economic growth and accumulation altered, new modes of social regulation were discovered and constructed that allowed the state to navigate a delicate path that satisfied the respective interests of varied social actors. Recognizing that any settlement of social relations into spatial form is necessarily temporary, Hay and Jessop (1995: 305) emphasize the 'constantly evolving spatial forms of accumulation and regulation', the dynamic of spaces of governance and regulation, since these can never be more than a temporary fixing of the contradictory social relations of the economy in a particular spatial form. Put another way, in a variety of historically geographically specific ways, the state seeks simultaneously to avoid the dangers of accumulation, fiscal, and legitimation crises. Accumulation crises could be triggered by a flight of capital to more favourable, profitable locations if the economic environment deteriorated, fiscal crises by state expenditure rising too far as a share of national income (with the added

---

[4] Again there are important differences among members of the 'school', as Boyer makes clear, but for present purposes these matter less than the features they share in common.

risk of inducing capital flight), and legitimation crises as a result of it falling too low, leading to significant fractions of the population challenging the right of the state to act in the ways that it did.

Thus, for regulationists the key role for the national state was to discover an appropriate coupling of social mode of regulation and economic growth model to constitute and reproduce a viable regime of accumulation, simultaneously meeting the competitive demands of various social groups while keeping diverse crisis tendencies within manageable limits. Subsequent developments in regulationist thought have emphasized that regulation is a multi-scalar process and that there are important governance mechanisms and institutions in civil society as well as within the state (see, e.g. Jessop 1997). However, this does not deny the key role of the (national) state within such multi-scalar and complex systems of regulation. As such, firms seek to influence state policies at various regulatory scales and shape the form and content of such modes of regulation, seeking to construct them in ways that favour and help secure their interests (recognizing that this involves firms competing among themselves to shape state policy agendas). A problem with regulationist approaches, however, is that they have little to say about how transition from one regime of accumulation and mode of regulation to another takes place—how, for example, this reflects the political strategies of firms and their articulation with those of other social actors. There is a seemingly seamless shift from one regime of accumulation and mode of regulation to another. Such a non-problematic transition sits uneasily with the messy complexity of the historical geographies of capitalist economies and their overdetermination as a result of struggles between social actors over (*inter alia*) the extent and form of state involvement in economy and society.

Recognizing this, the issue of firms seeking to act politically to shape state policy agendas can also be considered from a different theoretical perspective, that of Foucauldian concepts of governmentality (see, e.g. Rose 1996; Dean 1999). Governmentality is helpful in further understanding these issues because it emphasizes the ways in which the conception, scope, and content of state policies and other mechanism of government, governance, and regulation are imagined and defined and the ways in which policies are enacted and practised. As such, different modes of social regulation can be seen as expressions—and embodiments—of particular governmentalities. Rather than emphasize structures (although it is important not to forget or to underplay the significance of these structures), governmentality approaches emphasize practices and performances. As such, they may be useful in helping understand the messy transitions and translations from one regime of accumulation and mode of regulation to another which regulationist approaches tend to gloss over.

Governmentality is intrinsically linked to the activities of expertise, the role of which is not one of weaving an all-pervasive web of social control, but of enacting assorted attempts at the calculated administration of diverse aspects of conduct through the countless, often competing, local tactics of education, persuasion, inducement, management, incitement, motivation, and encouragement. Moreover, such activities are territorially demarcated. Space is an important element of governmentality because in order to govern it is necessary to render visible the space over which government is to be exercised. This is not simply a matter of looking at pre-given spaces: 'space has to be re-presented, marked out' (Thrift 2002: 205). This thereby locates the regulatory space of the state as one element in wider circuits of power and moves from a position that sees the state as simply an explanation of other events to one that regards the specific activities of the state as themselves to be explained. The black box of the state must be opened up in order to explain how it can perform with a degree of functional coherence. The focus is shifted to the co-evolution of the activities of the state and those of other political actors, including firms, as they seek to influence one another's actions and practices and it is by no means guaranteed that an (and even less so, the only) outcome of this process is a functional coherence in state activity. As Jessop (1990: 229) puts it, such internal coherence can only be achieved through the successful realization of specific 'state projects' which unites state agencies and officials behind a distinct line of action. Achieving such unity is thereby *always* a contingent matter. Even if it is achieved, however, there is no guarantee that such projects will always and only have their intended effects. State policies chronically produce unintended—as well as, or instead of, intended—outcomes and, as such, carry an immanent tendency to generate rationality crises. An emphasis on competing tactics and unintended consequences thus ties in neatly with ideas of crisis theories and a structural tendency to a crisis in crisis management precisely because of the inability to anticipate all the impacts of action. It suggests, for example, that in acting politically, not only states but also firms may produce effects other than those intended to further their own interest.

Jessop's strategic-relation theory (1990) of the state thus synthesizes elements of Foucauldian and neo-Gramscian thought. He draws together neo-Gramscian ideas as to how hegemonic practices are channelled through complex ensembles of institutions dispersed throughout civil society with Foucault's 'capillary' notion of power in theorizing the mechanisms of state power and knowledge and in seeking to account for *how* state power is developed and deployed. While there is a tension here in so far as neo-Foucauldians emphasize the autonomy of political discourse whilst neo-Gramscians are concerned to identify the economic and social bases of state power (MacKinnon 2000: 297), Jessop uses this tension to good effect. This is a view of power as fluid and relational, exercised from innumerable points within civil society, the economy, and the state, in productive networks of power that extend beyond the state. Nonetheless, Foucault privileged the role of the state (the 'macro-physics of power') as 'the point of strategic codification of the multitude of power relations ("the micro-physics of power") and the apparatus in which hegemony, meta-power, class domination and "sur pouvoir" are organised' (Jessop 1990: 239). For Jessop, then, the state is inscribed in all social relations and thus is simultaneously: a site of power; a generator of strategies and tactics; a product of strategies, so that the structure and modus operandi of the state is historically and geographically specific. Firms as a significant set of social actors are thus unavoidably caught up in and seek to shape, as well as being shaped and influenced by, the networks of power that impact upon state policies and in which these policies are embedded.

7.3 Constructing a New Mode of Governmentality and a New Mode of Social Regulation in North-East England in the 1920s and 1930s

In this part of the chapter, drawing on detailed empirical research in northeast England in the period from 1870 to 1946 (see also Carney and Hudson 1978; Hudson 1989), I illustrate how specific capitalist interests, acting collaboratively and cooperatively, shaped emergent forms of state policy, the transition from one mode of regulation to another (liberal to interventionist) as an integral part of the creation of a new governmentality regarding the relationships between capital and the state and the objects of state policy. This shows how major firms based in the region, after a period of struggle and uncertainty, came to adopt clear political strategies, not only to create and seek to administer new forms of state policy to underpin their interests but also to enrol other key social forces in the region—notably major trade unions—into a project that was represented as being (allegedly) in the regional interest, as serving the interests of all people resident in the region rather than simply specific private interests. Furthermore, this was a shift in the dominant conception of governmentality that was to have not only regional but also national effects and consequences as regions became the objects of specific state regional policies.

7.3.1 Liberal Ideology and Politics in the North-East, 1870–1914

The dominant mode of regulation in the north-east in this period was firmly grounded in liberal politics, in a governmentality that gave primacy to the market as a resource allocation mechanism, asserted the common interests of 'masters and men' and restricted the role of the state to the establishment, maintenance, and regulation of markets (see e.g. Moore 1974). Views as to the harmony of interests between 'labour and capital' were propounded extensively by the 'masters' in the region between 1870 and 1890 as part of a deliberate political strategy. They were closely tied to the institution of the practice of 'sliding scales', by which wages were cut by agreement in times of 'bad trade'. In order to function as intended, sliding scales required pliable trade unions, which nevertheless controlled the men, and an ideology that explained the naturalness and inevitability of wage cuts and the wrongness and futility of strikes. Liberal paternalism served as part of the mode of regulation and an elaborate set of rewards and sanctions helped moderate, Liberal men to become and remain trade union leaders.

However, these elaborate arrangements came under pressure by the mid-1880s. Fundamentally, this was because the sliding scale arrangements were sustainable only if periods of bad trade were not so severe as to force owners to make 'requests' of the union leaders that the men could not tolerate. In County Durham this is precisely what happened. Each crisis after 1890 weakened the hold of the progressive masters since they were driven to more severe measures to overcome the growing resistance of the men to wage cuts. The actions of the masters increasingly undermined the position of Liberal trade unionists and, conversely, gave opportunities for militants to further disturb the allegiances of the men, and provoke strikes and industrial action (see Gregory 1968: 68–81). Increasingly, the existing mode of regulation became untenable, as the concept of governmentality on which it was grounded became fragile and contested.

7.3.2 Seeking to Resolve Crises: The Politics of Reaction, 1918–36

By 1914 most of the main branches of economic activity in the Great Northern Coalfield, and in other similar UK regions, were interconnected via a variety of forms of inter-firm collaboration. These included: family ties; interconnecting directorships, trade associations, price-fixing rings, and employers' organizations that tied companies into interlocking coal combines (see Carney, Hudson, and Lewis 1977; Hudson 1989). Moreover, critically, the bulk of the capital of combines in the north-east was 'fixed' within the region in productive capacity (mines, machines, railways, and housing) or in activities associated with trade generated by production (ships, banks, port equipment, selling and dealing, insurance). This profoundly restricted the scope of their attempts to cope with the slump and depression of the interwar period.

Until 1921, combines in the region enjoyed booming profits, first in the war, then in a post-armistice speculative surge but, quite suddenly, boom conditions evaporated. This affected all the main companies in the region, some very severely. The majority of combine interests reacted in common. Locked into a Liberal governmentality, the problem as they saw it was that the war had 'distorted normal trade', while the solution lay in restoring the previous mode of regulation. As such, the appropriate policy was to cut wages and raise the number of hours worked and this was zealously applied across the north-east and in similar regions in the UK. The policy was relentlessly implemented. In the conditions of the 1870s wage cuts would have been followed by price cuts and a resolution of the crisis since commodities would have been cheapened sufficiently to restore profitability. However, in the 1920s there was a different outcome. The more vigorously the policies were applied, the more chronic unemployment intensified. In the Liberal world this could only happen because the cuts were not severe enough. Thus the failure of the policy in practice resulted in its intensification. However, these failures were accompanied by an active search for 'new' solutions appropriate to the new conditions. This accelerated after the general strike of 1926 when the dangers to social stability of single-minded wage cutting were amply demonstrated (especially to non-coal combine industrial and commercial interests in the UK: Gilbert 1976: chs. 10 and 11).

A variety of new policy innovations was explored as companies sought to construct new political strategies to combat the threat to their interests posed by crisis. These options included: mass lay-offs; capacity closures; amalgamation via merger and acquisition; cartel formation; labour transfer from areas of persistent unemployment; and, indicative of the depths of despair in discovering new policy solutions, the promotion of agricultural land settlement schemes to allow a degree of self-provisioning by the unemployed. Each of these policies was 'tried out' in the period after 1926 and, in practice, found to make things worse. Consequently, the Liberal mode of regulation and the conception of governmentality in which it was embedded were shattered in the north-east and elsewhere. However, by the mid-1930s no new coherent programme and mode of regulation had emerged to replace them. This was extremely serious, especially for those, such as the combines of the north-east which had much of their capital tied up in the Depressed Areas.

Although they had subscribed to the policies and politics of reaction in the 1920s and to the other policies outlined above, influential members of combines in the north-east were appalled at the damage done to their own interests (economic and political) by the failures of both the old mode of regulation and the politics of reaction that this failure set in motion. By 1936 there was evidence of an emergent alternative governmentality and a considerable commitment in the north-east (and also in Scotland, Wales, and Lancashire) to search for a new mode of regulation and 'new policies', to explore the possibilities for capital in selective state intervention and protectionism.

7.3.3 The Politics of Modernization, 1911–46

From an early stage, Chambers of Commerce in the north-east began to explore policy options that pre-figured a change in the dominant mode of regulation in the region (and beyond), seeking to attract inward investment to the area. The Chambers were formed by a combination of interests which included coalowners, shipowners, iron and steel masters, banks, shipbuilders, owners of chemical works, railway interests, dock companies, import and export agents, and public utility companies. The principal features of this combination of interests were twofold. First, ownership and control ran across all branches of production and activity in their specific subregions (Teesside, Tyneside, and Wearside) as well as the north-east in general. Second, and critically, the capital represented in the Chambers was mainly tied up *within the region*. It was therefore of great concern to the companies comprising the combines to ensure that conditions for continued capital accumulation in the region were reproduced. This required three conditions being met. First, gaining control over wage bargaining (through, e.g. the Northumberland and Durham Coal Owners' Association, the Shipowners' Association, North of England Iron and Steel Manufacturers' Association, and the North-East Engineering Trades' Employers Association). Second, the assembly and retention of labour forces (through colliery housing, housing trusts, and building societies). Third, establishing control over the formal political life of the region, via success in national and local government elections. At the time, political control was specifically regional in its focus because the assets of the combine owners were predominantly fixed in the region. There were also specific interests concerned to increase industrial activity. For instance, the rail companies had a direct interest in expanding traffic. The Port of Tyne Commissioners (a combination of shipowners, shipbuilders, and coal-owners) wished to increase use of the port and of the land they owned. Similarly, the public utilities wished to attract new industries to expand their markets. Finally, new industries would increase the rate income available to local authorities and so lessen the rate burden of existing concerns—all the main local authorities were linked into the Chambers. For these reasons, established interests in the region sought to construct a new governmentality, incorporating an interventionist mode of regulation that would redefine the relationships between capital and state, define the region as an object of regional policy, and accord a central role to the state in attracting new industries.

From the mid-1920s District Development Boards on Teesside, Tyneside, and Wearside also sought to promote such changes. By 1925 many industries in these areas were in a depressed condition. For example, on Tyneside this was especially so in shipbuilding and associated trades, shipping and the coal export trade. This greatly affected port interests, and the associated railway and public utility companies' interests. Thus, in that year the Tyne Improvement Commissioners (comprising representatives of the main private sector concerns with interests in the river, the Newcastle and Gateshead Chamber of Commerce, the public utility companies, and all local authorities in Tyneside) established the Tyneside Industrial Conference 'to consider the problem of industrial development' (Tyneside Industrial Development Board n.d.). The organization was run on lines similar to the Chambers of Commerce and its policy was to persuade 'industrialists' (including those located outside the UK) 'who contemplated *opening factories* in this country' to inquire to the Conference executive about '... *sites* for new works, facilities, rates and labour supply'. Its executive would provide a *coordinating* role, putting 'industrialists' in touch with the 'right people'. In 1935, following an Act of Parliament, the Tyneside District Board became the Tyneside Industrial Development Board. Between 1935 and 1939 over thirty new industries were established on Tyneside but their number was of less significance than the fact that they confirmed a qualitative shift in the dominant governmentality and mode of regulation in the region (and in similar regions eslewhere in the UK).

The policy of the Tees District Development Board was very similar to that of the Tyneside Industrial Development Conference, with one important addition which further elaborated the emergent new governmentality and the embryonic mode of regulation. It arose from the joint activities of the Teesside Chamber of Commerce and the Development Board between 1929 and 1936. This was the specific policy of central government trading estates to attract new industries. Again, this was to be the precursor of more general changes in national government policy and the emergence of a more interventionist mode of national state activity.

7.3.4 The New Programme of Regional Development, 1934–46

By the mid-1930s, therefore, combine and allied interests had successfully prosecuted a political strategy that had tentatively established policies which differed from those of earlier years. However, these policies and the new concept of governmentality in which they were embedded was neither widely accepted nor confidently proclaimed. Until the end of 1934 the new policies had grave limitations. First, they had neither involved nor even welcomed the intervention of central government departments. Second, trade union and Labour Party leaders in the region were hostile and had a recent record of sustained militancy. Finally, the new policies had conspicuously failed to stem the growing tide of unemployment by attracting new industries.

The establishment of a Commissioner for the Special Areas in England and Wales, indicative of a changing governmentality at national level, defining and representing 'Special Areas' as objects of state policy, altered the first of these limitations. The Commission strengthened organizations promoting the new policies. New Development Boards were encouraged (in south-west Durham and Hartlepool) and existing Boards given financial support. Moreover, funds were made available for a Regional Development Board and new executive organizations, funded via the Special Areas Act, were formed. These were especially important as avowed 'experiments' in implementing the new policies because the main advocates of these policies took charge of the operation of the executive organizations (and their budgets) as well as of the rejuvenated and new development boards

One of the most important policy innovations was the formation, in 1935, of the North-East Development Board (NEDB) under the Chairmanship of Lord Ridley. The initial aim of the organization was to allow '... the exchange of opinions and concerted action on non-party lines by representatives of a great variety of interests who have no other common meeting ground'. As such, the Board sought to overcome the limited class basis of support for the new regional development policies, although its early policy and composition were similar to those of the other development boards. The main issue identified by the NEDB at this time was 'to further on behalf of each and every part of the Area, the development of new industries and the revival and extension of existing industries in the area'.

By 1938 the Board had become an important coordinating institution in the region. Board activities had included a publicity campaign designed to make more widely known the opportunities and facilities for industrial development within the region, attempts to encourage the expansion of industries already established there and to attract new ones, and recommendations to the Government to expedite the improvement of the social and economic conditions of the north-east (Royal Commission on the Geographical Distribution of the Industrial Population 1938). By this time, the NEDB membership included several Labour Members of Parliament, many local authority representatives, and several trade unionists and members of the Industrial Advisory Council, although the latter served as individuals and not as representatives of their organizations.

The assimilation of Durham County Council (DCC) and the Durham Miners' Association (DMA) into the NEDB, alongside long-standing foes of Labour such as the coalowners, very soon after both DCC and the DMA had been militantly hostile to the National Government, was little short of remarkable. What remains questionable is their commitment to building a consensual regional policy. Subsequent events suggest that the industrialists/employers made the main policy innovations and set the political agenda for the emergent new mode of regulation whereas the trade unions and local authorities accepted the policies but played a minor role in their formulation.

Even so, by 1938 a 'regionalist' cross-class alliance was being established but dominated by major companies and other capitalist concerns seeking new ways out of Depression, often having tried and failed with the old remedies such as lockouts, evictions, blacklists, and wage cuts. As such, these companies were now central to an emergent mode of regulation in which their interests were hegemonic, represented as those of 'the region' (see Hudson 2001: ch. 8). The development boards appealed to a 'regionalist' sentiment, seeking to suggest that everyone in the north-east was 'suffering together' and all must unite to pull out of the Depression. For example, consumers in the region were urged to buy from north-eastern producers; import substitution was encouraged. There were, however, other elements. The most important of these, in the context of an emergent new governmentality, was that the NEDB had come to the tentative conclusion that state intervention to control industrial location was necessary. Some control had to be established over the new industries (such as car manufacturing, consumer electrical goods, and aircraft) that had expanded dramatically in the south-east in the interwar period. The NEDB was, however, in 1938 reluctant to specifiy how state control of industrial location should be established. However, that this view was being advanced, even tentatively, by leading figures regionally and nationally in the parties of the National Government was of central importance, while the Labour representation on the NEDB was unlikely to oppose such a proposal.

The grounds for consensus and the acceptance of the new governmentality by the Labour movement in the region had thus been established, albeit tentatively, by 1938. The arrangements were fragile, however, partly because of continuing Labour hostility and partly because the 'experimental' regional interventions of the National Government had not eradicated Depression, even through re-armament expenditure. Moreover, the NEDB could only innovate policy as thought and not as practice as it had scant financial resources. Beyond those, implementation depended on influencing the actions of others—central government, the agencies set up by the Commissioner for the Special Areas and local authorities, though the latter were still badly affected by the financial disasters of the Depression.

7.3.5 The Northern Industrial Group

The NEDB was wound up, probably in 1940, but the policy that it had tentatively adopted was made much more elaborate in 1943 by the same industrial interests and employers, together with some major trade unionists who had been involved in the NEDB's activities. In 1943, a new combination of these interests was formed, the Northern Industrial Group (NIG).

The Group was formed by a small number of regional notables (associates of Lord Ridley, a major influence in the economy and politics of the region) who met in 1943 to discuss the problems that would arise on the 'reconversion' of the regional wartime economy to a peacetime economy. Their discussions resulted in the circulation of a draft document to other employers and trade unionists which, after further discussion was published in 1943 as 'Considerations Affecting PostWar Employment in the North East'. There was clear continuity of constituent members between the pre-war NEDB and the new NIG and, equally importantly, a clear continuity with, but amplification of, the policies and views expressed on behalf of the NEDB by Lord Ridley in evidence to the Royal Commission in 1938.

This publication set out an elaborate programme around which all the signatories had sunk their differences. There were several elements to the programme. First, the change from war to peace economy should ensure continuity of employment in each part of the country. Second, in this transition period unemployment in the north-east should be alleviated by schemes for public works. Third, a stable level of employment in the 'heavy industries' must be assured by national policy. Taken together, these three policies suggest that the Group not only saw that state intervention would be necessary both for the short-period 'reconversion' of national and regional economies to peacetime production but also that such intervention *ought* to occur and be instrumental in achieving economic and social ends. The second policy was a continuation of the work feebly sanctioned before the war but the Group envisaged it as involving a much enlarged public expenditure. The third policy would directly benefit all the main signatories of the Report, including union leaders in the 'heavy industries'. The Group clearly welcomed enhanced state intervention in the economic and social life of the region and had a clear view as to the form that this intervention ought to take, based upon the wartime experience of its members who had been given positions of executive power in the state apparatus. Thus, Lord Ridley was the Controller of the Ministry of Production in the region, other NIG signatories controlled the administration of coal production, shipping, engineering, iron and steel, and chemicals. These experiences helped erode the 'old' Liberal opposition to state involvement in economy and society and further underpinned the transition from a liberal to an interventionist mode of regulation. However, although the newly converted supporters of state intervention in the region included trade unionists, it is by no means clear that the new enthusiasm for state intervention extended to the Labour Party. This was because a considerable radicalization was occurring in the rank and file of the Labour Party, which was pressing for what were regarded as socialistic uses of state power.

The fourth point in the programme was that future government policy should recognize that 'the large scale transference of population from the North East to other areas is socially and economically undesirable'. However, the Group firmly supported the view that population should be relocated *within* the region, with finance for this provided by central government to carry out the local reorganization of housing and industry in areas such as south-west Durham. Such policies aimed to retain or make available labour to satisfy the general requirements of accumulation as well as the specific requirements of individual companies.

The other main aspect of the programme of interest here concerned 'new industries': 'in order to ensure adequate employment a policy of diversification of industry for the North East must be adopted'. This could only be brought about by enhanced state intervention in the location of industry. Pre-war Liberal reservations about state 'interference' in the market and in 'freedom' of businessmen to do as they pleased were swept aside in a confident appeal to 'the national interest', which was ill-served by the overconcentration of new industry in London. 'Government-' sponsored factories, trading estates, related measures to overcome labour problems, and government intervention to reduce freight rates, ought to be allied to a strict control over the location of new factory space. This would be achieved by using control over materials' allocation evolved to regulate the war economy.

This latter set of policies, especially the strong support for physical controls over the location of industry, was, compared to the pre-war period, radical. It was based on the realization by capitalist interests with most of their assets still tied up in the region that expansion of sales and revenues was likely to be most rapid if the 'heavy' industries were 'kept' buoyant by government policy, combined with a government sponsored injection of new firms. If the price to be paid was further state control, this was acceptable. This remarkable shift from the old 'Liberal' fear of state intervention, with capital calling for a new interventionist mode of regulation, reflected the confidence of its private sector proponents that they could shape the activities of the state to their own commands and requirements.

The NIG elaborated on its 1943 programme, especially in response to the 1944 White Paper on Employment Policy (Ministry of Labour 1944). In its November 1944 'Memorandum on the Government White Paper on Employment Policy', the Group set out its policy as to how the 'Development Areas' should be administered The White Paper on Employment Policy suggested that in Development Areas, there would be regionally organized branches of the departments concerned with industrial location policy. The Group Memorandum responded to these proposals as follows: 'We would like to emphasize strongly that success depends upon quick decision and that this will not be obtained unless the various Government Departments in Whitehall delegate full authority to their regional representatives ... '

However, this administrative decentralization would not, in the Group's contention, be effective unless other changes were made. Not only did the Group consider it '... to be of vital importance that the Government regional organisation should have effective executive responsibility' but such an organization should '... maintain close contact with and ... be advised by a parallel group representing employers, employees and other interests in the area.... The Northern Industrial Group and the North East Development Association *because of their widely representative character* and the work which they are already carrying out, can advise in many ways any Government regional organisation which may be established' (NIG 1944: 11, emphasis added). This remarkable change in the conception of the most appropriate governmentality and new mode of regulation clearly reflected the perception by the NIG that it had successfully prosecuted political strategies that secured the interests of private capital in the north-east.

7.4 Concluding Comments

The formation of the NEDB and its reappearance as the NIG allied to the North-East Development Association were the results of political action by combine interests to discover a viable programme of regional development as an integral component of a new mode of regulation, encompassing a radical shift towards an interventionist state. As such, it reflected a qualitative shift in conceptions of governmentality. By 1944 the combine interests had their programme, the aims of which were:

... (a) to develop and promote the prosperity of existing industry in the North East, including the basic industries on which the Region depends for the greater part of its employment.
(b) to encourage commercial, technical and industrial research with a view to developing ancillaries to the basic industries and to help to establish new industries and so give a wider spread of employment by a greater diversity.
(c) to advise and co-operate with the Government and other bodies in respect of industrial development and needs of the Region in relation to Local and national plans with the object of maintaining a high Level of employment throughout the Region. (NIG 1946: 3)

Moreover, by 1944, this programme had obtained very broad support in the Labour movement in the region. The major capitalist interests in the region had succeeded in defining their specific interests as the general interest of all in the region, or making their interests hegemonic. This reflected astute political action and tactics by these companies and their representatives. Indeed, such was the confidence of the NIG that in 1944 it was, in effect, advocating the establishment of an entirely new form of government, a new mode of regulation in which the main government departments would be decentralized, have considerable autonomy, and be 'advised' by the Group and the NEDA. This prospect rapidly disappeared, however, with the demise of the wartime Coalition Government.

In the early days of the subsequent Labour government, the double-edged character of the Group's new position was revealed. If the government could be directed by capital to introduce certain policies favourable to combine interests, what might a government directed by socialists do? Might such a government not entirely demolish the carefully evolved NIG programme by taking the 'commanding heights' of the regional and national economy out of private hands entirely? This possibility had not been contemplated until 1945 and in response to it, combine interests had to rediscover elements of the Liberal mode of regulation and of the politics of reaction that had seemed to be utterly ineffective when it seemed that a permanent broad consensus on a full employment programme of regional development and national economic policy had been reached. This sharply illustrated that political strategies and tactics that seemed to have been extremely successful in protecting and developing private sector interests via new forms of state involvement with economy and society could produce unexpected, unintended, and unwanted effects and provoke attempts to re-impose former modes of regulation and concepts of governmentality.

References

Boyer, R. (1990). *The Regulation School: A Critical Introduction*. New York: Columbia University Press.

Carney, J. and Hudson, R. (1978). 'Capital, Politics and Ideology: North East England, 1870–1946', *Antipode*, 10(2): 64–78.

—— ——, and Lewis, J. (1977). 'Coal Combines and Inter-regional Uneven Development in the UK', in D. Massey and P. Batey (eds.), *Alternative Frameworks for Analysis*. London: Pion.

Dean, M. (1999). *Governmentality, Power and Rule in Modern Society*. London: Sage.

Gregory, R. (1968). *The Miners and British Politics, 1906–1914*. Oxford: Oxford University Press.

Hay, C. and Jessop, B. (1995). 'Introduction: Local Political Economy; Regulation and Governance', *Economy and Society*, 24: 303–6.

Holloway, J. and Piciotto, S. (eds.) (1978). State and Capital: A Marxist Debate. London: Arnold.

Hudson, R. (1989), *Wrecking a Region: State Policies, Party Politics and Regional Change in North East England*. London: Pion.

—— (2001). *Producing Places*. New York: Guilford.

Jessop, B. (1990). *State Theory: Putting Capitalist States in Their Place*. Cambridge: Cambridge University Press.

—— (1997). 'Capitalism and Its Future: Remarks on Regulation, Government and Governance', *Review of International Political Economy*, 4: 561–81.

MacKinnon, D. (2000). 'Managerialism, Governmentality and the State: A Neo-Foucauldian Approach to Local Economic Governance', *Political Geography*, 19: 219–314.

Ministry of Labour (1944). *Employment Policy*, Cmd. 6527, HMSO.

Moore, R. (1974). *Pitmen, Preachers and Politic*. Cambridge: Cambridge University Press.

Northern Industrial Group (1943). *Considerations Affecting Post-War Employment in the North East*. Newcastle upon Tyne.

—— (1944). *Memorandum on the Government White Paper on Employment Policy*. Newcastle upon Tyne.

—— (1946). *Objects, Organisation Methods*. Newcastle upon Tyne.

Poulantzas, N. (1975). *Classes in Contemporary Capitalism*. London: New Left Books.

—— (1978). *State, Power, Socialism*. London: New Left Books.

Rose, N. (1996). 'Governing Advanced Liberal Democracies', in A. Barry, T. Osborne, and N. Rose (eds.), *Foucault ad Political Reason: Liberalism, Neo-Liberalism and the Rationalities of Government*. London: UCL Press, pp. 37–64.

Royal Commission on the Geographical Distribution of the Industrial Population (1938). *Minutes of Evidence*, 18th Day, 31st March, HMSO.

Thrift, N. (2002). 'Performing Cultures in the New Economy', in P. du Gay and M. Pryke (eds.), *Cultural Economy: Cultural Analysis and Commercial Life*. London: Sage.

Tyneside Industrial Development Board (n.d.). *Tyneside Story*. Newcastle upon Tyne.

Von Braumühl, C. (1978). 'On the Analysis of the Bourgeois Nation State Within the World Market Context', in J. Holloway and S. Piciotto (eds.), *State and Capital: A Marxist Debate*. London: Arnold.

Part V

The Firm in Place

8

Studying the New Economy: An Activity Specific Approach to the High-Tech Firm

Mia Gray

8.1 Introduction

The growth of high-tech industries in the USA has engendered much hyperbole about the behaviour, structure, and dynamic potential of the high-tech sector from the popular media, public policy circles, and academia.[1] Despite all the attention, there is a great deal of misinformation surrounding high-tech industries and their effect on regional growth. Although geographers and planners have often enriched the debate, they have also, at times, added to some of the confusion about high-tech industries and regional growth due to their assumptions surrounding the high-tech firm and their minimization of broader institutional explanations. This chapter attempts to revisit some of the main assumptions surrounding the industry, the nature of the firm, and how we study the high-tech firm, and suggests ways around the current impasse.

The last two decades in geography and planning have seen a flourishing literature develop around the issues of industrial production and regional development. While much of the European literature has focused on craft-based innovative industries, American studies have focused much more

---

[1] High-technology industries are defined as those with 'greater than the national average of engineers, engineering technicians, computer scientists, mathematicians, and life scientists' (Glasmeier 1991: 19). Glasmeier identifies over fifty high-tech industries, broken down to a four digit SIC level, using this criterion, including computers, microelectronics, aerospace, and pharmaceuticals (Glasmeier 1991).

on the growth and success of high-tech innovative industries. High-tech was particularly enticing to US scholars because of its exceptional growth and, perhaps even more important, its tendency to agglomerate and become anchored in a region (Scott 1988*a*; Saxenian 1996).

In both the craft and high-tech cases, academics theorize that innovative firms are increasingly dependent upon social, institutional, and economic factors that are interwoven at the regional level into a local 'world of production' (Storper 1993). Over the years, a large body of literature built up around the regional development, structure, location, and organization and competitive strategies of high-tech industries in the USA (Hall and Markusen 1985; Scott and Angel 1987; Scott 1988*b*; Glasmeier 1991; Scott 1992; Gray, Golob, and Markusen 1996; Saxenian 1996; Markusen, Campbell, and Detrick 1999; Lyons 2000).

Although this literature has produced many insights into regional change and firm behaviour, all too often it is marked by a problematic treatment of the high-tech firm that obscures the relationship between industrial growth and regional change. This chapter critiques some of the existing approaches to high-tech regional growth. After reviewing some of the popular regional growth theories and their application to high-tech regions, this chapter highlights their strengths and weaknesses. I argue that the approach often used to explore the relationship between regions and the high-tech growth is flawed. I use a case study of the biopharmaceutical industry to argue that high-tech firms are much more variable and fragmented than many studies show. Firms can exhibit agglomeration alongside decentralization and are much more fractured than often portrayed—they tend to employ multiple strategies and face multiple external constraints. Many industry studies underestimate institutional variation between regions and tend to minimize institutional factors more generally.

The micro-level approach elaborated in this chapter—an activity specific approach—is one way to tease out the more complex nature of the high-tech firm. It minimizes the problems involved by following a product through each corporate activity, wherever the activity takes place. I argue that to understand firm behaviour and the decision-making process surrounding firm strategy formulation and implementation, we must break down the firm into its functional parts—development, production, and realization processes—and understand the strategic choices and locational opportunities for each separate activity. Organizationally, this means we assume each process may display its own strategy, separate from other functions. Spatially, this means we must study high-tech firms in regions other than new industrial spaces, such as mature regions and rural regions.[2]

I use two case studies of the biotechnology and pharmaceutical industries in the USA to develop an activity specific approach to firm strategy and location in the innovative drug sector.[3] For this study, I conducted a series of interviews with firms, trade associations, trade unions, and market analysts in 1997. I followed these up with additional interviews with market analysts in 2000. Since I am interested in all employment connected with getting the drug to market, wherever possible I conducted interviews with every firm that handled an activity associated with the drug. This is a major change from the way high-tech industries are usually studied and explicitly draws upon concepts and theories on spatial division of labour and commodity chains (Massey 1984; Sayer and Walker 1992; Gereffi and Korzeniewicz 1994).

8.2 Theories of Innovative Industries and Regional Change

The current emphasis on high-tech industry may be a relatively recent phenomenon, but the focus on innovation is not new. From Kondratieff's long waves to Vernon's product cycles, scholars have been trying to link innovation and economic growth. Since other studies have reviewed these theories in more detail (see, e.g. Sternberg (1996) and Gray and Parker (1998)), this chapter will focus on only two variants: flexible specialization and new industrial spaces, because of the large impact they have had on subsequent scholarship in the field.

The theory of flexible specialization has been extremely influential in the debate over industrial and regional change. This theory emphasizes process innovation in networks of small firms in *traditional* industries. This occurs when intensified rivalry, technological change, and market

---

[2] I define a *mature* region as one that retains the physical, institutional, and cultural legacy of a current/previous dominant industry (often, but not always, an oligopoly) whose effects remain strong enough to minimize the redeployment of these assets in another industry. Firms in these ageing, dominant industries often leave their indelible mark on a region by structuring labour-management relations, local labour markets, and the prevailing industrial system. By the same reasoning, a *new* region is one without a strong legacy from a previous round of industrialization. This does not imply the region had no pre-existing economic history, but that the previous activity has left a malleable set of assets, to be moulded and shaped by another industry.

[3] I rely on techniques pioneered in social science case study research (Yin 1984) and corporate interviews to study the firm (Schoenberger 1991; Healey and Rawlinson 1993; Markusen 1994).

segmentation drive firms to constantly innovate and to remain as flexible as possible to avoid being rigidly locked into a particular technology, process, or product industries (Piore and Sabel 1984; Best 1990). This system of production is marked by severe vertical disintegration, as firms specialize in one particular aspect of the production process, as well as sectoral agglomeration, since firms need spatial proximity to respond quickly. The spatial component of the theory stresses not only agglomeration but also, implicitly, an emphasis on mature regions. Scholars of this approach emphasize that mature regions provide a highly skilled labour force, which encourages new firm formation, venture capital, and socialized forms of risk sharing (Becattini 1978; Brusco 1982; Schmitz 1992; Zeitlin 1992). However, the great majority of the case studies in this approach are of European mature regions. It is still debatable to what extent new regions outside Europe can supply the same inputs and institutions.

Economic geographers in the 1980s drew heavily upon the phenomenon of flexible specialization to argue that this mode of development could also exist in new regions *outside* Europe, as a result of educational institutions, government investment, or sheer accident (Scott 1988a; Storper and Scott 1992; Storper 1993). This 'new industrial spaces' school tries to explain the agglomeration of production and research establishments in the USA. Like the flexible specialization model, these theorists contend that fragmented demand undermines mass production and that changing technology allows firms to respond to uncertain demand.

Spatially, however, the new industrial spaces literature differs sharply from the flexible specialization literature. Although still emphasizing agglomeration, the new industrial spaces theorists argue that mature regional economies offer an inhospitable environment to innovative industrial practices. The vertical integration and centralized control exhibited by dominant firms in mature regions precludes effective responses to the increasing volatility of markets and changing technologies (Saxenian 1996). Thus, emerging firms, particularly those firms based on flexible production, find the rigidity of the industrial practices in mature regions untenable. Additionally, like Massey (1984), the new industrial spaces theory contends that mature industrial regions' history of unionization, high wages, labour militancy, and rigid labour relations creates an aversion towards such regions in firms choosing a new location.

Agglomeration functions both to lower transaction costs (Scott 1988a, 1988b) and to spatially link research, manufacturing, and commercialization functions in new industrial spaces. This proximity is necessary for concurrent engineering and incremental process changes (often emanating from the shop floor). Thus, the new industrial spaces theory places particular emphasis on the nature and location of research and production and the relationship between the two.

Finally, like the flexible specialization theory, the new industrial spaces theory contends that industrial innovation is a social process. This means that innovation is not a process solely internal to the firm, but requires a regional network-based industrial system that promotes collective learning and flexible adjustment among the small enterprises with complementary specialties.

The new industrial spaces theory has been influential with scholars following America's high technology industries. Scott's original thesis, and the many studies that used the reasoning and assumptions embedded within it, helped to define how scholars today view high-tech industries in the USA. Many studies seem to support the new industrial spaces thesis that firm strategy in high-tech sectors revolves around flexibility, vertical disintegration, agglomeration, and thus, the need for regions without a strong industrial legacy. Support for this is found in Saxenian's work (1996) on Silicon Valley and Route 128 as well as Scott's own work on the semiconductors industry in Silicon Valley, the aerospace industry, and electronic system houses (Scott and Angel 1987; Scott 1988*b*; Scott and Mattingly 1989; Scott 1992). Additionally, industries such as biotechnology (Willoughby 1993*a*, 1993*b*; Prevezer 1997), the film industry (Storper 1994), medical complexes (Llobrera, Meyer, and Nammacher 2000) and software (Schweikhardt 1993), have been put forward as ones that have created their own flexible accumulation ensembles.

One of the fundamental weaknesses with the new industrial spaces school is its limited institutional analysis. This omission weakens its explanatory power and limits its ability to capture the complexity of the behaviour and strategy of the high-tech sector. Many scholars offer an implicit critique of the assumptions embedded in this literature when they highlight the institutional context in which firms make location decisions. For example, Markusen and her co-authors argue that high-tech firms' strategic and locational choices in the USA were structured by the state's defence spending during the Cold War (Markusen *et al.* 1991).

Ignoring institutional differences is particularly problematic because many scholars have applied the lessons learned from case studies in one country to regional economies in other countries without exploring how the different institutional structures affect replicability. This is seen most clearly when the new industrial spaces theorists use the European cases of flexible specialization to explain the growth of high-tech regions in the USA.

Activity Specific Approach to the High-Tech Firm

The other fundamental problem with the new industrial spaces school is their reliance on a simplified view of the firm—treating the firm as a unified entity with one overarching strategy. Most firms are not unified, but rather are fractured entities where different functions often promote different agendas. While some work has been exemplary in exploring the fractured nature of the firm (Schoenberger 1997; Feldman 2000), most economic geographers have ignored the issue. This problem is seen most clearly in Scott's emphasis (1988*a*) on transaction cost theory to explain agglomeration (see Henry 1992). Although minimizing transaction costs clearly does play a role in firm strategy and location, other factors motivate firm behaviour including minimizing sunk costs and risk, alliances and networks within districts and over distance, and interpreting information through the filter of corporate cultural identity (Clark 1994; Gray et al 1996; Schoenberger 1997).

Therefore, the theory cannot explain how firms construct strategy around issues such as location, partnering, and outsourcing and how they make decisions about different corporate activities (research, development, manufacturing, and marketing). In other words, the emphasis on vertical disintegration, agglomeration, and co-engineering explicitly assumes that all functions are tied to the research function. The implicit argument seems to be, where there is research, there is production, and specialized services. In reality, a firm's different activities can be involved in different production systems, each with their own strategic and locational logic. That is, some functions will simultaneously occur in regional networks, while other activities take place in international networks, while yet others are external-hierarchical functions (Gray, Golob, and Markusen 1996; Massey 1984). This sort of variation is hard to explain within a purely transaction cost framework.

Additionally, the theory does not capture the potential for separate firm functions to develop different strategies. For example, the research and development function may be motivated by competition in new product development and speed to market, while the manufacturing function is motivated by traditional cost-cutting concerns. More counter-intuitively, sometimes the *same* functions can be motivated by different concerns. For instance, one part of manufacturing might follow a 'high road' or advanced production systems approach, while other parts of manufacturing in the same industry might follow the 'low road' of cost competition. The new industrial spaces model does not capture any of these possibilities and, in fact, loses the complexity of firm strategy and the fundamental importance of differentiation (within firms). Firms do not all follow the same strategy—even ones in the same industry and country, using the same technology, can react differently (Massey 1984). Often, firms are responding to other factors beyond those identified in the new industrial spaces theory, such as their regulatory environment, funding options, legitimacy on Wall Street, and previous commitments of capital.

This narrow view of the firm also leads to a limited spatial analysis. Most studies of high-tech industries in the USA are weakened by their limited spatial analysis. Although there are notable exceptions (Saxenian 1996; Hendry, Brown, and Defillippi 1999), most high-tech locational studies analyse an industry only within a particular region, rather than looking at how firms in the industry interact with many regions. This type of approach does highlight firm behaviour in new industrial spaces but ignores it in mature regions, or other regional types, and thus, overemphasizes growth in new regions.

Finally, the assumption of agglomeration leads many regional studies of high-tech industry to focus almost solely on the location of headquarters and R&D (Howells 1990*a*, 1990*b*; Taggart 1991; Thorburn 1998). Scholars justify this narrow focus by arguing that the location of R&D promotes further rounds of research, which enhance *regional* R&D capacity. However, while R&D capacity is an important indicator of a firm's innovative potential, it is not the only (or necessarily the best) signal of a region's well-being. Some scholars' overemphasis on the research function leads them to underestimate the importance of other components of the production process—pilot manufacturing, commercial manufacturing, marketing, and distribution—which may be just as, or even more, important to the economic health of a region.

Regional employment is contingent on the other elements of the production process that firms maintain in each region. Thus, the location of firms in emerging industries involves more than simply tracking R&D capabilities. This suggests that mature regions may play a role in some firm strategies and that mature regions can benefit from high-tech growth, even if the R&D function is located elsewhere, by strengthening other components of the industry's production and commercialization ensemble.

8.3 The Biopharmaceutical Industry

The US drug-producing industry in 1995 comprised almost 1,500 firms, in both traditional pharmaceutical firms and in the newer biotechnology sector. Together, the industry had worldwide sales of roughly $99 billion and roughly 262,000 US workers (US Department of Labor 1993; Standard and Poor's 1996; PhRMA 1997). Firms in both subsectors tend to show strong agglomeration effects, since they require access to skilled labour, suppliers, and specialized business services (Feldman 1985; Fineberg *et al* 1993; Feldman and Schreuder 1995; Gray 1996; Schreuder 1996).

The industry remained an extremely stable oligopoly with almost no entry into the industry throughout much of the post-war period.[4] However, in the last twenty years the rise of the biotechnology sector—with its new technology, new firms, and new locations—upset the traditional stability of the drug-producing industry. The more traditional pharmaceutical firms tend to cluster in New Jersey/New York region, the Upper Midwest, and Puerto Rico; while biotech firms cluster in Northern and Southern California, Boston, and the New Jersey/New York region.

In earlier work, I disaggregated the biopharmaceutical industry into research, development, initial pilot production, intermediate chemical production, and final product production, domestic and foreign marketing activities. I then followed all thirty-two Food and Drug Administration (FDA) approved biotechnology drugs, my proxy for innovation in the field, through each process (Gray 1999). I showed that almost all of the innovation had come from emerging biotechnology firms outside the traditional pharmaceutical sector. The majority of these biotech firms emerged and located their research facilities in new drug-producing regions, while a minority emerged in mature drug-producing regions. However, downstream activities showed a more complicated pattern, with many functions, such as production and marketing, split between firms in new and mature regions (Gray and Parker 1998; Gray 1999). I showed that when the biopharmaceutical industry is treated in this manner, the spatial and organizational structure of the sector suggest a *multi-centred* industry emerging, rather than the exclusive growth of the new regions at the expense of the mature ones.

This section explores the reasons why some biotech firms choose to locate their pilot production, advanced manufacturing, and marketing operations in new regions, usually close to their headquarters and R&D functions, while others choose to locate them in mature regions. I use the case studies to analyse the choices firms made concerning the siting of

---

[4] The one exception was a small Mexican firm, Syntex. The company initially developed the first versions of cortisone, estrogen, and progestogen, and within a few years this led to the development of the first birth control pill. By the mid-1960s, Johnson & Johnson, Searle, and Parke Davis all licensed the technology for oral contraception pills from Syntex, which also had its own birth control pill. The company had broken into the elite oligopoly.

Activity Specific Approach to the High-Tech Firm

downstream functions. I chose three products as cases, each of which represents a different firm strategy. I chose some cases where products were developed in the new spaces of drug-production and others where products were developed in mature regions that have a long history of drug production. I follow a firm's decision surrounding a particular biotech product (not for every product, since firms often change strategy from product to product) and highlight a firm's location decisions regarding downstream functions.

8.4 Case 1—Alferon N: Niche Marketing and Growing Pains

The first case examines a product developed by Interferon Sciences, a small firm in the New York/New Jersey region. Interferon Sciences was founded in 1980, based on its work in alpha interferon.[5] The company is small, with only seventy-seven employees. Their one product, Alferon N, gained FDA approval in 1989.

The company benefits from its location in the mature region, finding it easy to recruit skilled workers and to fill many management positions with ex-pharmaceutical executives. Their strategy is shaped by many external factors, including appealing to Wall Street analysts, overcoming regulatory hurdles, and attaining scale economies. The company's initial strategy was to subcontract out many downstream functions but, unhappy with the results, they are now attempting a more integrated strategy. The company conducts R&D and advanced manufacturing in the region but a large pharmaceutical firm in the Midwest conducts the high volume manufacturing. Dissatisfied with a licensing agreement for domestic marketing, the firm recently took this function back in-house, while retaining numerous licensing deals for foreign marketing.

A majority of the company (53%) is owned by National Patent Development Corporation. Although National Patent does not play an active role in the company, preferring a 'hands off' approach, they do provide Interferon Sciences with certain legal, financial, and administrative services. More significantly, Interferon Sciences and National Patent share office, warehouse, and laboratory space.

---

[5] Interferons are naturally occurring proteins that contribute to the body's natural defences against foreign substances. One type of interferons, alpha interferons have become pre-eminent in biotech research. In 1995, it is estimated that the worldwide market for alpha interferons is $1.5 billion.

199

The company's strategy is to use Alferon N to show potential investors the company's capabilities, to leverage more funds, and then to develop more products. In interviews, company officers explained their strategy: they wanted to use the approval of Alferon N to 'prove themselves' to potential investors, whether or not the drug sold well. The president of the firm explained:

> It was an important strategic move to quickly and successfully take a product through clinical trials, so we went with the easiest indication, even though it's a product with a small market. That put us in good stead on Wall Street and showed that, although we're a small company, we can take a drug through the approval process.

After proving their ability in this manner, they could use their newfound legitimacy to raise funds to support clinical trials for other indications. They were successful in this and issued a series of stock offerings (private and public) in the early 1990s.

Interferon Sciences knew that Alferon N had only a small- to medium-sized potential market and that it might be a few years before they made substantial profits. This situation is common for emerging biotech firms—in 1996 only 9 of the top 100 biotech firms reported a profit (Griffith 1998). However, even with low expectations, product sales were disappointing and, in 1997, Interferon Science had still not achieved profitability and, in fact, had a loss of $22 million.

Interferon Sciences officials claim that the firm emerged in New Jersey because the founders lived there and the presence of the pharmaceutical industry made it easy to hire managers and employees. More importantly, the firm located many functions in the New York/New Jersey region because the company depends on the agglomeration economies provided by the traditional pharmaceutical industry. The high calibre of the labour force is a particular benefit to the firm. At interview, the president cited 'the excellent labour pool—in scientists, technicians, and manufacturing' as the reason the 'area works for us'.

The firm emerged in New Jersey and locates all its research and development facilities in the region. The president stated: 'We do like to keep R&D close by—there's no real distinction between headquarters and research, at least for a small biotech.' Most of their research is focused on gaining FDA approval to treat other illnesses or 'indications' with the same drug. Until recently, most of their work has revolved around the final phases of two additional FDA trials for Alferon N, one to treat HIV-infected patients and one to treat Hepatitis C.

The company's manufacturing is also based in New Brunswick, New Jersey, very close to their headquarters and laboratories. It conducted its own pilot runs and at first used its upgraded pilot plant to produce commercial runs. The company expanded its commercial production facilities by 50 per cent in 1991 and substantially improved its manufacturing process.

The company keeps its advanced production in the New Jersey area because of the skilled scientific and manufacturing workforce in the area. The human resource manager explained:

> We couldn't go to somewhere like Puerto Rico. Maybe under different circumstances, but hiring and training is so easy here. We get people from the pharmaceutical industry ... the process is a bit different, but it's close enough that it's an easy transition for workers.

The president of the firm confirmed this, saying that, 'the presence of the big pharma firms is important. You need that pool of talent. We look for researchers around the nation, but here, its easy to get great process engineers and good production workers.'

This seems to hold only for the firm's advance production operations, the process whereby they create the active ingredients. The high-volume manufacturing—the formulation and packaging—is contracted out to Abbott Labs, located in Chicago. Abbott then uses Sandofi-Winthrop McPherson, located in Kansas, to finish the product. One of Abbott's investor relations officers offered a comparative advantage explanation for the location. She pointed out that, 'we could produce it in a number of places, as long as costs aren't out of line. It just so happens that's where the extra capacity is.'

Marketing has been a major problem for the company. The company sold exclusive marketing and distribution rights to Purdue Pharma in the Midwest, an affiliate of the Purdue Frederick Company, in 1988. Company officials felt Purdue had the clout and resources to maximize sales of the drug. Purdue had the global marketing and distribution system already in place and had the resources to take Alferon N through the approval process in other countries. However, dissatisfied with Purdue's marketing efforts, the company reacquired all of the marketing rights from Purdue in 1996. The president of the firm explained:

> The deal with Frederick Purdue didn't work because Frederick Purdue was not marketing it right. They increased their sales force from 150 reps to 300 reps, but the sales stayed constant. They sell as much of it now with no real marketing as when it was their product.

In 1996, the company set up its own marketing department and hired a vice-president of marketing, with many years experience in the traditional pharmaceutical firms.

The company will still not attempt to market internationally themselves. The new marketing director argued that marketing internationally requires, 'a scale of operations that is impossible for a small firm to maintain', and yet, biotech firms need to maximize their income while products remain under patent. So small biotech firms like Interferon Sciences license the product to larger pharmaceutical firms, which incur little extra cost to market another drug through their pre-existing marketing and distribution system. Interferon Sciences has entered into a number of development and marketing agreements around the world: Fujimoto Diagnostics of Osaka, Japan, has bought the development and marketing rights for the Japanese market; Andromaco, of Mexico City, has already gained regulatory approval in Mexico and will market and distribute the drug; and Cell Pharm GmbH, in Hanover, will seek regulatory approval, market, and distribute the drug in Germany. The firm is continuing to look for potential partners to develop and market Alferon N in other countries.

Interferon Sciences wants to control the sales of their product but the firm cannot profitably market only one drug. The sales of a single product, particularly a product with a small market, cannot support the necessary infrastructure. The company's strategy of resuming control over domestic marketing of Alferon N is based on the assumption that the firm's other products will be approved, so that the firm can realize scale economies in sales and marketing.

In anticipation of additional product approvals, the company again expanded manufacturing. The production operations manager explained that the push for expanded production came from the market and from the institutional environment. First, they needed to be ready for increased demand. Second, the regulatory requirement demands early commitment to a particular manufacturing process. He explained it was necessary since, '... the FDA has changed. They're stricter in their manufacturing oversight. Now, you must have your facilities before approval. It can be risky.'

To allow it to handle domestic distribution, the company also struck a deal with Alternate Site Distributors, a subsidiary of Bergen Brunswig Corporation, a large pharmaceutical distributor. Alternate Site Distribution will establish a wholesale distribution programme, run a clinician and customer product information line on the product, and run a reimbursement programme. These functions are considered too complex for the company to provide for itself.

However, Interferon Sciences suffered a severe set-back in early 1998. The FDA did *not* approve Alferon N for the treatment of HIV, as it had hoped and expected, but ruled that the drug required further testing. In response, the company went through a massive restructuring and laid off about 25 per cent of its workforce, mostly in manufacturing. A few months later, the firm also received discouraging results from the Hepatitis C tests, which led to yet further layoffs and restructuring.

This leaves the firm in a weakened position. The problem is that unpredictable technology, uncertain product approval, and unsteady investment flows make it difficult to establish their reputation and a market presence which the firm needs to survive. Despite the recent bid to increase control over the marketing of Alferon N, and even if the drug is eventually approved to treat other illnesses, it now seems likely that the firm will have to turn to a third party to commercialize its products. The idea of becoming a more integrated firm has become much harder for it to realize.

To summarize, Interferon's decisions about retaining and siting different functions have changed over time. It has always kept research, prototyping, and advanced manufacturing near its headquarters in New Jersey and subcontracted out the high volume production. However, after licensing away the marketing rights to Alferon N, it renegotiated the deal and resumed marketing operations themselves. It assumed it could realize economies of scale with future FDA approvals. Thus, the FDA rejections came as a particular blow. Now the firm will have difficulty retaining its independence from the traditional pharmaceutical firms.

Its location in New Jersey, a mature drug-producing region, seems to satisfy the needs of Interferon Sciences. In particular, the skilled labour force, trained in drug production, if not biologics, seems to benefit the firm. Overall, it seems to find the pharmaceutical presence a boon, suggesting that biotech firms can benefit from the agglomeration economies created by the pharmaceutical firms.

8.5 Case 2—B. Humulin and Neupogen and the 'Research Engine'

The second case is Genentech, one of the oldest and most profitable biotechnology firms in the USA, which emerged in the San Francisco Bay Area (Lee and Burrill 1996). The firm was founded in 1976, one of the founders being a professor at the nearby University of California, San Francisco. The firm issued its first public offering on the stock market in

1980 and received FDA approval for its first product in 1982. A string of other approvals soon followed. In 1997, Genentech's total revenue was over $1 billion and its profit was $129 million.

This case covers two of Genentech's products to highlight the full range of the firm's strategies. Humulin, an early product, was developed by Genentech, but all the downstream functions were licensed to a traditional pharmaceutical producer in a mature region. For its best seller, Neupogen, on the other hand, the firm kept all downstream functions except for foreign manufacturing. More often than not, Genentech has followed the first strategy and traded away the development, manufacturing, and marketing rights for its products. However, it has developed the capacity to commercialize and domestically market a product itself should it think the payoff commensurate with the risk.

The company has been a powerhouse in the industry—performing the initial research on twelve of the thirty-two FDA approved products and is popularly dubbed the 'research engine' of the industry. Indicative of the structure of the sector, it manufactures only four of these products. The remaining products have been licensed to firms in the traditional pharmaceutical industry.

Genentech's first product, Humulin, is a recombinant form of human insulin. The FDA approved the product for treatment of diabetes in 1982. Although Genentech raised roughly $35 million in its initial public offering on the stock market, it was rapidly using this capital to fund ongoing research projects. The company felt unable to both develop the new drug and continue to fund other research. The director of business and corporate development explained: 'We couldn't develop that [Humulin] by ourselves at the time—we didn't have the money, the infrastructure, the know-how....' Instead, Genentech reached a deal with Mid-West based Eli Lilly & Co. whereby Eli Lilly would take the product through clinical trials, develop the manufacturing process, manufacture, and market the product.

Eli Lilly used its engineers, steeped in the chemically based pharmaceutical tradition, to develop a manufacturing product, pilot the production process, and get the process approved by the FDA. Part of the reason why Genentech felt unable to develop the product itself was the difficulty in scaling up the new, and not fully understood, large proteins to commercial scale. The production manager at Genentech explained:

Making a recombinant protein is a very complicated process. You have all these problems being able to express the product in appreciable quantities, commercially scaleable quantities, and then you have to scale that up. So, it's not as straight forward as a chemical process.

However, the Lilly engineers were able successfully to apply the expertise gained in the chemical process to the new recombinant process.

A second factor was that Eli Lilly had the financial resources to fund the development cycle. The director of business development explained that:

> It's a huge development effort to undertake, making a new process for a protein and scaling it up. It's probably one of the most expensive parts of bringing a product to market. Eli Lilly had the funding. They could support a large and complicated effort to find a way to manufacture the protein at commercial scale.

Eli Lilly developed the drug, built the pilot plant, and the final commercial manufacturing plant in Indianapolis, Indiana. Eli Lilly has recently invested heavily in upgrading all its advanced manufacturing facilities in Indiana to more flexible specifications. Its production manager explained that the company policy is to develop and manufacture the active ingredients of the majority of its products in Indiana. Humulin was no exception and in fact, 'we felt it was particularly important to have it close enough for the engineers to fiddle with it, because it was new—we hadn't made proteins before'. The final part of the manufacturing process, the formulation and packaging, occurred in two locations, Indianapolis and Mexico, respectively.

Genentech also sold marketing rights to Eli Lilly. The final agreement stipulated that Lilly would have full marketing rights over Humulin in return for royalties and benchmark payments. Lilly would market the product in the USA, in Europe, Asia, and all other markets. From Lilly's point of view, marketing the product was relatively simple and inexpensive since it already had marketing and distribution channels that spanned the globe. Because of economies of scale, adding an additional drug did not require much additional personnel or infrastructure. On the other hand, as the investor relations manager pointed out, if Genentech were to market the drug by itself, 'we would have had to start from scratch—open offices, just for the one product line'.

Over the years Humulin became one of the most profitable biotech therapeutic drugs ever. In 1995, its worldwide sales were $665 million. However, the general feeling among those I interviewed at the company was that Genentech could have struck a better deal. The case went into litigation and was settled only after years of legal proceedings.

The next time Genentech had a drug with a huge potential market; it followed a very different strategy. Nutropin, an injectable human growth hormone, was approved for a succession of different indications between 1993 and 1997. Realizing the size of the potential market, Genentech decided to develop, manufacture, and domestically market the product itself. Development, pilot production, and commercial manufacturing occurred in the city of South San Francisco. When asked why it located research, pilot and manufacturing production in close proximity, the director of business development replied:

> It really is a very complicated process and there needs to be really close communication between the people developing the processes and the people who are actually developing the drug from the clinical standpoint and pharmacological standpoint.

More recently, Genentech moved Nutropin's manufacturing operations to the periphery of the region. The new facilities are located in Vacaville, a small city in the Sacramento valley, about eighty miles east of San Francisco. The director of business and corporate development stressed that Genentech sited the new operations in an accessible but inexpensive location where it 'can still draw upon the great base of people coming from the universities, and also lower our manufacturing costs. We're still keeping manufacturing close so that our development people can get back and forth—that's important.'

When asked why the firm has kept the development and manufacturing of Nutropin while simultaneously negotiating away the manufacturing and marketing rights of other new products, the director of business and corporate development explained that it depends on the expected size of the market and whether the product 'fits' Genentech. He said:

> If it's a new product and it's an awesome strategic fit and has some really big market potential, we would keep it ourselves. If it's an opportunity over a couple of hundred million, say $300 million at peak, in market opportunities and it's a good strategic fit, it's probably something that we'd be interested in developing here.

Thus, although Genentech has developed its own development and manufacturing capacity, it employs it only when the perceived rewards are large enough to justify the cost and risks involved.

Even in this case, Genentech will not market the products abroad. It still does not possess the necessary international marketing and distribution channels. Instead of trying to market internationally themselves, in 1990 it teamed up with a large Swiss pharmaceutical firm, Roche Holdings, whose American headquarters are in New Jersey. Roche bought 66 per cent of Genentech for $2.1 billion and now has the 'right of first refusal' on foreign marketing rights for future Genentech products. If Roche declines a particular product, Genentech is free to find another partner to

Activity Specific Approach to the High-Tech Firm

market the product abroad. The director of business and corporate development commented:

> It's really hard to build from the ground up the infrastructure to do worldwide development and commercialisation of drugs. You can't afford it. So what you do is a deal like we did with Roche.... We just plug right into them and let them take care of it and they pay us a royalty.

To summarize, Genentech has more often than not traded away the development, manufacturing, and marketing rights for its products, using the licensing fees from smaller products to fund ongoing research. However, it does have the capacity to commercialize and domestically market a product should it think the potential sales are worth the risk.

Genentech emerged in a new drug-producing region because of the university ties of one of the founders. However, Genentech's strategy of licensing the manufacturing and marketing activities means that the products have often been developed, manufactured, and marketed elsewhere, often by firms in mature regions. When the company does retain control over downstream functions, it performs all the functions in the new region to increase communication between the activities, although increasingly these operations are located on the periphery of the region.

8.6 Conclusion

The case studies explored in this chapter illustrate the complexity of firm strategy in an emerging industry and highlight the pitfalls of assuming a particular strategy simply because a firm belongs to the high-tech sector. Instead, the case studies show that numerous strategies are pursued by firms in the *same* industry, using the *same* technology. They also show the strength of following each firm activity separately. Following *each product by function* highlights what might otherwise be lost in such a study: that strategies differ by product even in the same firm. Studies that assume vertical disintegration and agglomeration or downsizing and dispersion tend to miss this intra-firm variation.

The ability to disaggregate our approach also helps disentangle other issues. Much of the literature on high-tech industries assumes low barriers to entry, based on the software industry. But this certainly is not universal within the high-tech sector. In fact, the barriers to entry in the biopharmaceutical industry are still very high and the challenge of the new technology has allowed entry only into research and manufacturing functions. In one sense, each corporate activity (particularly drug approval and marketing) has its *own* barrier to entry, and overcoming one does not ensure the surmounting of the next. Small biotech firms, pressed for cash, often do not have the resources to pursue research, regulatory approval *and* marketing.

The cases explored here demonstrate that, even relatively successful biotech firms that have broken into drug research and advanced manufacturing, still face great barriers to entry for regulatory approval and marketing functions. These functions, particularly the latter, require such large amounts of resources that small firms must often turn to larger ones with bigger budgets to accomplish them. Only the established pharmaceutical firms or the firms with a few blockbuster drugs, have the resources necessary to set up the global and national marketing networks to comfortably take products through the approval process.

The traditional pharmaceutical firms are able to benefit from this since the downstream functions are compatible across the two sectors. Drugs based on biotechnology have the same downstream needs as traditional drugs. This allows the pharmaceutical firms to add the new products at minimal costs due to economies of scale and allows them to maintain their comparative advantage in these areas.

The analysis also shows that firms in both mature and new regions benefit from agglomeration economies. It would appear that the engineering–manufacturing link is important, as theorized, to firms in both types of region. This means that advanced manufacturing functions are kept near R&D. But, as the Genentech–Eli Lilly example shows, pharmaceutical R&D can easily substitute for biotech R&D. However, contrary to the new industrial spaces literature, it seems that firms can gain agglomeration benefits from locating in either new or mature regions. The fact that some biotech firms are successfully researching and producing drugs in mature regions, and are able to use the same labour pool and management experts as the pharmaceuticals, demonstrates that mature regions are providing the inputs necessary for small firm formation and growth. Biotechnology firms in newer areas seem to benefit from the presence of each other, while biotechnology firms in mature regions are similar enough to the pharmaceutical firms to benefit from the presence of the older firms. Respondents from firms in both mature and new, emerging regions spoke of a good labour pool being an important factor in their location. Biotech firms in mature regions found it easy to cross-train pharmaceutical workers, which shows that the industry work-process differs, though not to such an extent that the pharmaceutical industry's 'resources' could not be redeployed.

Activity Specific Approach to the High-Tech Firm

To summarize, new market entrants are using multiple strategies to get around the considerable barriers to entry. Some firms attempt integration while others specialize in a core function. Many firms try to gain attention with early approval and marketing of niche drugs. It seems that only having a 'blockbuster' drug gives a firm the resources to overcome the barriers surrounding many downstream functions. When firms develop drugs with smaller potential markets, they license them to the pharmaceutical producers. The pharmaceutical producers can profitably market smaller products, since they can exploit their existing scale economies, while the smaller firms use the royalties to fund more research (hopefully, the next time leading to a blockbuster). This strategy is seen most easily in Genentech's decisions about which products to keep in-house.

The strategy that a firm chooses is often due to the pressure exerted by external forces, rather than rational internal decision-making. The regulatory state and stock market financiers, in particular, play an important role. Firm strategy lies at the boundary between intended managerial aims and the threats and opportunities created by these other actors. Firms in this fledging industry or subsector are fundamentally shaped by forces outside of their control, such as 'the mood of Wall Street', changes in the regulatory system, or the success of competitor products. These factors often force the biotech firms to make decisions regarding licensing that do not fit their stated strategies. In this way, firms often license their products to pharmaceuticals not as part of a larger strategy but in response to immediate needs.

Another important external institutional factor affecting firms' strategies is the numerous ways that the state shapes the market and the terms of competition in the industry. The state supports university research and creates demand through the inclusion or exclusion of a drug on the Medicare formulary lists. This is a particularly important point for the biotech firms with orphan products that have a limited market yet command monopoly rents. The state also determines the regulatory environment: the FDA approves new drugs and certifies production processes and manufacturing sites. Dealing with FDA requirements often disadvantages the new, small firms that do not possess the resources, expertise, and knowledge to successfully negotiate the process. Again, this encourages small biotech firms to license or sell their products to the traditional pharmaceutical firms.

Certainly, taking a more nuanced look at the biotech industry, through a micro-level, activity specific approach, challenges many assumptions made in the literature surrounding high-tech firms in the USA. It upholds the need for agglomeration of many functions found in both the new industrial spaces and the flexible specialization literatures. However, breaking the firm down into its functional processes highlights that the external economies found in mature regions can substitute for those found in new regions.

Much of the work on high-tech industries in the USA is influenced by the new industrial spaces literature. The assumptions about the firm that run through the thinking of this school means that these theories have difficulty explaining how firms construct strategy around issues such as location, partnering, and outsourcing, and how they make decisions about different corporate activities.

As can be seen above, the activity specific approach is able to offer a more nuanced vision of the firm. It does not assume a firm has one overarching strategy that is executed without problem, but looks for the variation within a firm and between firms. The approach also shows that while high-tech firms are concerned with minimizing costs and the co-location of certain functions, this is balanced by many other considerations such as financing, regulations, and access to markets. Instead, decisions about location, partnering, and outsourcing are not always the intended strategy of the firm, but often the outcome of complex interplay of forces internal and external to the firm.

Acknowledgements

The author would like to thank Ann Markusen, Ron Martin, Peter Maskell and Rolf Sternberg for their help and insightful comments.

References

Becattini, G. (1978). 'The Development of Light Industry in Tuscany', *Economic Notes.* 5–6.

Best, M. (1990). *The New Competition. Institutions of Industrial Restructuring.* Cambridge: Polity Press.

Brusco, S. (1982). 'The Emilian Model: Productive Decentralisation and Social Integration', *Cambridge Journal of Economics*, 6(2): 167–84.

Clark, G. (1994). 'Strategy and Structure: Corporate Restructuring and the Scope and Characteristics of Sunk Costs', *Environment and Planning A*, 26(1): 9–32.

Feldman, J. (2000). 'Civilian Diversification, Learning, and Institutional Change: Growth Through Knowledge and Power', *Environment and Planning A*, 31(10): 1805–24.

Feldman, M. (1985). 'Biotechnology and Local Economic Growth: The American Pattern', in P. Hall and A. Markusen (eds.), *Silicon Landscapes*. Boston, MA: HarperCollins.

—— and Schreuder, Y. (1995). *Initial Advantage: The Origins of the Geographic Concentration of the Pharmaceutical in the Mid-Atlantic Region*, Unpublished manuscript. Carnegie Mellon University and University of Delaware.

Fineberg, D., Gilmore, R., Krantz, J., Llanes, M., Miller, R., Mann, U., and Schmitt, B. (1993). *The Biopharmaceutical Industry in New Jersey: Prescriptions for Regional Economic Development*, Unpublished report. New Brunswick: Rutgers University, Dept. of Urban Planning and Policy Development.

Gereffi, G. and Korzeniewicz, M. (1994). *Commodity Chains and Global Capitalism*. London: Greenwood Press.

Glasmeier, A. (1991). *The High-Tech Potential: Economic Development in Rural America*. New Brunswick, NJ: Transaction Publishers.

Gray, M. (1996). *New Jersey Prospects: The Pharmaceutical Industry in a New Age*, Working Paper #113, Center for Urban Policy Research, Rutgers University, New Brunswick.

—— (1999). *An Activity Specific Theory of Firm Location in Innovative Industries: The Case of the Biotechnology Industry*, Unpublished dissertation. Rutgers University.

—— and Parker, E. (1998). 'Industrial Change and Regional Development: The Case of the US Biotechnology and Pharmaceutical Industries', *Environment and Planning A*, 30(10): 1757–74.

—— Golob, E., and Markusen, A. (1996). 'Big Firms, Long Arms, Wide Shoulders: The "Hub-and-Spoke" Industrial District in the Seattle Region', *Regional Studies*, 30(7): 651–66.

Griffiths, V. (1998). 'Genzyme Follows Prescription for Profitability', *Financial Times*, 5 March: 35.

Hall, P. and Markusen, A. (eds.) (1985). *Silicon Landscapes*. Boston, MA: Harper Collins.

Healey, M. and Rawlinson, M. (1993). 'Interviewing Business Owners and Managers: A Review of Methods and Techniques', *Geoforum*, 24(3): 339–55.

Hendry, C., Brown, J., and Defillippi, R. (1999). 'Regional Clustering of High-technology-based Firms: Opto-electronics in Three Countries', *Regional Studies*, 34(2): 129–44.

Henry, N. (1992). 'The New Industrial Spaces: Locational Logic of a New Production Era', *International Journal of Urban and Regional Research*, 16(3): 375–96.

Howells, J. (1990*a*). 'The Internationalization of R&D and the Development of Global Research Networks', *Regional Studies*, 24(6): 495–512.

—— (1990*b*). 'The Location and Organization of Research and Development: New Horizons', *Research Policy*, 19(2): 133–46.

Interferon Sciences (1998). *Annual Report*. New Brunswick, NJ.

Keeble, D. and Wilkinson, F. (1999). 'Collective Learning and Knowledge Development in the Evolution of Regional Clusters of High-technology SMEs in Europe', *Regional Studies*, 32(4): 295–303.

Lee, K. and Burrill, S. (1996). *Biotech 97 Alignment: The Eleventh Industry Annual Report*. Palo Alto, CA: Ernst and Young LLP.

Llobrera, J., Meyer, D., and Nammacher, G. (2000). 'Trajectories of Industrial Districts: Impact of Strategic Intervention in Medical Districts', *Economic Geography*, 76(1): 68–98.

Lyons, D. (2000). 'Embeddedness, Milieu, and Innovation Among High-technology Firms: A Richardson, Texas, Case Study', *Environment and Planning A*, 32(5): 891–908.

Markusen, A. (1994). 'Studying Regions by Studying Firms', *Professional Geographer*, 46: 477–90.

—— Lee, Y.-S. and DiGionanna, S. (eds.) (1999). *Second Tier Cities. Rapid Growth Beyond the Metropolis*. Minneapolis, MN: University of Minnesota Press.

—— Hall, P., Campbell, S., and Detrick, S. (1991). *Rise of the Gunbelt, The Military Remapping of Industrial America*. New York: Oxford University Press.

Massey, D. (1984). *The Spatial Division of Labour*. London: Routledge.

PhRMA (Pharmaceutical Research and Manufacturers of America) (1997). Reporters Handbook: Key Industry Facts About PhRMA. www.phrma.org/key-industry-facts-about-phrma/>.

Piore, M. and Sable, C. (1984). *The Second Industrial Divide*. New York: Basic Books.

Prevezer, M. (1997). 'The Dynamics of Industrial Clustering in Biotechnology', *Small Business Economics*, 9(3): 255–71.

Saxenian, A. (1996). *Regional Advantage: Culture and Competition in Silicon Valley and Route 128*. Cambridge, MA: Harvard University Press.

Sayer, A. and Walker, R. (1992). *The New Social Economy: Reworking the Division of Labour*. Oxford: Blackwell.

Schmitz, H. (1992). 'Industrial Districts: Model and Reality in Baden-Wurttemberg, Germany', in F. Pyke and N. Sengenberger (eds.) *Industrial Districts and Local Economic Regeneration*. Geneva: International Institute for Labor Studies.

Schoenberger, E. (1997). *The Cultural Crisis of the Firm*. Cambridge, MA: Blackwell.

—— (1991). 'The Corporate Interview as a Research Method in Economic Geography', *Professional Geographer*, 43(2): 180–9.

Schreuder, Y. (1996). 'The German American Pharmaceutical Business Establishment in the New York Region', *Environment and Planning A*, 30(10): 1743–56.

Schweikhardt, G. (1993). *Development of Technology-Based Companies Around the Puget Sound*. Seattle: Economic Development Council of Seattle and King County.

Scott, A. (1988a). *New Industrial Spaces*. London: Pion.

—— (1988b). 'Flexible North America and Production Systems and Regional Development: The Rise of New Industrial Spaces in Western Europe', *International Journal of Urban and Regional Research*, 12(2): 171–86.

—— (1992). 'The Role of Large Producers in Industrial Districts: A Case Study of High-technology Systems Houses in Southern California', *Regional Studies*, 26(3): 265–75.

—— and Mattingly, D. (1989). 'The Aircraft and Parts Industry in Southern California: Continuity and Change from the Inter-war Years to the 1990s', *Economic Geography*, 65(1): 48–71.

—— and Angel, D. (1987). 'The US Semiconductor Industry: A Locational Analysis', *Environment and Planning A*, 19(7): 875–912.

Sternberg, R. (1996). 'Regional Growth Theories and High-tech Regions', *International Journal of Urban and Regional Research*, 20(3): 518–38.

Standard and Poor's (1996). *Healthcare: Pharmaceuticals, Industry Survey*, New York.

Storper, M. (1993). 'Regional "Worlds" of Production: Learning and Innovation in the Technology Districts of France, Italy, and the USA', *Regional Studies*, 27(5): 433–55.

—— (1994). 'The Transition to Flexible Specialisation in the US Film Industry: External Economies, the Division of Labour and the Crossing of Industrial Divides', in A. Amin (ed.), *Post-Fordism, A Reader*. Oxford: Blackwell.

—— and Scott, A. (1992). 'Industrialization and Regional Development', in M. Storper and A. Scott (eds.), *Pathways to Industrialization and Regional Development*. London: Routledge.

—— and Walker, R. (1989). *The Capitalist Imperative: Territory, Technology, and Industrial Growth*. New York: Blackwell.

Taggart, J. H. (1991). 'Determinants of the Foreign R&D Locational Decision in the Pharmaceutical Industry', *R&D Management*, 21(3): 110–12.

Thorburn, L. (1998). 'Innovation by Australian Biotechnology Companies', *Australasian Biotechnology*, 8(5): 280–8.

US Department of Labor, Bureau of Labor Statistics (BLS) (1993). *Current Employment*. Washington, DC: Economic and Statistics Administration.

Willoughby, K. (1993*a*). 'The Local Milieus of Knowledge-based Industries: What Can We Learn From a Regional Analysis of Commercial Biotechnology', in J. Brotchie, P. Hall, E. Blakely and Batty M. (eds.), *Cities in Competition*. Cheshire, UK: Longman.

—— (1993*b*). *Technology and the Competitive Advantage of Regions: A Study of the Biotechnology Industry in New York*, Monograph 44. Berkeley, CA: Institute of Urban and Regional Development, University of California, Berkeley.

Yin, R. (1984). *Case Study Research: Design and Methods*, Applied Social Research Methods Series 5. Beverly Hills, CA: Sage

Zeitlin, J. (1992). 'Industrial Districts and Local Economic Regeneration: Overview and Comment', in F. Pyke and W. Sengenberger (eds.), *Industrial Districts and Local Economic Regeneration*. Geneva: International Institute for Labor Studies.

9

Learning Firms in Learning Regions: Innovation, Cooperation, and Social Capital

Bjørn T. Asheim

9.1 Introduction: Post-Fordism as Learning Economies

At the heart of post-Fordist regional economic growth is the operation of the 'learning' firm in the 'learning' region. The purpose of this chapter is to explore this concept of the firm and the processes that shape it in the context of the transition to post-Fordism under conditions of globalization. In a globalizing learning economy, understanding innovation as interactive learning implies that cooperation is necessary to make firms and regions competitive. Building social capital is a key strategy in promoting such cooperation—within firms, networks of firms, and regions. Social capital can arise both from civicness and from organizational and institutional innovation. But, while the latter can be built, the former can only be built on. Therefore, central to the promotion of cooperation and organizational and institutional innovation is the formation of 'learning' organizations. However, successful learning organizations need the strong involvement of their workers (the micro-level), horizontal cooperation between firms in networks (the meso-level), and a bottom-up, interactive regional innovation system (the macro-level). When combined with organizational and institutional innovations at different administrative levels, these relationships can create learning regions (Asheim 1996). The interlinking of cooperative partnerships, ranging from work organizations inside firms to 'development coalitions', is strategically important to realize the benefits of learning-based competitiveness (Amin and Thrift 1995a; Ennals and Gustavsen 1999; Asheim 2001).

For Lundvall and Johnson (1994: 26) the 'learning economy' refers to the contemporary post-Fordist economy dominated by ICT (information and communications technology), reflexive work organizations, and innovation-based compeititon. Lundvall (1996) has argued that the concept of the learning economy can be used in two interconnected ways, as a theoretical perspective on the economy, and as a reference to a particular economic period when knowledge and learning have become particularly important (Lundvall and Borras 1999). However, these new circumstances require new theoretical understandings, and it is to begin the development of these understandings that is the aim of this chapter.

9.2 Alternative Models of Capitalism: Coordinated Market Economies

In his book, *The Corrosion of Character. The Personal Consequences of Work in the New Capitalism* (1998), Richard Sennett discussed some of the consequences, especially for the well-educated middle class, of being exposed to the flexible labour market of the global economy. He described a new situation in which people are no longer able to plan careers after graduation, but are instead confronted by an unstable, insecure labour market in which skills are rapidly exhausted. Sennett focused on the middle-class, professional labour market typical of Silicon Valley, where speed of change and the challenges of world class competition have created internal labour markets where 'the winner takes all'. However, because the rate of new firm growth is high, new job opportunities in these markets are continuously being created. As a result, individuals' periods of unemployment are often short, and aggregate unemployment remains low. But the overall problem remains, people have lost control of their life situations and life projects in new, numerically flexible labour markets.

These labour markets are strongly polarized. Unskilled workers in low-paid service jobs, are exposed to the same type of numerical flexibility, but with neither the personal gains of prestigous high-paid jobs nor the power gained from higher education. So, while the well-educated middle class now feels powerless, the working class is both powerless and vulnerable (Asheim and Clark 2001).

However, Sennett's analysis (1998) must be placed in context. For Soskice (1999), Sennett's 'new capitalism' refers to a 'liberal market economy', with *numerical* labour market flexibility, which he contrasts with a 'coordinated market economy', with *functional* labour market flexibility. In addition, these two alternative views of new capitalism need to be set against two contradictory tendencies evident in processes of economic globalization. First, there is the *neo-Fordist* tendency, a development path that originated as the new international division of labour in the 1970s. It involves worldwide sourcing and input price minimization in line with the principle of *comparative advantage*, aided by transportation and communication innovations and the liberalization and deregulation of international trade and financial markets. Second, there is the *post-Fordist* tendency, the learning economy development path, based on the dynamic principle of *competitive advantage*. It rests on 'making more productive use of inputs, which requires continual innovation' (Porter 1998: 78) promoted by supporting regulatory and institutional frameworks. Competitive advantage is, therefore, based on exploiting unique competencies and resources to sustain innovation. Firms, regions, and nations compete on what they have that is unique compared to their competitors. Coordinated market economies might typically be associated with the post-Fordist tendency, while they can exhibit both tendencies depending on what sectors (i.e. high-tech, capital intensive versus low-tech, labour intensive) are being examined.

Soskice (1999) has also argued that different national institutional frameworks support different forms of economic activity. Thus, while coordinated market economies have their competitive advantage based on diversified quality production, liberal market economies are most competitive in industries that are radically innovative. From a comparison of coordinated market economies (such as Sweden, Germany, and Switzerland) and liberal economies (such as the USA), Soskice suggested that the coordinated economies performed best in the production of 'relatively complex products, involving complex production processes and after-sales service in well-established industries' (e.g. the machine tool industry). In contrast, liberal market economies performed best in industries producing complex systemic products, such as IT and defence technologies and advanced financial and producer services, where scientific knowledge is important (Soskice 1999: 113–14). However, in the liberal market economies, such as that of the USA, the low-end labour market, in low-tech, labour-intensive industries creates only unskilled, low-paid jobs, with workers suffering poverty, low living standards, and alienation, a situation that has been recognized by both Porter (1990) and Lazonick (1994).

Thus, the institutional competitive advantage of coordinated market economies appears to be based on the constant upgrading of existing industries and technological trajectories (e.g. in manufacturing industries). This upgrading is the product of interactive innovation that involves long-term cooperation—between workers and firms, between firms, and between firms and the knowledge infrastructure—to create interactive learning.

To illustrate the historical and social background of a coordinated market economy, the example of the economic development of Norway and the rest of Scandinavia in the last century, provides interesting historical evidence. Contemporary Norwegian society is characterized by egalitarian social structures with a low level of conflict both in society and in the workplace. Educational levels are high, the culture is essentially homogenous, and equality is both an ideal and in most cases a reality. Social control is well developed, and social cohesion is strong. Ideals of social justice and solidarity are strong, as is the protestant ethic in both work and consumption. Trade unions are representative and cooperative minded, and political life is very stable (Nylehn 1995). This cooperative tradition is embedded in long established and contemporary structures in Norwegian society.

In the Norwegian (and Scandinavian) case, it was the causal effects of socio-structural factors (i.e. agrarian and educational reforms and a relatively even distribution of land and income) and political-institutional structures (i.e. the political mobilization and organization of the peasantry and the labour class together with a stable political framework) that have been seen as positively contributing to rapid industrialization and economic development. To Mjøset (1983), these socio-structural factors amounted to a 'configuration of development' that went so far as to determine the effect of factors such as natural resource endowment, population size and density, infrastructure, trade policy, direct foreign investments, technology transfer, and so on, on economic growth. And, it is precisely these egalitarian social structures that are highlighted in international comparative studies as the important causes behind the rapid industrialization and economic development in the Scandinavian countries compared with the development in other parts of the European periphery (Berend and Ranki 1982; Senghaas 1985).

The importance of non-economic factors for the performance of an economy points, therefore, to sociocultural (i.e. institutional) as well as political-institutional (i.e. organizational) structures, which incorporate historical and territorial dimensions. Here, the concept of *social* capital is particularly relevant. The concept of social capital extends both the classical economic concept of capital as *physical* capital (i.e. assets that generate income) and the neoclassical economic concept of *human* capital, which focuses on the importance of education and the training of the labour force, to capture the role of *social* and *cultural* aspects of economic performance 'encompassing the norms and networks facilitating collective action for mutual benefit' (Woolcock 1998: 155). Social capital can depend on the level of 'civicness' in civil society as well as on the degree of formal organization in the public sphere. According to Putnam, social capital means 'features of social organization, such as networks, norms, and trust, that facilitate action and cooperation for mutual benefit' (Putnam 1993: 35–6). As such, social capital can be viewed as a structural property of larger groups (Woolcock 1998). It is a set of shared and common values and expectations, obligations, and social norms which govern the behaviour of individuals in society (Greve 1999)—akin to what in other contexts has been called 'institutional thickness' (Amin and Thrift 1995*b*).

To sum up, it can be argued that in the Norwegian (Scandinavian) case of economic development, changes in the socio-institutional framework (e.g. educational reforms, political democratization, land reforms, etc.) had primacy in relation to changes in the techno-economic paradigm. In reality, this meant the promotion of *cooperation* in contrast to competition as the dynamic force of societal changes and the main driver of technological development. The same argument can be made for the Third Italy, where non-economic factors have been more important than techno-economic structures for the economic performance of the regions. This is the prespective of the learning economy that holds a central position in the new institutionalist perspective on regional development (Grabher 1993; Amin and Thrift 1995*b*; Lundvall 1996; Amin 1999).

9.3 Learning Economies, Learning Organizations, and Development Coalitions

It can be argued that the learning economies of the Nordic countries are paradigmatic examples of Soskice's coordinated market economies. The strategic role played by cooperation in a learning economy is underlined by the understanding of interactive learning as a fundamental aspect of the process of innovation (Asheim 1996). This broader understanding of innovation as a social, non-linear, and interactive learning process puts new emphasis on the role played by sociocultural and institutional structures in regional development. They are no longer vestigial remnants of pre-capitalist civil societies. They are necessary prerequisites for regions to be innovative and competitive in a post-Fordist learning economy. If these observations are correct, the implication is that new 'forces' are now shaping technological development in capitalist economies, modifying the nature and importance of competition between firms. Obviously, the contradictions inherent in the capitalist mode of production persist. But, as Lazonick (1993) has argued with reference to Porter's empirical evidence (1990), 'domestic cooperation rather than domestic competition is the key determinant of global competitive advantage. For a domestic industry to attain and sustain global competitive advantage requires continuous innovation, which in turn requires domestic cooperation' (p. 4). Cooke (1994) supports this view, emphasizing that, 'the co-operative approach is not infrequently the only solution to intractable problems posed by globalization, lean production or flexibilisation' (p. 32).

Porter emphasizes that the reproduction and development of competitive advantage requires continuous innovation, which in a learning economy is conceptualized as a contextualized interactive learning process, promoted by clustering, networking, and inter-firm cooperation. This view of innovation means that all elements of firms and business organizations can be sources of innovation, irrespective of their size, position within larger organizations, R&D intensity, location, or whether they are SMEs. This broadly based process implies that it is possible to find productive and innovative firms enjoying competitive advantage in global markets in all branches and sectors of coordinated market economies. It goes some way towards explaining the seemingly paradoxical situation of low-tech industries, for example the furniture industry, flourishing and reproducing their international competitive advantage in high-cost countries such as Denmark, Germany, and Italy. Nevertheless it is important to re-emphasize that the diffusion, exploitation, and utilization of knowledge is dependent on the socio-institutional framework of coordinated market economies rather the workings of techo-economic subsystems (Freeman and Perez 1986).

The operation of learning economies underlines the importance of cooperation based on dynamic, flexible, learning organizations. A dynamic, flexible 'learning organization' can be defined as one that facilitates the learning of all its members and has the capacity to continuously transform itself by rapidly adapting to a changing environment through innovation (Pedler et al. 1991; Weinstein 1992). However, a problematic aspects of learning organizations, and indeed of learning economies in general, is the emphasis that is placed on 'catch-up' learning (i.e. learning by doing and using) based on incremental innovation, and not on new knowledge creation and radical innovation. Ekstedt et al. (1999) have recognized the limitations of incrementalism in learning organizations and have argued that 'it will not lead to a major change in organisational structure or to a radical shift in organising patterns. It is more likely that an incrementally developed learning organisation will do "more of the same" although with time it might do so more effectively' (p. 43). Indeed, incremental product and process innovation does not offer the prospect of long-term economic growth within a learning economy, nothwithstanding 'the tremendous importance of incremental innovation, learning by doing, by using and by interacting in the process of technical change and diffusion of innovations' (Freeman 1993: 9–10). Processes of knowledge creation are, therefore, pivotal in successful learning organizations and economies.

However, the concept of the development coalition offers a model of the learning organization that goes beyond the limits of incremental learning, when that organization is placed in a more nuanced societal context. Development coalitions can be understood as bottom-up, place-based, horizontal cooperation involving a wide range of actors including, workers and managers within firms, networks of firms and organizations, and the general mobilization of resources in a broader societal context to initiate and promote learning-based processes of innovation, change, and improvement (Ennals and Gustavsen 1999). As an expression of the idea of learning organizations, development coalitions are fluid, transnational, and continuously reshaping themselves to meet new challenges. Essentially, however, they are made up of horizontal relationships, constituting channels through which information flows, experiences are compared, and new solutions are worked out by extracting the best out of a broad range of experiences and ideas. Such coalitions can also be formed on many different levels, from small workplaces, to both small and large networks and regions, to whole nations (Ennals and Gustavsen 1999).

To build on the work of Ennals and Gustavsen (1999), the principal characteristic of a learning organization that is part of a development coalition is its ability to change—'to *change* its patterns, to continuously transcend what is, to take on new shapes, new forms' (Ennals and Gustavsen 1999: 16). Thus, learning organizations organized as development coalitions have features that are distinctive in comparison to other forms of learning organizations that transcend the problems of incremental learning. The establishment of those coalitions involves not only cooperation but also planned collective action among groups of firms (Sabel 1992). As such they represent a form of social capital embedded in formal organizations at the system level of society, which contrasts with social capital that is rooted in civicness.

9.4 Micro-level Learning: The Learning Firm as a Development Coalition

The concept of the learning firm and the learning organization envisages enterprise growth being created through knowledge and learning, at the same time, creating new, enriching, and empowering forms of work (Hudson 1999). In their development of the concept, Lundvall and Johnson (1994) have argued that, 'the firm's capability to learn reflects the way it is organised. The movement away from tall hierarchies with vertical flows of information towards more flat organisations with horizontal flows of information is one aspect of the learning economy' (p. 39). However, Hudson sees little evidence of this labour market empowerment in the liberal market economies of the UK and USA, seeing no reduction in the relative significance of 'the alienated and deskilled mass worker' (Hudson 1999: 60).

However, the socio-technical approach to organization theory, has shown that flat and egalitarian organizations have the prerequisites for flexibility and learning, and have the capacity to become learning organizations, not least because of their strong engagement with their functionally flexible, central workers (Asheim 1996). These structures have the capacity to build trust and to mobilize and diffuse informal or tacit, non-R&D based, knowledge (Herrigel 1996), while authoritarian, hierachical structures encourage employees to keep relevant information to themselves (You and Wilkinson 1994). Learning firms use inter-firm networking and intra-firm horizontal communication to enhance learning capabilities. But, to remain competitive they must continually reproduce themselves through innovation. The innovation process is itself based on collective learning both inside the business enterprise and within networks of cooperating firms.

This structure and functioning of the learning firm shows through clearly in the Scandinavian coordinated market economies, especially in their experience with 'Kalmarism' as it contrasts with 'Fordism', 'Neo-Taylorism' and 'Toyotism' (Leborgne and Lipietz 1992). Indeed, 'the process of continous improvement through interactive learning and problem-solving, a process that was pioneered by Japanese firms, presupposes a workforce that feels actively committed to the firm' (Morgan 1997: 494). Brusco (1996) has gone on to argue that it was through such worker commitment and high levels of worker participation that firms in the industrial districts of Emilia-Romagna were able, 'to be efficient and thus competitive on world markets' (Brusco 1996: 149). And, Brusco et al. (1996) have maintained that, 'experience in Emilia-Romagna has demonstrated that competitiveness on global markets is not a contradiction to high labour cost, high incomes and a fair distribution of income; on the contrary, we would claim that a fair income distribution is a necessary condition (although not sufficient) for consensus, and consensus and participation are an indispensable prerequisite for economic success' (p. 35).

However, the cooperative participation of labour has to be on a broad scale for it to have a significant and lasting effect on firms' innovativeness and competitiveness. All workers in a firm have to be involved in the continuous improvement of its operations to increase productivity and quality in the pursuit of growth. In this way, collective learning stands in contrast to individual learning, where the improved skills of the individual are traded on the labour market at a given price (Lazonick and O'Sullivan 1996; Storper 1997). According to Lazonick and O'Sullivan (1996), innovative firms need to create social organizations to enable collective learning to occur. Thus, the 'firm' in learning economies is still the basic unit of production, even if project-based forms of organizing have gained in importance in the 'new industries' of the media, journalism, and advertising, for example (e.g. Sennett 1998, Grabher 2002a, 2002b).

There is, therefore, the possibility for the negotiated involvement of labour in the firms of a flexible, learning economy. This is a possibility with which Leborne and Lipietz (1992) disagree. They argue that such, 'collective involvement and flexibility are incompatible ... [because the] ... external rigidity of the labor market [is] associated with the negotiated involvement of workers (p. 339). However, Porter (1990) points out that in general, 'labor–management relationships are particularly significant in many industries because they are so central to the ability of firms to improve and innovate' (p. 109). It might, therefore, be argued that characteristically Norwegian society is a culture in which cooperation is both recognized and valued as an important part of local social capital, and this has positive consequences at both the micro-level of the firm, in terms of the loyalty, flexibility and positive attitudes of workers, and at the macro-level of society in terms of the social regulation of the labour market.

The presence of social capital in the form of a strong tradition of cooperation adds to the high level of human capital in the workforce in a synergistic way, and represents an international competitive advantage (not still fully exploited, according to Porter), not least because it means decisions can be implemented swiftly because they have been arrived at by concensus. This way of bringing society inside the firm in learning organizations, based on participation, cooperation, and regulation, is an alternative way of achieving the fusion of economy and society (Piore and Sabel 1984) compared to the industrial district model, in which the firm is embedded in the spatial structures of social relations (Sforzi 2000). These contrasting models of contextualizing the firm also reflect the alternative interpretations of social capital, that is, as rooted in the 'civicness' of communities (in industrial districts) or through formal organizations at the system level of societies (development coalition).

9.5 Meso-level Learning: The Learning System as a Development Coalition

The importance of horizontal forms of cooperation in promoting innovation highlights the qualitative aspects of networking, and more specifically the governance structure of networks. Through networking, the aim is to create, 'strategic advantages over competitors outside the network' (Lipparini and Lorenzoni 1994: 18). However, to achieve this goal it is important that the networks are organized in line with the principle of the 'strength of weak ties' (Granovetter 1973). Grabher has argued that, 'loose coupling within networks affords favourable conditions for interactive learning and innovation. Networks open access to various sources of information and thus offer a considerably broader learning interface than is the case with hierarchical firms' (Grabher 1993: 10). A bottom-up, interactive innovation model is an example of such a network, characterized by loose coupling that broadly stimulates creativity among its member firms and institutions.

New, post-Fordist ways of organizing industrial production can take various forms. The specific form of industrial organization resulting from close inter-firm networking is represented by 'quasi-integration' (Leborgne and Lipietz 1988). Quasi-integration refers to relatively stable relationships between firms, where the principal firms aim to combine the benefits of both vertical integration and vertical disintegration in their collaboration with suppliers and subcontractors (Haraldsen 1995). According to

Leborgne and Lipietz, 'quasi-integration minimises both the costs of coordination (because of the autonomy of the specialised firms or plant), and the costs of information/transaction (because of the routinised just-in-time transactions between firms)'. Moreover, 'the financial risks of R&D and investments are shared within the quasi-integrated network' (Leborgne and Lipietz 1992: 341). They also maintain that the more horizontal are the ties between the partners in a network, the more efficient is the network as a whole. As Håkansson (1992: 41) emphasizes, 'collaboration with customers leads in the first instance to the step-by-step kind of changes (i.e. incremental innovations), while collaboration with partners in the horizontal dimension is more likely to lead to leapwise changes (i.e. radical innovations)'. More generally, Leborgne and Lipietz (1992: 399) argue that, 'the upgrading of the partner increases the efficiency of the whole network'.

This form of networking between firms can be described as a change from the domination of vertical relations between principal firms and their subcontractors to horizontal relations between principal firms and suppliers. Patchell refers to this as a shift from production systems to learning systems, which implies a transition from, 'a conventional understanding of production systems as fixed flows of goods and services to dynamic systems based on learning' (Patchell 1993: 797). Such institutionalization of a continuous organizational learning process involves a redefinition of a firm's relations to its major suppliers based on the recognition that 'a network based on long-term, trust-based alliances could not only provide flexibility, but also a framework for joint learning and technological and managerial innovation. To be an integral partner in the development of the total product, the supplier must operate in a state of constant learning, and this process is greatly accelerated if carried out in an organisational environment that promotes it' (Bonaccorsi and Lipparini 1994: 144).

As a consequence of the increased awareness and recognition of intra- and inter-firm cooperation and networking as important factors in promoting international competitiveness, 'the issue of (extended) trust has come to the fore' (Humphrey and Schmitz 1996: 23). According to Lipparini and Lorenzoni (1994), 'a high dose of trust serves as substitute for more formalised control systems' (p. 18). In this context, a critical question concerns how possible it is to develop the necessary extended trust as the basis for inter-firm cooperation and networking in order to sustain collective efficiency, defined as, 'the competitive advantage derived from local external economies of joint action' (Humphrey and Schmitz 1996:

28). This is of special importance in the context of cooperation at different levels of the innovation process. Lundvall and Borras (1999) maintain that, 'at each of these levels agents and individuals communicate and co-operate. They need to develop a common language and modes of interpretation and, above all, trust in order to overcome some of the uncertainties characterising the innovation process' (p. 30).

In a study of the Lyon region in France, Lorenz (1992) has shown that trust and cooperation among firms can be intentionally created through a 'partnership' strategy, which is based on establishing long-term relationships between firms and their subcontractors concerning the volumes, prices, and quality of work. From a study in the USA, Sabel (1992) has pointed to the possibility of creating trust by bringing in consultants to enable groups of firms to redefine their collective interests so as to pave the way for what he called 'studied trust'. But, at the same time, he warned us that this, 'does not prove that there is even one sure ... way to actually extend trust when the actors believe it is in their interest to do so'. It is indeed questionable whether the intentional creation of trust between networked firms can ever be 'embedded' in the same way as the 'mutual knowledge and trust' of Marshallian industrial districts.

Agglomerations as learning systems have two advantages in the production of trust. First, manufacturers do not only have to rely on their own experience but can exploit the experience of others. Second, agglomerations facilitate joint actions, with the potential to build institutional trust. 'Schemes or centres which promote, assure and certify quality are unlikely to emerge without joint initiatives from foresighted manufacturers' (Humphrey and Schmitz 1996: 33). And, in general, 'physical proximity guarantees frequently scheduled meetings, where face-to-face communication enhances the sharing of tacit knowledge' (Nonaka and Reinmöller 1998: 415).

However, the importance of trust as the basis of inter-firm cooperation in order to create competitiveness does not in itself guarantee an adequate level of innovativeness in the long run. Even so, factors such as trust among firms in the local cluster and loyalty among the workforce can be of great significance in forming close and innovative inter-firm networks with customers and suppliers/subcontractors as well as establishing flexible and learning intra-firm organizations, which are of strategic importance in fostering the competitive advantage of firms and regions (i.e. Marshall's agglomeration economies). On the other hand, as argued by Lundvall (1996), 'it will not be possible to preserve a reasonable degree of trust without a minimum of social cohesion. As the social basis for learning is eroded, the rate of change will slow down. This is one reason why the analysis of the learning economy cannot neglect the social dimension and also why any policy strategy aiming at promoting the learning economy must have a new New Deal as an integrated part' (Lundvall 1996: 17).

When the cultural diversity of Europe is added to the empirical evidence that entrepreneurships and innovation are unevenly spread across its geography, it is clear that not all cultural settings possess or produce social capital. More specifically, it is evident that it is impossible to apply the 'industrial districts' model of social capital formation in southern Italy owing to the lack of trust and the dominance of 'strong ties' in that part of Italy. Certainly, social capital has developed more or less organically in specific historical and geographical settings. But, in the Third Italy, this 'spontaneous' development has been assisted by institution-building and the development of an intermediate governance structure that can act as a positive environment for enterprise development (Bianchi 1996). The implication is, therefore, that policy initiatives have the capacity to build social capital by promoting and stimulating the collective capacity for cooperation and networking. Indeed, examples of such initiatives can be identified in the Third Italy, in Denmark, and in Norway.

9.6 Macro-level Learning Organization: The Learning Region as a Development Coalition

As part of the perspective that recognizes innovation as culturally and institutionally contextualized, strategic elements of learning emerge as localized rather than placeless processes. As such, they are an important part of the knowledge base and infrastructure of firms and regions, both configured by and configuring historical trajectories of economic change. This view is supported by Porter, who argues that, 'competitive advantage is created and sustained through a highly localised process' (Porter 1990: 19). But, localized learning is based not only on tacit knowledge, but also on 'sticky', codified knowledge which, it can be argued, also constitutes contextual knowledge. This is 'disembodied' knowledge and know-how (not embodied in machinery), that is generated by the positive externalities of the innovation process. Generally, it is based on a high level of individual skill and experience, a collective technical culture, and a well-developed institutional framework. These factors are highly immobile in geographical terms (de Castro and Jensen-Butler 1993), and represent

Innovation, Cooperation, and Social Capital

important contextual conditions that are able to foster innovativeness and competitiveness (Asheim 1999).

It can be argued that this contextual, disembodied knowledge combined with place-specific 'untraded interdependencies, (i.e. 'a structured set of technological externalities which can be a collective asset of groups of firms/industries within countries/regions' (Dosi 1988: 226)) can constitute the material basis for the competitive advantage of regions in the globalizing learning economy, even if their industrial structures are dominated by more traditional, low to medium high-tech sectors as in the Third Italy and parts of Scandinavia. Thus, with global competition in post-Fordist learning economies driven by the principle of competitive advantage, 'the building of a "home base" within a nation, or within a region of a nation, represents the organizational foundation for global competitive advantage' (Porter 1990, cited in Lazonick 1993: 2). In this context it is important to emphasize that, 'whilst knowledge in the form of embodied technical progress can be exported independently of social institutions, such knowledge in its disembodied form cannot be absorbed independently of such institutions' (de Castro and Jensen-Butler 1993: 3). The rationale behind promoting regional endogenous development is precisely, 'to use ... social organization to generate innovation and economic development' (Lazonick and O'Sullivan 1995: 4).

The concept of the 'learning regions' has been applied in at least three different contexts. It was first introduced by economic geographers in the mid-1990s (Florida 1995; Asheim 1996), to emphasize the role played by cooperation and collective learning in regional clusters and networks to promote the innovativeness and competitiveness of firms and regions in the globalizing learning economy (Asheim 1997). The approach was inspired by the rapid economic development of the Third Italy, and drew attention to the importance of cooperation between small firms in industrial districts and between firms and local authorities as a mechanism for achieving international competitiveness (Asheim 1996). The second approach expressed more directly the idea of learning and learning economics, and originated in the writings of new evolutionary and institutional economics on the knowledge- and learning-based economy. It argued that 'regional production systems, industrial districts and technological districts are becoming increasingly important' (Lundvall 1992: 3), and found support in Porter's view (1998) of the strategic importance of clusters. The third and most recent approach conceptualized learning regions as region-based development coalitions. It has been developed by members of the socio-technical school of organization theory, building on their knowledge of how to establish learning organizations through broadly based particiapation at the regional level (Ennals and Gustavsen 1999).

All three approaches underline the important role of innovation, intra- and inter-firm networks at the regional scale, and the building of social capital in post-Fordist learning economies. However, while the economic geography and evolutionary economics approaches emphasize innovation, the action research approach focuses mainly on the necessity for broad participation. Merging these approaches provides a more coherent model of the processes that generate economic growth and employment through social cohesion and 'learning firms' within 'learning regions'. Thus, it is an important task to merge these approaches in order to obtain a coherent model or policy framework for formulations of partnership-based development strategies in order to achieve economic growth, employment generation as well as social cohesion, as expressed by the idea of the learning firm in a learning region.

Such an extension of the idea of forms of territorial organization deepens and widens the notion of cooperation within agglomeration. The original and simplest form of cooperation within a cluster can be described as the territorially integrated input–output relationships that occur within value chains. These relationships can be supported through informal social networking or through arm's-length market transactions within industrial districts. A deeper form of cooperation occurs with the purposeful, functional integration of value chain collaboration and the building of competence networks between collaborating firms. While proximity is central to the operation of cluster-based input–output relations, the emergence of competence networks represents a step towards more systemic and planned forms of cooperation, and the strengthening of horizontal forms of cooperation, which more efficiently promote learning and innovation. The further development of more systemic forms of cooperation occurs when integrated learning or innovation systems are established and extend across time-space incorporating both the economy and the state. Or, as Nonaka and Reinmöller have put it, 'the concepts of clusters of industrial districts and networks are also attempts to describe interorganizational phenomena. Industrial districts are accumulations of interdependent companies located near each other (the condition of proximity). Networks are a concept focused on interorganizational relations. . . . Unlike the concept of industrial districts, the concept of networks does not necessarily entail the condition of proximity' (Nonaka and Reinmöller 1998: 406).

It is argued here that the conceptualization of innovation supportive regions as 'development coalitions' draws together all previously identified forms of integration—that is, territorial, functional, and system integration—together with the social integration of both society and lifeworld. In such coalitions, it is the coexistence and copresence of actors in space and time that is of vital importance as, 'all participants must do their best to gain an understanding of others, to pool insights and strive for joint solutions' (Ennals and Gustavsen 1999: 16). Pivotal to this deepening and widening of cooperation within regions is the strategic role played by social capital.

9.7 Conclusion: Social Capital and Alternative Capitalism

In this chapter it has been argued that, under the right conditions, interactive learning has the capacity to promote and sustain regional competitive advantage and growth within local economies. At the core of these conditions are cooperation and non-market and non-economic factors, including social capital, trust, and a tissue of supportive institutions (Putnam 1993). According to Lazonick (1991), 'history shows that the driving force of successful capitalist development is not the perfection of the market mechanism but the building of organizational capabilities' (Lazonick 1991: 8). Those capabilities, it is suggested here, are fostered by trust and the building of social capital at the regional scale within firms, networks of firms, and public-sector/private-sector relationships. However, the discussion has shown that learning-based, endogenous regional development also requires specific socio-cultural and socio-economic structures that are found only in certain places. Typically, those places are the well-off regions of developed countries, that have the techno-economic and political insitutions of coordinated market economies rather than of liberal market economies.

Therefore, though it has been suggested that there is the potential to generate learning within regions through the use of appropriate policy instruments, it is important to bear in mind that the learning firms/learning regions model of regional economic growth is not universally applicable.

Following Lundvall (1996), it would appear that learning in a coordinated economy can generate endogenous growth in some regions without restricting the growth potential of other regions. Indeed, a policy of strong competition, building on innovation and differentiation strategies within networks of large and small firms, together with interactive, localized learning and continuous innovation in industrial and territorial clusters, has the potential to promote learning and knowledge creation, and an innovation-based learning economy. Such a dynamic learning economy populated with learning firms offers the vision of a long-term growth-oriented kind of capitalism that is able to generate development *in* as well as *of* regions.

References

Amin, A. (1999). 'An Institutionalist Perspective on Regional Development', *International Journal of Urban and Regional Research*, 23: 365–78.
—— and Thrift, N. (1995*a*). 'Territoriality in the Global Political Economy', *Nordisk Samhällsgeografisk Tidskrift*, 20: 3–16.
—— —— (1995*b*). 'Institutional Issues for the European Regions: From Markets and Plans to Socioeconomics and Power of Association', *Economy and Society*, 24: 41–66.
Asheim, B. T. (1996). 'Industrial Districts as "Learning Regions": A Condition for Prosperity?', *European Planning Studies*, 4(4): 379–400.
—— (1997). 'Learning Regions in a Globalised World Economy: Towards a New Competitive Advantage of Industrial Districts?', in M. Taylor and S. Conti (eds.), *Interdependent and Uneven Development: Global-local Perspectives*. Aldershot, UK: Ashgate, pp. 143–76.
—— (1999). 'TESA bedrifter på Jæren—fra et territorielt innovasjonsnettverk til funksjonelle konserndannelser?', in Isaksen, A. (ed.), *Regionale innovasjonssystemer. Innovasjon og læring i 10 regionale næringsmiljøer, STEP-report R-02*, The STEP group, Oslo, 131–52.
—— (2001). 'Learning Regions as Development Coalitions: Partnership as Governance in European Workfare States?', *Concepts and Transformation, International Journal of Action Research and Organizational Renewal*, 6(1): 73–101.
—— and Clark, E. (2001). 'Guest Editorial: Creativity and Cost in Urban and Regional Development in the "New Economy" ', *European Planning Studies*, 9(7): 805–11.
Berend, I. and Ranki, G. (1982). *The European Periphery and Industrialization, 1780–1914*. Cambridge: Cambridge University Press.
Bianchi, P. (1996). 'New Approaches to Industrial Policy at the Local Level', in F. Cossentino et al. (eds.), *Local and Regional Response to Global Pressure: The Case of Italy and Its Industrial Districts*, Research Series 103. International Institute for Labour Studies, Geneva, 195–206.
Bonaccorsi, A. and Lipparini, A. (1994). 'Strategic Partnerships in New Product Development: An Italian Case Study', *Journal of Product Innovation Management*, 11(2): 135–46.

Brusco, S. (1996). 'Global Systems and Local Systems', in F. Cossentino et al. (eds.), *Local and Regional Response to Global Pressure: The Case of Italy and Its Industrial Districts*, Research Series 103. International Institute for Labour Studies, Geneva, 145–58.

—— et al. (1996). The Evolution of Industrial Districts in Emilia-Romagna', in F. Cossentino et al. (eds.), *Local and Regional Response to Global Pressure: The Case of Italy and Its Industrial District*, Research Series 103. International Institute for Labour Studies, Geneva, 17–36.

Castro, E. de and Jensen-Butler, C. (1993). *Flexibility, Routine Behaviour and the Neo-Classical Model in the Analysis of Regional Growth*. Denmark: Department of Political Science, University of Aarhus.

Cooke, P. (1994). 'The Co-operative Advantage of Regions', Paper presented for the conference on 'Regions, Institutions, and Technology: Reorganizing Economic Geography in Canada and the Anglo-American World', University of Toronto, September 1994.

Dosi, G. (1988). 'The Nature of the Innovative Process', in G. Dosi et al. (eds.), *Technical Change and Economic Theory*. London: Pinter Publishers, pp. 221–38.

Ekstedt, E. et al. (1999). *Neo-Industrial Organising. Renewal by Action and Knowledge Formation in a Project-Intensive Economy*. London: Routledge.

Ennals, R. and Gustavsen, B. (1999). *Work Organisation and Europe as a Development Coalition*. Amsterdam–Philadelphia: John Benjamin's Publishing Company.

Florida, R. (1995). 'Toward the Learning Region', *Futures*, 27(5): 527–36.

Freeman, C. (1993). 'The Political Economy of the Long Wave', Paper presented at EAPE 1993 conference on 'The Economy of the Future: Ecology, Technology, Institutions', Barcelona, Spain, October.

—— and Perez, C. (1986). 'The Diffusion of Technical Innovations and Changes of Techno-Economic Paradigm', Paper presented at the conference on 'Innovation Diffusion', Venice, Italy, March.

Grabher, G. (1993). 'Rediscovering the Social in the Economics of Interfirm Relations', in G. Grabher (ed.), *The Embedded Firm. On the Socioeconomics of Industrial Networks*. London: Routledge, pp. 1–31.

—— (2002a). 'Cool Projects, Boring Institutions: Temporary Collaboration in Social Context', *Regional Studies*, 36: 205–14.

—— (2002b). 'The Project Ecology of Advertising: Tasks, Talents and Teams', *Regional Studies*, 36: 245–62.

Granovetter, M. (1973). 'The Strength of Weak Ties', *American Journal of Sociology*, 78(6): 1360–80.

Greve, A. (1999). 'The Role of Social Capital in the Development of Technology', Paper presented at a conference on 'Mobilizing Knowledge in Technology Management: Competence Construction in the Strategizing and Organizing of Technical Change', Copenhagen, Denmark, October.

Haraldsen, T. (1995). 'Spatial Conquest—The Territorial Extension of Production Systems', Paper presented at the Regional Studies Association conference on 'Regional Futures: Past and Present, East and West', Gothenburg, May.

Herrigel, G. (1996). 'Crisis in German Decentralised Production: Unexpected Rigidity and the Challenge of an Alternative form of Flexible Organization in Baden Württemberg', *European Urban and Regional Studies*, 3(1): 33–52.

Hudson, R. (1999). 'The Learning Economy, the Learning Firm and the Learning Region: A Sympathetic Critique of the Limits to Learning', *European Urban and Regional Studies*, 6(1): 59–72.

Humphrey, J. and Schmitz, H. (1996). 'Trust and Economic Development', *Discussion Paper* No. 355, Institute of Development Studies, University of Sussex.

Håkansson, H. (1992). *Corporate Technological Behaviour. Co-operation and Networks.* London: Routledge.

Lazonick, W. (1991). *Business Organization and the Myth of the Market Economy.* Cambridge: Cambridge University Press.

—— (1993). 'Industry Cluster Versus Global Webs: Organizational Capabilities in the American Economy', *Industrial and Corporate Change*, 2: 1–24.

—— (1994). 'Creating and Extracting Value: Corporate Investment Behavior and American Economic Performance', *STEP-report*, No. 20, The STEP group, Oslo.

—— and O'Sullivan, M. (1995). 'Organization, Finance and International Competition', *Industrial and Corporate Change*, 4: 1–49.

—— —— (1996). 'Sustained Economic Development', *STEP-report* No. 14, The STEP group, Oslo.

Leborgne, D. and Lipietz, A. (1988). 'New Technologies, New Modes of Regulation: Some Spatial Implications', *Environment and Planning D: Society and Space*, 6: 263–80.

—— —— (1992). 'Conceptual Fallacies and Open Questions on Post-Fordism', in M. Storper and A. J. Scott (eds.), *Pathways to Industrialization and Regional Development.* London: Routledge, pp. 332–48.

Lipparini, A. and Lorenzoni, G. (1994). 'Strategic Sourcing and Organizational Boundaries Adjustment: A Process-based Perspective', Paper presented at the workshop on 'The Changing Boundaries of the Firm', European Management and Organisations in Transition (EMOT), European Science Foundation, Como, Italy, October.

Lorenz, E. (1992). 'Trust, Community, and Cooperation: Toward a Theory of Industrial Districts', in M. Storper and A. J. Scott (eds.), *Pathways to Industrialization and Regional Development.* London: Routledge, pp. 195–204.

Lundvall, B.-Å. (1992). 'Introduction', in B.-Å. Lundvall (ed.), *National Systems of Innovation.* London: Pinter Publishers, pp. 1–19.

—— (1996). 'The Social Dimension of the Learning Economy', *DRUID Working Papers*, No. 96-1, Aalborg University, Aalborg.

—— and Borras, S. (1999). *The Globalising Learning Economy: Implications for Innovation Policy.* Luxembourg: Office for Official Publications of the European Communities.

—— and Johnson, B. (1994). 'The Learning Economy', *Journal of Industry Studies*, 1(2): 23–42.

Mjøset, L. (1983). 'Norge i utviklingsteoretisk lys', *Tidsskrift for samfunnsforskning*, 24: 565–76.
Morgan, K. (1997). 'The Learning Region: Institutions, Innovation and Regional Renewal', *Regional Studies*, 31(5): 491–503.
Nonaka, I. and Reinmöller, P. (1998). 'The Legacy of Learning. Toward Endogenous Knowledge Creation for Asian Economic Development', *WZB Jahrbuch 1998*, 401–33.
Nylehn, B. (1995), 'Kan "ledelse på norsk" være et konkurransefortrinn?', *Bedre Bedrift*, 3: 43–6.
Patchell, J. (1993). 'From Production Systems to Learning Systems: Lessons from Japan', *Environment and Planning A*, 25: 797–815.
Pedler, M. et al. (1991). *The Learning Company*. London: McGraw-Hill.
Piore, M. and Sabel, C. (1984). *The Second Industrial Divide: Possibilities for Prosperity*. New York: Basic Books.
Porter, M. (1990). *The Competitive Advantage of Nations*. London: Macmillan.
—— (1998). 'Clusters and the New Economics of Competition', *Harvard Business Review*, November–December: 77–90.
Putnam, R. (1993). *Making Democracy Work*. Princeton, NJ: Princeton University Press.
Sabel, C. (1992), 'Studied Trust: Building New Forms of Co-operation in a Volatile Economy', in F. Pyke and W. Sengenberger (eds.), *Industrial Districts and Local Economic Regeneration*. Geneva: International Institute for Labour Studies, pp 215–50.
Senghaas, D. (1985). *The European Experience. A Historical Critique of Development Theory*. Leamington Spa, UK: Berg Publishers.
Sennett, R. (1998). *'The Corrosion of Character. The Personal Consequences of Work in the New Capitalism*. New York: W. W. Norton.
Sforzi, F. (2000). 'Learning from Industrial Districts: The Firm as a "bit of society" ', Abstract of paper for a workshop on 'The Firm in Economic Geography', University of Portsmouth, UK, March.
Soskice, D. (1999). 'Divergent Production Regimes: Uncoordinated and Coordinated Market Economies in the 1980's and 1990's', in Kitchelt et al. (eds.), *Continuity and Change in Contemporary Capitalism*, Cambridge: Cambridge University Press, pp. 101–34.
Storper, M. (1997). *The Regional World. Territorial Development in a Global Economy*. New York and London: The Guilford Press.
Weinstein, O. (1992). 'High Technology and Flexibility', in Cooke, P. et al. (eds.), *Towards Global Localisation*. London: UCL Press, pp. 19–38.
Woolcock, M. (1998). 'Social Capital and Economic Development: Toward a Theoretical Synthesis and Policy Framework', *Theory and Society*, 151–208.
You, J.-I. and Wilkinson, F. (1994). 'Competition and Co-operation: Toward Understanding Industrial Districts', *Review of Political Economy*, 6(3): 259–78.

Part VI

Theorizing the Firm—Afterword

10
Theorizing the Firm in Economic Geography

Päivi Oinas

10.1 Introduction

Until very recently, economic geographers have not engaged strongly with the theory of the firm. One section of the literature in this field has focused on the firm in the abstract as an actor that participates in the broader social and economic processes of regions and places (Lagendijk and Oinas 2005: 8–9). Another section of that literature has focused on the specificities of particular firms in particular industries and localities, but has a limited theoretical perspective on why those firms behave the way they do. The chapters of this volume are forward-looking and future-oriented and build on this disciplinary history to challenge current thinking on the theory of the firm.

Firms are extraordinarily diverse. That diversity covers the corner bakery, a cousin's one-man accounting firm, or a local construction company. It also includes major corporations, like Sony, who when they laid off 7 per cent of their worldwide employment in 2005 axed 10,000 jobs. It embraces those less tangible entities, such as consultants, who make money by telling others how to make money, or the Internet-based businesses such as eBay whose business idea is to provide a platform for others to do business. Some firms produce tangible goods while others, like financial firms, provide intangible services. Still others are well-known as consumer brands while others function as seemingly invisible nodes in complex production systems. What is more, this difference and diversity among firms is multiplied by the impact and legacy of past decisions and past strategies, and by the nature of the time- and place-specific environments from which they have emerged, with their different cultural values, beliefs and practices, different tastes, laws, rules and regulations, that lead them to operate according to different principles.

In short, firms are different, and they function differently. The reasons for these differences, and the societal consequences of the actions of each type of firm, obviously need explanation. This has been the focus in economic geography: to understand and explain the circumstances under which certain types of firm have operated in particular ways with particular geographical outcomes. It is a focus that has been sharpened in recent years, and it is evident in many of the chapters in this volume. However, confining economic geography's explanatory ambition to this contextual focus alone evades the questions posed in the introduction to this volume: what is the firm; how should it be conceptualized; and how should its behaviour be theorized? There are no simple answers. In compiling this volume, we have felt it enough at this stage to ask questions and raise issues that a future research agenda will need to address.

If firms are to be taken as something more than case studies or type examples of socio-economic processes, then the general question to be addressed by economic geographers is what characteristics of firms are shared by the wide array of forms that the firm exhibits? And why do we have the firms that we have? This question, posed in many different ways, has been a continuous source of discussion and debate among economists, management scholars, organization theorists, and other social scientists. But, there is no clarity between disciplines as to how the different approaches relate, there is no comprehensive theory. As Michael Taylor suggests in the opening chapter to this book, the theory of the firm is at best a collection of 'fragments'. While scrutinizing four central approaches to the firm in economics, Gibbons (2005: 201) charges that it is 'difficult to understand their commonalities, distinctions, and potential combinations'. In other words, it is difficult to see how the fragments fit together. It is like building a puzzle when you know you have only some of its pieces. Why is this so? It is largely, I would argue because theories represent disciplinary conventions concerning how to go about conceptualizing and explaining particular phenomena. They derive from worldviews that have been moulded through the practice of doing research from particular perspectives, often by several generations of scholars. The traditions typically remain distinct from each other, and there are no generally accepted criteria or rules to guide how one way of theorizing might be

Theorizing the Firm in Economic Geography

played out against others across the social science disciplines. The firm is a many-sided object. No one theory or disciplinary perspective captures all of its sides or aspects, and none provides explanations of all its aspects simultaneously. Theories of the firm are crafted from particular perspectives that are necessarily only partial, and they focus on different and sometimes quite discrete aspects of the firm.

If, however, we only have such 'fragments' of different perspectives, does this mean that we do not have a full grasp of what the firm is? This may be the conclusion that we have to draw from current levels of understanding of the firm. It is possible that those fragments might be used to construct a comprehensive conceptualization and a related theoretical structure that might 'explain' aspects of the firm that we regard as key to understanding this societal institution. Then again, Hodgson (2002: 43) has observed that this is not a common aspiration: in the economics literature, for example, 'it is repeatedly proclaimed that all attempts to define "the firm" are fruitless'. He is critical of such proclamations and notes that '[t]his licensed imprecision promotes habits of conceptual vagueness and terminological sloppiness that have prevailed in the business and economic literature ever since' (Hodgson 2002: 43). Such confusion does not make these literatures particularly attractive. Similarly, the often narrow approaches to the firm in economics, with overly limiting assumptions, have been condemned by economic geographers, and this condemnation is evident in the chapters of this book (see also Taylor and Asheim 2001; Maskell 2001a; Yeung 2005).

What then is the way forward? What is economic geography's way to theorize the firm? What we argue in this volume is that economic geographers should not shy away from participating in the collective attempt to theorize the firm. There is a need to formulate definitions and provide explanations that fit their particular needs as social scientists attempt to understand the firm from a spatial perspective and in a spatial context. This argument might be considered modest, but it needs to be made. The point is that there is no theory 'out there' that could be found and picked up to serve our purposes. Nevertheless, there are many approaches that can be used as 'entry points' to understanding and explaining the behaviour of the firm in a spatial context. Through such an entry point, it is possible to venture into explaining aspects of firms as well as developing ideas on to how to construct a fuller picture. Other social scientists are as confused as we are concerning the usefulness of different, fragmented theories of the firm and how they relate one to another. Economic geographers need to participate in a collective project that promises no quick answers. But, as late-comers to the project, the obvious questions to be asked are: how do we develop an economic geography perspective to the firm, and what distinctive contribution can the discipline make to the project?

Against these questions, the remaining sections of this chapter explore a number of pertinent issues. Section 10.2 draws together a series of observations on attempts to identify a theory of the firm in two other research areas, Austrian economics and the National Business Systems (NBS) literature. Section 10.3 takes up Peter Maskell's answer (2001a) to his own question: 'what kind of theory of the firm suits economic geography and why?' His reply was that the evolutionary competence-based theory suits economic geography best. I will briefly comment on this approach in light of the chapters of this volume which helps us see that even if it accommodates many of the ideas presented in the chapters, it still remains a 'fragment', a partial view. Section 10.4, explores a number of examples of how definitions are formulated in various research traditions, and suggests that the various partial theories of the firm are bolstered by the partial definitions that they employ. It is, as a consequence, difficult to find a comprehensive definition of the firm that would fit economic geographers' broad interests. In the light of these discussions, Section 10.5 suggests that a comprehensive account on the firm appropriate to the needs of economic geographers might take as its starting point a view of the firm as a multi-dimensional coordination problem.

10.2 Searching for a Theory of the Firm

Economic geographers are not the only representatives of a research field lacking an established conceptualization and a theory of the firm on which theoretical insight can be accumulated. Austrian economists, for example, have recently explicitly tackled the problem that they do not have a theory of the firm that suits their research programme (see, e.g. Witt 1998, 1999, 2000; Ioannides 1999). It is informative to observe the spirit in which such a theory has been sought. Ioannides (1999), for instance, engages in an exploration of what an Austrian perspective on the firm would have to look like, in order to be acceptable both as 'Austrian' and as a 'theory of the firm'. The Austrian tradition attributes to *the entrepreneur* the role of the equilibrating or coordinating agent in the economy, and their analysis relies on methodological individualism. As Ioannides (1999: 77) puts it, 'an Austrian perspective must be capable of describing the firm as an institution that is created through the entrepreneurial action of individuals; an action which is subjectively motivated and carried out in conditions of radical uncertainty and ignorance.' The relevant theory of the firm, then, is developed on the basis of Kirzner's notion of entrepreneurial behaviour.

Similarly, we may ask what an economic geographical perspective on the firm would have to look like, in order to be acceptable both as 'economic geographic' and as a theory of the firm. Obviously, economic geography is a different intellectual endeavour from, for example, Austrian economics. The latter has recently been going through a dynamic process of development, but it is still a relatively distinct research programme within economics (Boettke 1999: 3). Economic geography does not have such clear intellectual footing in one particular approach to the economy, and thus it is not possible to state as clearly what would be the fundamental theoretical foundation of a theory of the firm in our field. As also clearly reflected in the contributions to this volume, contemporary economic geography is intellectually a broadly ranging sub-discipline within human geography. First, it is subject to the influences that affect developments within geography. Second, it is a very flexible field. Its history is marked by constant accommodation of ideas from neighbouring disciplines. Although relatively distinct intellectual roots may be detected in its earlier history (see Scott 2000, 2004), it is presently evolving very strongly under a variety of disciplinary influences stemming from literatures as diverse as institutional and evolutionary economics, regulation theory, political science, economic and organizational sociology, management science, cultural anthropology, and cultural studies.

While the efforts of Austrian economists differ from those of economic geographers, we might compare our field with another stream of research that shares many of the concerns that economic geographers feel comfortable with, namely the NBS research programme (e.g. Whitley 1992, 1999, 2002; Morgan, Whitley, and Moen 2005). The NBS literature provides an institutional account of national differences in the operating principles and outcomes of various market economies. It is increasingly interested in institutional change, and seems to be adopting evolutionary ideas. The literature has shown through empirical comparisons that even if globalization seems to create pressures towards convergence and the adoption of 'best practices', these tendencies nevertheless produce divergent national 'models' in different national settings. This is obviously a view that is shared among institutionalists across disciplines, many economic geographers included. Bjørn Asheim (Chapter 9), for instance, building on a related literature on 'varieties of capitalism' (see Soskice 1999; Hall and Soskice 2001) underscores that (in the Nordic countries) 'the diffusion, exploitation and utilization of knowledge are dependent on the socio-institutional framework of coordinated market economies rather than narrowly on the workings of techno-economic subsystems'. However, while institutional environments in various ways condition— by enabling and constraining—the operation of business firms, the very same firms, by their strategic decision-making and subsequent operations, also influence the way their respective 'business system' develops; they contribute to the evolutionary path of the business systems of which they are a part (Moen and Lilja 2005; Oinas 2005).

Since some economic geographers feel comfortable with this manner of institutional thinking about the economy, it is interesting to consider what kind of theoretical approach to the firm this literature might pick up. In what appears to be an attempt to identify a theoretical account of the firm for the purposes of the NBS literature, Morgan (2005*b*), advocates the RBV of the firm, building on the ideas of Penrose (1959) and Richardson (1972) (see also Michael Taylor's Chapter 1 in this volume). Morgan does not provide explicit criteria for choosing this approach, but he argues that it 'has three key insights for our understanding of changing capitalisms. First, it sees firms as actively developing and growing in the context of their environment, both using existing institutional resources but also searching for new combinations of resources that can strengthen firm uniqueness. Second, it identifies the engine of growth with the development of core capabilities through new combinations of resources inside the firm and through interactions outside the firm; this in turn relates to the centrality of innovation processes to firm growth. Third, it emphasizes the limitations to growth emerging from problems of managerial coordination.' (Morgan 2005*b*: 416) Suited to economic geographers' view of the firm as multiply embedded in its environments, geographically as well as socially, this approach is emphatically 'as concerned with the internal generation of distinctive collective competences as with the operation of external environments' (Morgan 2005*a*: 1–2).

Then, if Austrians need to build a firm around the opportunity-recognizing entrepreneur, and the NBS literature needs to construct a view of a dynamic firm that evolves alongside the surrounding society, the economic geographers' challenge is to portray the dynamic firm in its multiple and changing regional environments. Economic geographers share the view along with many other social scientists, many institutionally oriented economists included, that firms are social entities that operate in particular societal contexts where they evolve, as active agents, along and in interaction with other elements of the society—a process that Giddens (1984) called *structuration*, or what has recently been referred to as *co-evolution* (Volberda and Lewin 2003). Additionally, it is in the nature of geographical inquiry to concretely *place* the firm in its geographical surroundings, leading to accounts of the significance of location, local social relations, relations over space, as well as on broader spatial scales. Indeed, it remains the role of geographers to provide a systematic inquiry into the significance of the spatial context. What might then be an appropriate approach to the firm?

10.3 What Kind of Theory of the Firm for Economic Geography?

Peter Maskell (2001*a*: 337) has explicitly posed the questions 'what kind of theory of the firm suits economic geography and why?' He generates answers to these questions by invoking two suitability criteria (Maskell: 338). The first criterion concerns rationality assumptions, and he suggests that economic geographers are likely to accept theories that assume bounded (rather than complete) rationality of economic agents. His second criterion concerns the question whether the theory gives theoretical significance to the spatial context in which the firm is placed. His conclusion is that the elements of the evolutionary competence-based theory of the firm 'are all directly applicable also at the regional or national level'. His elaboration of the second criterion appears to involve an inconsistency in that he suggests that 'elements highlighted in the theory should not only be valuable when addressing issues on the level of the firm, but should be applicable and useful when studying the economic dynamics of localities, regions, nations, or continents' (Maskell: 338). The inconsistency is that it cannot be required that a theory of the firm should be applicable at any level other than that of the firm: a theory of the firm does not need to explain anything else but the firm. It is true that 'taking the competence view of the firm to the aggregate level of the locality' (Maskell: 339) is possible, but then it is no longer a theory of the firm but a theory of the locality (or cluster; see Maskell 2001*b*; Malmberg and Maskell 2002). It follows that *this* criterion stating that a theory should be 'directly applicable also at the regional or national level' (Maskell 2001*a*: 339) cannot be used to rule out other theoretical approaches, say, the property rights theory or transaction cost economics. Nevertheless, what is intended by the second criterion is sound per se, namely that, in order to suit economic geography, the theory of the firm should 'give theoretical significance to the spatial context in which the firm is placed' (Maskell 2001a: 338). And this furthermore suggests that any theory of the firm that we adopt as economic geographers should be compatible with our theories of those entities—places, regions, cities, clusters, etc.—in which we study firms. Going further, it can be suggested that to appropriately theorize the development or 'evolution' of regions and their economies, we need to theorize the economic agents that give direction to that evolution (Oinas 1995; Maskell 2001a: 340). That is, we should develop the firm-related foundations of the processes involved in regional development. A vital aspect of this basic tenet is that such a theory should account for the external relations of firms with agents and processes at multiple scales and in historical time. These may not be surprising points as such—and the chapters of this volume provide ample evidence for them—but they are worth erecting as fundamental precepts to theoretical thinking on the firm in economic geography. The resources approaches would appear to offer a useful foundation on which to build a theory of the firm in economic geography.

Versions of the resources approach to the firm,[1] emphasizing different aspects of resources, have recently grown remarkably popular within the strategic management and industrial organization literatures as well as among economists pursuing evolutionary ideas. Versions of it have also been embraced by a handful of economic geographers (e.g. Maskell et al. 1998; Maskell and Malmberg 1999; Oinas 1999, 2002; Oinas and van Gils 2001; Pinch et al. 2003; Bathelt and Glückler 2005). Judged by popularity, then, it would appear to be a plausible path to follow to develop a theory of the firm in economic geography. Interestingly, it also seems to capture a range of items in which economic geographers are interested, including those broached in the chapters of this volume. For instance, the successes

---

[1] Note that for the related approaches that in the literature are referred to as 'the resource-based view of the firm', the 'knowledge-based theory', or the 'capabilities' or 'competences', 'approach' or 'perspective' or the like I am here using the term *resources approach*. This is for the following reasons. First, the fundamental idea is that superior *resources* is what brings firms sustained competitive advantage in competition against other firms on the markets of goods or services. Competences/capabilities, and their upgrading via learning/innovation are a key resource, and cognitive capabilities or the ability to acquire and enhance relevant knowledge for firm-specific competitive purposes is the key factor behind firm success. These all, as well as tangible resources which should not be forgotten, conveniently fall under the term 'resource'. Second, it is debatable whether it is a fully fledged *theory* in terms of including a clearly specified explanandum ('sustained competitiveness') and explanantia (the mechanisms through which specific uses of resources lead to sustained competitiveness of kinds of firm in kinds of competitive circumstance). Rather, I see it as an *approach* that is being vividly developed, aiming to gain more understanding of these issues.

Theorizing the Firm in Economic Geography

and misfortunes of the various tiers of firms involved in the Birmingham gun-making system (Michael Taylor and John Bryson, Chapter 3) can be explained through the vocabulary of the resources approach: the skills, competencies and power-providing resources of the different tiers of firms in production as well as in negotiating and implementing contracts, and responding to changes in demand. Equally, Michael Taylor's discussion (Chapter 4) of 'coalitions of people who in very particular circumstances of time and place deploy bundles of assets to generate personal wealth to the best of their collective ability' resonates deeply with Penrose's work (1959). The entrepreneurial and managerial capacity to coordinate collective agency to strive for strategic goals can also be seen as a key resource for firm competitiveness. So too is their capability to create credible narratives to legitimize strategic decisions internally and externally; to mobilize external resources such as those of investors (Phillip O'Neill, Chapter 5; Ann Markusen, Chapter 6; and act in conjunction with the state as a regulator and a potentially experimental policymaker (Ray Hudson, Chapter 7). Additionally, the argument that firm success, especially its ability to learn, can be regarded as a function of its societal surroundings, as Bjørn Asheim (Chapter 9) explains, is intrinsically in line with and extends the resources approach. Similarly, Mia Gray's discussion (Chapter 8) of the differential geographical locations of different functions of the pharmaceutical firms that she studies can be approached from a resources perspective. The resources to carry out different production functions in firms (research, development, stages of production, domestic and foreign marketing, distribution) are derived from and nurtured by the different locations; for firms to function successfully, an environmental fit is required. Coordinating the diverse internal capabilities needed to perform different functions and matching those functions with locations where the functions can be carried out most successfully is a significant firm competence (cf. Oinas 1999; Oinas and van Gils 2001). Finally, if firm boundaries are not fuzzy, even though that is what has been suggested (Oinas, Chapter 2), from a resources perspective it means that it is possible to give a resource-based explanation to the question of where the firm's boundaries are, i.e. what is meaningful to coordinate inside the firm and outside the firm (see Langlois 2002). Though only briefly developed here, these examples show the potential for economic geographers to apply and extend the resources approach (see also Taylor, Chapter 1, and the literature he refers to; Morgan 2005*b*).

Michael Taylor is, however, critical of the resources approaches in Chapter 1 of this volume, seeing them as fragmentary perspectives on the firm comprising 'bulked-up empirical microprocesses' removed from the specificities of historical time. As such, they too are only one set of perspectives on the firm amongst a host of others. Indeed, it might be illuminating to explore the same empirical circumstances of the dynamics of firms in a region or a set of regions from a number of theoretical perspectives—transaction costs, behavioural, competences, knowledge and evolutionary, for example—to see what differences of interpretation and insight emerge. With our present understanding of the relations of these various theories, however, it is difficult to see how to integrate such complementary analyses. As has frequently been complained, economists' assumptions and those of economic geographers, among others, are so different that these different academic communities seem to live in different worlds (see the discussion in Martin 1999). Even though it has been shown that economists' assumptions are merely devices to isolate phenomena for the purpose of making claims about causal relations (e.g. Mäki 2004; Marchionni 2004), we still do not have a good methodological grasp on how to integrate ideas in models and theories originating in very dissimilar conceptual frameworks and research styles.

10.4 Defining the Firm

It can be suggested from this discussion that there is a need to generate a more comprehensive theory of the firm in the social sciences (a situation that is particularly apparent in economic geography), to guide the framing of questions about firms and their behaviour as agents in societies and in regions. It is important to recognize from the outset, however, that the practice of *defining* the firm is different in different theoretical traditions. It appears that often, a definition very closely reflects the perspective from which a theory is developed. In effect it conflates an aspect of the firm with the firm in its entirety. If this is true about all theories of the firm, it suggests that definitions of the firm are as partial as are the theories or approaches they stem from.

There is evidence that supports this claim. In the property rights perspective, for example, 'the firm is defined in terms of the assets it owns' (Grossman and Hart 1986: 692). This narrow definition fits the quest to explain contractual relations between unequal partners based on ownership of non-human assets. In an entirely different framework, Nooteboom (2000), who is interested in the role of the firm in processes of learning and innovation in the economy, defines the firm as a 'focusing device'. In order to achieve common goals, 'a firm must direct and align perception, understanding, and evaluation by the people connected with it' (2000: 71).

Because these two approaches focus on different aspects of the firm, it appears that the firms they study are entirely different entities. It is an aspect of the present nature of theorizing in economics and related fields. What a firm 'is', depends on what is being explained and what questions are being asked. Whether this is a satisfactory situation is open to question. Consider Nooteboom's definition, for example. It leaves room for further questions concerning the firm. People striving towards a common goal can 'get focused' in arrangements other than those within the firm. They do not need to be connected to the same firm (or to any firm at all for that matter). Something else is needed to make a social arrangement that is a 'focusing device' also a firm. For this, we need greater theoretical clarity. In this context, economists' discussions of asset ownership, incentives, alignments of interests, production and transaction costs, and so on, have a contribution to make without necessarily providing a complete explanation.

Holmström and Roberts (1998) recognize the problem of using overly limited theories to understand the firm. They propose taking a broader view of the firm than has been customary in transaction cost economics and property rights theory:

Firms are complex mechanisms for coordinating and motivating individuals' activities. They have to deal with a much richer variety of problems than simply the provision of investment incentives and the resolution of hold-ups. Ownership patterns are not determined solely by the need to provide investment incentives, and incentives for investment are provided by a variety of means, of which ownership is but one. Thus, approaches that focus on one incentive problem that is solved by the use of a single instrument give much too limited a view of the nature of the firm, and one that is potentially misleading. (Holmström and Roberts 1998: 75)

They observe that 'firms are poorly defined in property rights models and it is not clear how one actually should interpret the identities of [firms]' (Holmström and Roberts 1998: 79). Consequently, they recognize the need to work out a fuller definition of the firm—though they wrote contemporaneously with colleagues with starkly opposing views. Masten, for instance, took a strong stand:

For what it is worth, my current view is that clarity and precision would be best served if we stopped seeking a theory of *the* firm altogether and accept that the word 'firm' is just a generic term for a range of commonly observed organizational arrangements. Rather than debate whether the firm is defined by the employment relationship or the assets it owns or a nexus of contracts, we would be better off if we content ourselves with constructing theories of ownership, of employment relations, or of contracting, as the case may be. In doing so, we would also bring economic theory into closer alignment with the law. Although the word 'firm' has quasi-legal origins—deriving from *firmare*, meaning 'to ratify by signature', which eventually came to designate a 'commercial house' or 'business'—the word currently has no specific legal meaning or ramifications. Instead, the law construes 'firm' as synonymous with 'business entity or enterprise', defined, in turn as an 'investment of capital, labor and management in an undertaking for profit' (Black's Law Dictionary, 5th edn., 1979). While the concept of the firm will remain a useful abstraction for certain purposes, the term is one that serious students of economic organization would probably do well to avoid. (Masten 1998: 58–9)

Here, one might think that Masten is intellectually exasperated, or that he fails to see what is implicit in his own text, namely that often a definition merely corresponds to the aspect of the firm that is a theory's object of analysis.

All definitions are not similarly narrow, however. Chesterman's definition (1977: 46–7; see Michael Taylor and John Bryson, Chapter 3; Michael Taylor, Chapter 4) includes a broader set of relevant aspects, but then again leaves out those taken up, for instance, by Nooteboom (2000) and Taylor (Chapter 4). A firm, according to Chesterman, has to fulfil six criteria: it must have a line of business; the repetition and continuity of activity; the employment of assets; the involvement of two or more people as owners, managers and workers; a degree of autonomy; and entitlement to surplus profits, and Taylor and Bryson (Chapter 3) use this definition to identify firm types in their study. Finally, Whitley (1987: 126) portrays firms as 'interdependent, semi-autonomous economic agents which are able to control and direct the uses of resources by virtue of delegated property rights in ways which make a difference to economic and social outcomes', highlighting the economic nature of the firm as well as its societal agency (see Päivi Oinas, Chapter 2). This definition is broad, and is at the level of his work on business systems, but like others, it is also partial.

The point is made tentatively here, though to some extent it is obvious: different theories developed from different perspectives shed light on different aspects of the firm, and are thus also defined from that perspective, in line with their immediate explanatory purposes. But what are such purposes in economic geography, a sub-discipline with diverse interests and a broad scope? Since the field does not have a range of existing traditions that within themselves self-evidently approach the firm as 'assets', 'a nexus of contracts', 'social relations', or any other such partial representation, it might be open to attempts to understand the firm in its complexity, to think of what is essential about the firm *as a firm* in comprehensive terms. If we go on from what we have in the various chapters in this volume, the definition of the firm might include ideas of collective agency, drawn together and operating in compliance with the law, and aiming to reach goals spelled out by an implicit or explicit, but nevertheless evolving strategy. Its operation requires the existence of an organization, aligning of interests and creating incentives (which are not necessarily only pecuniary), and involves the challenges of coordinating the varied and constantly evolving individual, collective, and material resources, both internal and external to the firm, including resources that come with the institutional environment of the firm, and potentially in more than one location. And it would have to be observed that the firm is intended to function on the basis of profit created by its operation. This list is no more than a tentative outline of the range of issues that could be included in or implied by a more comprehensive definition of the firm. Economic geographers and other social sciences would seem inclined to share an interest in developing such a comprehensive perspective to the firm. It would provide a common ground for relevant questions to be asked about the firm and a platform for integrating analyses that aspire to answer those questions.

10.5 The Firm as a Multidimensional Coordination Problem

The items in any list of factors that are significant for defining the firm—like the one attempted above—have to do with the fundamental problem that any social entity has, namely the problem of coordination. Successfully solving the coordination problem makes 'competitive' firms. Competitiveness is a woolly concept in itself, but ultimately it boils down to firms' abilities to survive in market competition—notwithstanding the possibility of some institutionally acceptable periods of loss making, as Markusen (1999: 878) has pointed out. Surviving in the market requires that all of a firm's resources are put to the use of serving this end, no matter what strategy has been chosen to achieve it. Gearing all resources to serving the goal of survival involves the coordination of non-human assets as well as individual and collective competencies, whilst acknowledging not only economic constraints related to scarcity of resources but also the various human, social, and societal constraints involved in the undertaking.

Recognizing the multiple aspects of this coordination problem helps us see why, for instance, the presently popular 'communities of practice' approach (Lave and Wenger 1991; Amin and Cohendet 2004) offers only a very limited view of *the firm* even though it is certainly helpful in explaining firm *success*. Particularly, groups involved in 'communities of practice', or 'epistemic communities' (Cowan, David, and Foray 2000: 234) are concerned with the voluntary and collaborative accumulation of a common stock of expert knowledge (see Michael Taylor, Chapter 4), that is, these groups' activities are coordinated around *similar* knowledge. This is necessary for the maintenance and updating of the diverse competencies firms need to carry out their different functions. To coordinate a firm in its entirety, in contrast, involves the coordination of the *diversity* that emerges from bringing together various areas of expert knowledge. These areas include the various stages of production as well as marketing and distribution as Mia Gray describes (Chapter 8), but also strategic management, organizational design, human resource management, accounting and finance, public relations, and government lobbying (many of which feature in the other chapters of this volume). The key competence in firms, then, is the ability to orchestrate the whole process, and keep all areas of expert knowledge tuned to each other. Even if a firm comes up with an outstanding technological solution, but tries to use it in a product that is poorly designed or marketed, it will not succeed. No wonder governing coalitions in firms may be only temporary and managers at times stay on board only for a fleeting period (Michael Taylor, Chapter 4).

The portrayal of a firm as a 'bundle of coordination problems' still involves various perspectives. Many of those have been discussed in the chapters of this volume. Externally, the formal institutional environment helps coordinate firm action via legal and regulatory structures (cf. Ann Markusen, Chapter 6; Ray Hudson, Chapter 7). Within those structures, deals are made and sealed by contracts that fix formal aspects of relations between firms (Michael Taylor and John Bryson, Chapter 3). Such activities take time and effort and, according to the TCE (transaction cost economics) perspective, it is transactions costs that determine whether some activities are coordinated within a firm or are contracted out. Furthermore, the accumulation of knowledge is coordinated informally in communities of practice (Michael Taylor, Chapter 4). Informal institutions coordinate firm action by means of shared values, beliefs, myths, conventions, and so on (Bjørn Asheim, Chapter 9). Diverse function-specific narratives in firms also help hold a firm together even at times of change, and they help legitimize firms' actions externally (Phillip O'Neill, Chapter 5; Ann Markusen, Chapter 6). Additionally, understanding, for instance, the role of leadership is helpful, and so is the significance of incentive schemes for various employee groups. Other perspectives can be added. Research in the future will have to go into understanding how different firm coordination problems are solved in relation to each other, and how this understanding can grow into a more comprehensive explanatory structure that is concerned with the whole of the firm and not merely aspects of it.

If all existing theories provide but one perspective on the firm, then great effort is needed to integrate and find commonalities and complementarities between these perspectives. Certainly there are deficiencies in existing theories, and either empirical evidence or the resources of complementary theories can be drawn upon to make progress. The critical review presented by Michael Taylor (Chapter 1) is pertinent in this respect as it outlines the historical and explanatory relations among a selection of key approaches to the firm. The similarities and differences between these approaches are also outlined and discussed in the literature more broadly (see, e.g. Gibbons 2005; Langlois, Yu, and Robertson 2002*a*, *b*, *c*). Foss (2005), however, appears to be one of the very few scholars who have seriously begun to think about the difficult task of possibly integrating diverse approaches to the firm. The undertaking is far from completed, however. For economic geographers, it is only beginning. It is a necessary beginning since otherwise the discipline does not have a strong theoretical grasp of a key agent inducing change in the places, regions, and countries that it studies.

References

Amin, A. and Cohendet, P. (2004). *Architectures of Knowledge. Firms, Capabilities, and Communities*. Oxford: Oxford University Press.

Bathelt, H. and Glückler, J. (2005). 'Resources in Economic Geography: From Substantive Concepts Towards a Relational Perspective', *Environment and Planning A*, 37: 1545–63.

Boettke, P. J. (1999). 'Is There an Intellectual Market Niche for Austrian Economics?' *Review of Austrian Economics*, 11(1/2): 1–4.

Chesterman, M. (1977). *Small Businesses*. London: Sweet and Maxwell.

Cowan, R., David, P., and Foray, D. (2000). 'The Explicit Economics of Knowledge Codification and Tacitness', *Industrial and Corporate Change*, 9: 211–53.

Foss, N. J. (2005). *Strategy, Economic Organization, and the Knowledge Economy*. Oxford: Oxford University Press.

Gibbons, R. (2005). 'Four Formal(izable) Theories of the Firm?', *Journal of Economic Behavior and Organization*, 58: 200–45.

Giddens, A. (1984). *The Constitution of Society. Outline of the Theory of Structuration.* Cambridge: Polity Press.

Granstrand, O., Patel, P., and Pavitt, K. (1997). 'Multi-technology Corporations: Why they have "Distributed" Rather than "Distinctive" Core Competences?', *California Management Review*, 39: 8–25.

Grossman, S. and Hart, O. (1986). 'The Costs and Benefits of Ownership: A Theory of Vertical Integration', *Journal of Political Economy*, 94: 691–719.

Hall, P. and Soskice, D. (2001). *Varieties of Capitalism*. Oxford: Oxford University Press.

Hodgson, G. M. (2002). 'The Legal Nature of the Firm and the Myth of the Firm-Market Hybrid', *International Journal of the Economics of Business*, 9(1): 37–60.

Holmström, B. and Roberts, J. (1998). 'The Boundaries of the Firm Revisited', *Journal of Economic Perspectives*, 12(4): 73–94.

Ioannides, S. (1999). 'Towards an Austrian Perspective on the Firm', *Review of Austrian Economics*, 11(1/2): 77–97.

Langlois, R. N. (2002). 'Modularity in Technology and Organization', *Journal of Economic Behavior and Organization*, 49: 19–37.

—— Yu, T. F.-L., and Robertson, P. (2002a, b, c). *Alternative Theories of the Firm*, Vols. I, II, III. Cheltenham, Edward Elgar.

Lagendijk, A. and Oinas, P. (2005). 'Localisation, External Linkages, and Explaining Local Development', in A. Lagendijk and P. Oinas (eds.), *Proximity, Distance and Diversity: Issues on Economic Interaction and Local Development*. Aldershot, UK: Ashgate, pp. 3–22.

Lave, J. and Wenger, E. (1991). *Situated Learning: Legitimate Peripheral Participation*. Cambridge, UK: Cambridge University Press.

Mäki, U. (2004). 'Realism and the Nature of Theory: A Lesson from J. H. von Thünen for Economists and Geographers', *Environment and Planning A*, 36(10): 1719–36.

Malmberg, A. and Maskell, P. (2002). 'The Elusive Concept of Localization Economies: Towards a Knowledge-based Theory of Spatial Clustering', *Environment and Planning A*, 34: 429–49.

Marchionni, C. (2004). 'Economic Geography Versus Geographical Economics: Towards a Clarification of the Dispute', *Environment and Planning A*, 36(10): 1737–53.

Markusen, A. (1999). 'Fuzzy Concepts, Scanty Evidence, Policy Distance: The Case for Rigour and Policy Relevance in Critical Regional Studies', *Regional Studies*, 33(9): 869–84.

Martin, R. (1999). 'The New "Geographical Turn" in Economics: Some Critical Reflections', *Cambridge Journal of Economics*, 23: 65–91.

Maskell, P. (2001a). 'The Firm in Economic Geography', *Economic Geography*, 77(4): 329–44.

—— (2001b). 'Towards a Knowledge-based Theory of the Geographical Cluster', *Industrial and Corporate Change*, 10: 921–43.

—— Eskelinen, H., Hannibalsson, I., Malmberg, A., and Vatne, E. (1998). *Competitiveness, Localised Learning and Regional Development. Possibilities for Prosperity in Open Economies*. London: Routledge.

—— and Malmberg. A. (1999). 'Localised Learning and Industrial Competitiveness', *Cambridge Journal of Economics*, 23: 167–85.

Masten, S. E. (1998). 'The Three Great Puzzles of the Firm', in S. G. Medema (ed.), *Coasean Economics: Law and Economics and the New Institutional Economics*. Dordrecht, the Netherlands: Kluwer, pp. 51–63.

Moen, E. and Lilja, K. (2005). 'Change in Coordinated Market Economies: The Case of Nokia and Finland', in G. Morgan, R. Whitley, and E. Moen (eds.), *Changing Capitalisms?* Oxford: Oxford University Press, pp. 352–79.

Morgan, G. (2005a). 'Introduction: Changing Capitalisms? Internationalization, Institutional Change, and Systems of Economic Organization', in G. Morgan, R. Whitley, and E. Moen (eds.), *Changing Capitalisms?* Oxford: Oxford University Press, pp. 1–18.

—— (2005b). 'Institutional Complementarities, Path Dependency, and the Dynamics of Firms', in G. Morgan, R. Whitley, and E. Moen (eds.), *Changing Capitalisms? Internationalization, Institutional Change, and Systems of Economic Organization*. Oxford: Oxford University Press, 415–46.

—— Whitley, R. and Moen, E. (eds.) (2005). *Changing Capitalisms? Internationalization, Institutional Change, and Systems of Economic Organization*. Oxford: Oxford University Press.

Nooteboom, B. (2000). *Learning and Innovation in Organizations and Economies*. Oxford: Oxford University Press.

Oinas, P. (1995). 'Organisations and Environments: Linking Industrial Geography and Organisation Theory', in S. Conti, E. J. Malecki, and P. Oinas (eds.), *The Industrial Enterprise and its Environment. Spatial Perspectives*. Aldershot, UK: Avebury, pp. 143–67.

—— (1999). 'Activity-Specificity in Organizational Learning: Implications for Analysing the role of Proximity', *GeoJournal*, 49: 363–72.

—— (2002). 'Competition and Collaboration in Interconnected Places: Towards a Research Agenda', *Geografiska Annaler*, 84B(2): 65–76.

—— (2005). 'Finland: a Success Story?' *European Planning Studies*, 13(8): 1227–44.

—— and van Gils, H. (2001). 'Identifying Contexts of Learning in Firms and Regions', in D. Felsenstein and M. Taylor (eds.), *Promoting Local Growth: Process, Practice and Policy*. Aldershot, UK: Ashgate, pp. 61–79.

—— and Lagendijk, A. (2005). 'Proximity, Distance and Diversity: Issues on Economic Interaction and Local Development', in A. Lagendijk and P. Oinas (eds.), *Proximity, Distance and Diversity*. Aldershot, UK: Ashgate, pp. 307–31.

Patell, P. and Pavitt, K. (1998). 'The Wide (and Increasing) Spread of Technological Competencies in the World's Largest Firms: A Challenge to Conventional

Wisdom', in A. Chandler, P. Hagström, and Ö. Sölvell (eds.), *The Dynamic Firm*. Oxford: Oxford University Press, pp. 192–213.

Penrose, E. (1959/1995). *The Theory of the Growth of the Firm*, rev. edn., Oxford: Oxford University Press.

Richardson, G. (1972). 'The Organisation of Industry', *Economic Journal*, 82: 883–96.

Pinch, S., Henry, N., Jenkins, M., and Tallman, S. (2003). 'From "Industrial Districts" to "Knowledge Clusters": A Model of Knowledge Dissemination and Competitive Advantage in Industrial Agglomerations', *Journal of Economic Geography*, 3(4): 373–88.

Scott, A. J. (2000). 'Economic Geography: The Great Half-century', *Cambridge Journal of Economics*, 24: 483–504.

—— (2004). 'A Perspective of Economic Geography', *Journal of Economic Geography*, 4(5): 479–99.

Soskice, D. (1999). 'Divergent Production Regimes: Coordinated and Uncoordinated Market Economies in the 1980s and 1990s', in H. Kitschelt, P. Lange, G. Marks, and J. D. Stephens (eds.), *Continuity and Change in Contemporary Capitalism*. Cambridge: Cambridge University Press, pp. 101–34.

Taylor, M. and Asheim, B. (2001). 'The Concept of the Firm in Economic Geography', *Economic Geography*, 77(4): 315–28.

Volberda, H. and Lewin, A. (2003). 'Coevolutionary Dynamics Within and Between Firms: From Evolution to Co-evolution', *Journal of Management Studies*, 40(8): 2111–36.

Witt, U. (1998). 'Imagination and Leadership—the Neglected Dimension of Evolutionary Theory of the Firm', *Journal of Economic Behavior and Organization*, 35: 161–77.

—— (1999). 'Do Entrepreneurs Need Firms? A Contribution to a Missing Chapter in Austrian Economics', *Review of Austrian Economics*, 11(1/2): 99–109.

—— (2000). 'Changing Cognitive Frames—Changing Organizational Forms: An Entrepreneurial Theory of Organizational Development', *Industrial and Corporate Change*, 9(4): 733–55.

Whitley, R. (1987). 'Taking Firms Seriously as Economic Actors: Towards a Sociology of Firm Behaviour', *Organization Studies*, 8(2): 125–47.

—— (ed.) (1992). *European Business Systems. Firms and Markets in Their National Contexts*. London: Sage.

—— (ed.) (1999). *Divergent Capitalisms*. Oxford: Oxford University Press.

—— (ed.) (2002). *Competing Capitalisms: Institutions and Economies*. Cheltenham, UK: Edward Elgar.

Yeung, H. (2005). 'The Firm as Social Networks: An Organisational Perspective', *Growth and Change*, 36(6): 307–28.

Index

Abbott Labs 201
ABN Amro 138
accounting systems 123–4, 125, 126, 128, 139
  accrual 127, 133 n.
  divisional 66
  new 132, 133
accumulation strategy 138
acquisitions 107, 163, 164
  aggressive new strategy based on 105
  international debt-funded 132
  lull in 155
actor-network theory 89
adaptation 10, 11, 89
aerospace 150, 152, 195
  consequences for 163–4
  mega-mergers and 'pure play' prescriptions 153–7
agglomerations 153, 164, 192, 195, 196, 200, 203, 207, 208, 225
  assumption of 197
  local integration of small firms in 4
  need for 210
  notion of cooperation within 228
  sectoral 194
  state-based 162
  strong effects 198
Airbus 163
Aldrich, H. 42, 52, 53, 54
Alexander, M. 127
Alferon N 199–203
alienation 216, 221

Allen, G. C. 62
Allenstown 150
Alliant Tech 156
alpha interferon 199
Alternate Site Distributors 202
altruism 94, 98
Amatori, F. 91
ambiguity 53
Amin, A. 39, 42, 45, 54, 111
Anderson, Paul 132, 133, 134, 135, 137, 138, 139, 140
Anders, William 152
Andromaco 202
antitrust 161
apprenticeships 71–2, 73, 76, 102
  changes to 81
  regulated by statute 70
Araujo, L. 21, 63, 67
arbitrage 95
Argyris, C. 122 n.
Arizona 134, 159
arms exports 161
arms manufacture 61–84
artisans 62, 69, 70, 71, 72, 76
  negotiation between contractors, small masters and 73
Asahi Breweries Ltd 106
Asheim, B. 8, 16, 18, 89, 118 n., 239
Asia Pacific region 106
Asian family businesses 111
Aspin, Les 160

255

Index

asset management 151
asset specificity 6, 7
assets 36, 65, 98, 151, 246
   deployment, beginning to reap commercial rewards 106
   employment of 92
   intangible 9
   key 137
   minimally leveraged 126
   mobilizing and remobilizing 103
   mutually specific 47
   new high performing 134
   newly acquired 105
   observable 14
   passed from one coalition to another 103
   redeployment of 193 n.
   retained, returns available from 134
   rights to use and control 6
   sales of 134
   shared 51
   soft 139
   substantial write downs of 133
   tangible 9
assumptions 5
   embedded 195
   equilibrium 6, 22
   key 6
   rationality 243
Aston Group 96, 97
asymmetric information 8
Australia 126 n.
   see also BHP; Carlton; Elders; Henry Jones
Austrian economics 240–1, 242
autonomy 172
   individual agents 52
   political discourse 176
   relative 171 n.
   specialized firms 224
   see also semi-autonomy

background:
   educational, shared 107
   professional 109
   social, conformity of 109
bad trade 177
Badaracco, J. 40
balance sheets 133
   clean-out 135, 140
   restructured 134
banks 69
   foreign 137
Barbera, M. 128, 139
Barney, J. 5
barriers to entry 207, 208, 209
Bathelt, H. 18, 244
BDM Corporation 157
Bear Stearns 155
Behagg, C. 62, 73, 76
behaviouralism 7, 87, 89, 90, 92
beliefs:
   common 107
   cultural 238
benchmark payments 205
Berg, M. 62, 72
Bergen Brunswig Corporation 202
Berghoff, H. 72
best practices 241
Bethesda 157
Bhagat, S. 159
Bhidé, A. 22
BHP Ltd/BHP Billiton 105, 106, 117–18, 128, 130, 135–41
   reform of 131–5
bicycles 78–9
Billiton, *see* BHP
biopharmaceutical industry 197–9
biotechnology 193, 195, 197–8, 200, 202, 208
   one of the oldest and most profitable firms in USA 203
Birmingham (UK) 61–84, 245
Birnberg, J. G. 122 n.
birth control pill 198 n.
Black Country 69, 80, 81

Index

blockbuster drugs 209
boards of directors:
  core and peripheral members 111
  creation and construction of 105
  formation of 107, 108, 109
  incestuous arrangements 109
  selection of new members 108
  strategic role of 106, 107
Boeing 156, 159, 162, 163, 164
Boettke, P. J. 241
Bolton Committee (UK 1971) 92, 96
Bonaccorsi, A. 224
boom conditions 178
Booz Allen 155
Borras, S. 225
Boston 198
Boston Consulting Group 126 n.
bottlenecks 76
boundaries of the firm 17, 33–60, 67
  contracts and 64–7
  defining 87
  flexible specialization and 62–4
  indistinct, permeable and fuzzy 61
  multiple 21, 63, 66, 67
  specific 7
bounded rationality 6, 17, 87, 89, 243
  'thin' conception of 7, 8
bounty system 76, 81
Boyer, R. 173
brass founding 64
Braunmuhl, C. von 172
bribery 152
British government 71, 77, 78, 79
  Board of Ordnance 68, 69, 73, 74, 75
  Select Committee Report on Small Arms (1854) 75
Broken Hill Proprietary Company, *see* BHP
Brookings Institution 161
Brown, J. S. 139
Brulin, G. 45
Brusco, S. 222
BSA (Birmingham Small Arms) 77–9, 80, 81

Bush administration 160
business angels 100
business schools 107
Business Week 152
Butler, J. 5
buyer switching-costs 14

calculative practices 126
California 150, 157, 198
  see also Los Angeles; Sacramento; San Francisco; Silicon Valley
Campbell, A. 127
capabilities 14, 17, 67, 200
  cognitive 244 n.
  complementary 67
  indirect 67
  learning 221
  managerial 95
  replicated, readily available and ubiquitous 65
  see also organizational capability
capacity 74–5
  collective 226
  stretched to the limits 76
capital 69, 71, 87, 89, 95, 127–8, 171, 185
  cost of 133, 137
  externalization of 152
  finance 150, 152, 165
  flight of 173–4
  harmony of interests between labour and 177
  industrial 150, 152
  money 151
  mutual dependence between state and 172
  proprietary intangible 156
  return on 133, 151
  separation of the state from 172
  structural class relationship between labour and 169
  substantial upgrade funds 132
  suppliers of 164
  working, cost of 128

257

Index

captial (*cont.*)
  see also human capital; social capital; venture capital; *also under following headings prefixed* 'capital'
capital accumulation:
  conditions reproduced 179
  necessary to control or eliminate problems of 171
  smooth, undermining conditions needed for 170
capital gains 128
capital markets 153
  internal 66
capitalism:
  alternative 215–18, 229–30
  chronically recurring characteristic of societies 169
  conditions necessary for continued viability of 170
  firm as key agent of accumulation within 119
  inescapable bottom line 94
  long-term growth-oriented kind of 230
  new 216
  varieties of 242
capitalist behaviour 91, 92
capitalist reproduction 172
car industry 79
Carlton and United Breweries Ltd 105
Carney, J. 170, 176, 178
cartels 75, 178
cash flows 131, 133
  expected net returns 128
  free 127, 128, 137
  idle 123
  net positive 133
  restructured management 133–4
  underutilized 126
Casson, M. 65
Castro, E. de 227
causal power 18
causality 90

Cell Pharm GmbH 202
Chambers of Commerce 179, 180, 181
Chandler, A. D. 22, 90–1
change 49, 91
  economic 226
  firms as agents for 63
  institutional 152
  path-dependent process of 12
  regional 192, 193–7
  speed of 215
  understanding the geography of 18
  see also technological change
charisma 95
Chesterman, M. 71, 72, 80, 92, 248
Cheung, S. N. S. 81
Chicago 201
Chicago School 119
China 4
choices:
  discouraging mergers to ensure 160
  strategic and locational 195
  see also rational choice
City of London 107, 108
civicness 214, 218, 221, 223
Clark, G. 150
class system 109, 110
Clegg, S. 90, 99
Clinton administration 160, 161, 165
closures 134, 150, 157, 178
clusters 36, 94, 198, 219, 225, 228
  cooperation within 228
  flexibly-specialized 70
  place-based 4, 14, 15
  strategic importance of 227
coalitions 10, 92, 95–6
  and communities of practice 109–12
  development 215–29
  members paid in excess of opportunity costs 11
  purposive, goal-seeking 98
  region-based 227
  temporary 97–104, 110, 111, 112
  see also strategic coalitions

Index

Coase, R. 6, 37, 44 n., 52, 55, 81, 91
coercion 92
co-evolution 243
Cohen, K. 10
Cohendet, P. 54, 111
Cold War 195
collaboration 49, 51, 88, 224
  inter-firm 177–8
  suppliers and subcontractors 223
  value chain 228
collective action:
  goal-directed 42
  planned 221
collective agency 85–145, 245
commercialization 194, 207
Commissioner for the Special Areas (England and Wales) 181, 183
common understandings 120
communities of communities 88, 110
communities of practice 16, 52, 88, 250
  coalitions and 109–12
  inter-firm 54
comparative advantage 216
  maintaining 208
compensation 152
competencies 67, 87, 94, 98
  appropriate 95
  evolving need for appropriate skills and 96
  firm-specific 89
  unique 90, 216
competition 8, 153
  cost 196
  discouraging mergers to ensure 160
  ever-tightening 15
  firm seen as protective enclave from 12
  global 227
  innovation-based 215
  intensifying 105
  internal 49
  international market 123
  strong 229

  world class 215
competitive advantage 10, 63, 216, 224
  creating 61, 226
  global 219, 227
  institutional 217
  international 219, 223
  regional 229
  reinforcing 16
  reproduction and development of 219
  source of 87
  strategic importance in fostering 225
  sustained 226, 229, 244 n.
  well-recognized sources of 16
competitive heterogeneity 13, 14
  managerial competence a source of 15
competitiveness 51, 225, 249
  fostering 227
  global 222
  international 96, 224, 227
  key resource for 245
  matters of strategic significance to 47
  sustained 244 n.
complementarities 48, 49, 251
complete-contracts theory 6, 9, 13, 18, 20
conflict 10, 53, 89
  inter-group, individual action and 88
  low level of 217
  national and local union leaders 150
  political 171
conformity 109, 111
conglomerates 104
  inferiority of 156
  large, division of 128
consultants 126, 225, 237
contestation 89
contingency views 23, 165
contract law 91
contractors 66, 69, 73, 79
  defence 156, 161, 162
  longstanding ties with 67

Index

contracts 7, 8, 91, 162
  boundaries and 64–7
  employment 51–2
  exchanges mediated by 6
  guns, firms and 61–84
  legal, implicit or explicit 55
  market exchanges always involve 55
  prime, lost 157
  replaced by trust 63
  strong 62
contractual hazard 16
control 51
  centralized 112, 194
  external 49
  formal political life 179–80
  social 217
  state 185
  see also managerial control
Cooke, P. 219
Cooper & Goodman 77
cooperation 61, 62
  collective capacity for 226
  deepening and widening of 229
  horizontal 220, 228
  importance of horizontal forms of 223
  inter-firm 219, 224, 225
  intra-firm 224
  need to maximize 120
  promotion of 218
  recognized and valued 222
  role played by 227
  tradition of 217, 223
  systemic and planned 228
coordinated market economies 63, 215–18, 221
  socio-institutional framework 219, 242
  techno-economic and political institutions 229
coordination 20, 65
  costs of 224
  internal 42
  managerial 242
  multidimensional problem 249–51

tight 48
core competency 153
corporate raiders 132
cortisone 198 n.
costs 6, 7
  coordination 224
  cutting 158, 159, 196
  development 14
  economized 8, 16
  external 65
  labour 159
  learning 14
  opportunity 11
  sunk 196
  see also transaction costs
Council on Foreign Relations 163
Cowan, R. 250
Cowling, K. 40, 48
Coyte, R. 128, 139
creative destruction 95
creative tension 15
creativity 22, 223
creditors 11
cross-ownership 49
CS First Boston 155
CSFB 138
cultural evolutionary perspective 17, 18
culture(s):
  essentially homogenous 217
  organizational 53
  regional industrial 39, 41, 54
  shared 16
  technical, collective 226
Curwen, P. 11
custom(s):
  firm-specific 53
  social regulation of 73
cycle of discovery 96
Cyert, R. M. 5, 9, 10, 92

Darwinian selection 8
David, P. 250
Dean, M. 174

260

Index

debt:
  financing 105
  obligations 127
  restructured 133–4
  unmanageable 106
decentralization 111, 112, 192
  administrative 186
  problems inherent in 171
decision-making 22, 89, 192
  firm a site of 89
  impossibility of predicting or ascribing probabilities to outcomes 20
  interdependent 48
  internal structure 10
  judgmental 22
  problems of 90
  rational 89
  see also strategic decision-making
defence 154–5, 156, 164
  spatial restructuring 160–3
  spending on 93, 157, 195
demand 10
  fragmented 194
  inadequate treatment of 23
  irregular and erratic 73
  matching supply with 95
  stability of 77
  variations in 74
Denis, D. & D. 156
Denmark 219, 226
Department of Defense/Department of Justice (US) 161
Depressed Areas 179
Depression 182, 183
deregulation 105, 216
Deutsche Bank 138
Deutsche Bourse 137
Development Areas 185
Dicken, P. 40, 41, 42, 44, 46, 48, 49, 50, 51, 96, 118 n.
differences 237–8
differentiation 53, 119, 229

fundamental importance of 196
  intra-organizational 97
directorships, *see* boards of directors
discursive view 89, 92, 94
discursive-performative view 90
disintegration 48
distribution rights 201
distributional flows 117, 118, 119
distributional returns 138
District Development Boards 180, 181–2
diversification 78, 79, 165
  capacity to 10
  discount 156
  internally-financed 164
  policy of 185
  uncertain returns to 154
diversity 237–8
  cultural 226
divestitures 153, 155
  dual use-destroying 164
dividends 127, 128, 133
Doeringer, P. 66
Dore, R. 67
Dosi, G. 227
double-entry bookkeeping 123
Dow, G. 8
Dowdy, J. 161
downsizing 101, 102, 134, 152, 157, 207
downstream activities/functions 198, 199, 204, 209
Dubois, A. 21, 63, 67
Duguid, P. 139
Duke Energy Corporation Inc. 132 n.
Dunning, J. 9
Durham 177, 182, 185
  South-West 181
dynamic inequality 111
dynamic tension 15

earnings per share 133
East India Company 69
East South Central states 157
Eastleigh 102

Index

eBay 237
economic development 217, 218
 rapid of Third Italy 227
 social organization to generate 227
economic growth 173, 174
 academic and policy rhetoric as key agent in 36
 innovation and 193
 local 97
 path to, in local economies 61
 processes that generate 228
 rapid 4
 regional, post-Fordist 214
 understanding the geography of 18
economism 87
educational levels 217
efficiency 89, 224
 adaptive 14, 15
 allocative 65, 66
 collective 224
 compromised 7
 link between stock market prices and 156
 maximum, all decisions made to achieve 6
egalitarian social structures 217
Elders IXL Ltd 105
electronics firms 99–102, 109
Eli Lilly & Co. 204–5, 208
elites 108, 109
Elliott, John 105, 106
embeddedness 39, 41, 46, 87, 92, 96
 Polanyi's notion criticized 45
Emilia-Romagna 222
emotional commitment 53
Enfield 74–5, 77, 101
enforceable contracts 65, 73, 92
Ennals, R. 220, 229
Enron 126 n.
enterprise development 226
enterprise niches 20
enterprise segmentation model 21, 96
'enterprise terrain' 97

entrepreneurship 15, 22, 88, 92, 94
 aggressive 105
 ambiguity in the way interpreted 95
 fragmented 72
 serial and multiple 100
 specific attempt to incorporate into transaction cost 23
 time-specific and place-specific acts of 97
environmental damage 138
ephemeralization of jobs 97
epistemic communities 54, 250
equality 217
equilibrium 6, 19, 22
 intertemporal 20
Esso 102–3
estrogen 198 n.
ethnic connections 121
Euronext 137
EVA (economic value added) model 126 n., 127 n.
evolutionary theory 11, 12, 19
executive salaries/compensation 94, 152
exhaustion exit strategies 131
expansion 9
expectations 200
 convergent 16
 higher profit 151
 monetary reward 8
 shared and common 218
external relations 43
externalities 226, 227
 benefits of 4
externalization 17, 152

factor markets 81
 regional differences in 14
factors 69, 77, 79, 81
factors of production 95
Fagan, R. H. 105
family members 101, 111
 connections 121
 ties 62, 177–8

fashion 152–3, 156, 165
Fawley refinery 102–3
FDA (US Food and Drug Administration) 198, 199, 200, 202, 203, 204, 209
Federal Trade Commission 161
'fence sitters' 155
film industry 195
financial firms 149, 150–2, 164–5, 237
  spatial consequences of strategies 157–9
financial management narratives 117–45
financial markets 129, 130, 137
  global, competitively priced 135
  liberalization and deregulation 216
financial sector 151–3
  active pressures on industrial firms 153
Fiorina, Carly 35
FIRE (finance, insurance, and real estate sector) 151–2
firms:
  alternative conceptualization of 9–13
  defining 71, 246–9
  distinction between markets and 67
  family, federated 62
  financial narratives of 122–30
  first to acknowledge the growing complexity of 119
  high-tech, activity specific approach to 191–213
  learning 214–23
  legal 40
  limitations of conceptualizing as phenotype 90–7
  political/political actors in 147–88
  stylizing 87, 88, 89–90, 97, 109–10
  see also boundaries of the firm; small firms; theory of the firm
first-mover advantages 14
Flamm, Ken 161
flexibility 68, 72, 78, 195, 222, 224

flat and egalitarian organizations have prerequisites for 221
founded upon elasticity of small producers with limited capital 69
functional labour market 216
given way to standardized mass production 79
intensely competitive 76
limited routines 12
numerical 215
flexibilization 63
flexible accumulation 21
flexible specialization 21, 61, 70, 193, 194, 195, 210
  and boundaries of the firm 62–4
  hallmark of current era of 67
Fligstein, N. 43, 126
Florence, P. 72, 74
Florida 159
Foray, D. 250
Fordism 61, 77, 221
forex trades 137
formality 49
Fortune Global 500 list 131
Foss, N. 7, 8, 22, 37, 48, 52
Fosters Brewing Group Ltd 105, 106, 108, 111
Foucault, M. 170, 174, 175, 176
France 104, 225
Franco-Prussian war (1870–1) 78
Freeland, R. 43
Freeman, C. 220
Freeport-McMoRan Inc. 132 n.
French regulationist school 173
Frey, B. 8
Friedman, Milton 119
FTSE companies 108
  All-Share Index 135
Fujimoto Diagnostics 202
functionalism 7, 8, 16

Gadde, L.-E. 21, 63, 67
Galunic, C. 5, 7, 16, 17, 18

Index

game theory 155
gearing levels 134
Genentech 203–7, 208
General Accounting Office (US) 162
General Dynamics 152, 155, 157
genes 12
Georgia 159, 162
Germany 202, 216, 219
Ghoshal, S. 3, 8, 9, 14–16, 20
Gibbons, R. 37 n., 238, 251
Gibson-Graham, J. K. 120
Giddens, A. 243
Gilbert, M. 178
Gilbertson, Brian 138, 139, 140
Gingrich, Newt 162
Glasmeier, A. 191 n.
global funds 135–8
globalization 4, 90–1, 105, 161, 216
 accelerating 62
 only solution to intractable problems posed by 219
 pressures of 6
 problems associated with 63
 transition to post-Fordism under 214
Glückler, J. 18, 244
goals 52
 collective 10–11
 common 46, 247
 firm-specific 42
 implicit 94
 inconsistent 11
 shared 49
Goldberg, V. 67
Goldman Sachs 151
Goodman, John D. 77
Goodyear, Charles (Chip) 132, 133, 134, 135, 137, 139, 140
Goold, M. 127
Gosport 101
Gotbaum, Josh 160
governance 6, 8, 43, 77, 88, 123
 intermediate structure 226

governmentality 170, 174, 187
 constructing a new mode of 176–86
 space an important element of 175
Grabher, G. 222, 223
Granovetter, M. 39, 43, 46
Gray, H. Peter 152 n.
Gray, M. 193
Great Northern Coalfield 177
Gregory, R. 177
Grossman, S. 246
group contracting 68–74
 sustainability of 74–6
growth hormones 205
Grumman 158–9
Guetzkow, H. 122 n.
gun-making 61–84, 245
'Gunbelt' crescent 157
Gustavsen, B. 220, 229

Habermas, J. 172–3
Hahn, M. 15–16, 20
Håkansson, H. 224
Hall, P. 242
Hambrick, D. 106
Handy, C. 111
Hanover 202
Harrison, B. 51
Hart, O. 6, 8, 246
Hartlepool 181
Hay, C. 173
hedging 137
hegemonic practices 175
Henry, N. 196
Henry Jones IXL Ltd 105
Henwood, D. 151, 152, 153
Hepatitis C 200, 203
heterogeneity 19, 23
 see also competitive heterogeneity
Hicks, J. 20
hierarchies 44, 49
 managerial, problems of control within 88

264

Index

markets versus 87
transactions moved out of markets into 7
high-tech firms 191–213
HIH 126 n.
Hikino, T. 91
Hill, S. 107, 108
Himmelstrand, U. 45
HIV (human immunodeficiency virus) 200, 203
Hodgson, G. 12, 21, 44 n., 52, 55, 65, 66, 67, 87, 97, 110, 239
hold-up problem 49
Holloway, J. 172 n.
Holmström, B. 247
homogeneity 52
Honeywell 156
Hoopes, D. 13, 14
Hopwood, A. 122 n., 124, 125, 126, 129
HP (Hewlett-Packard) 35
Hudson, R. 170, 176, 178, 182, 221
Hughes 159, 163
human capital 218, 223
  not entirely specialized 10
Humphrey, J. 224, 225
Humulin 204–5
hybrid firms 21, 48, 63, 67

ICI 77
ICT (information & communications technology) 215
identification 17
  employment relations and 51–4
identity 16, 52
  firm-specific, individual and collective 53
  generic 37
IMF (International Monetary Fund) 165
imitation 14
implicit agreements 50–1
income distribution 222

incomplete-contracts theory 6, 8, 9, 12, 16, 18, 19, 20, 64–5, 90
indebtedness 159
independence 49, 70
India 4
Indianapolis 205
individualistic behaviour 52
indivisibilities 47, 48, 51
Industrial Advisory Council 182
industrial districts 39, 66, 67, 70, 162 n., 222, 223, 225, 226
  arm's-length market transaction within 228
  clusters of 228
  importance of cooperation between small firms in 227
industrial firms 150–2
'industrial swarming' 72
industrialization 64, 193 n.
  import replacement policies 105
  rapid 4, 217
inefficiencies 7
informality 49
information:
  embodied 9
  full, relative absence of 153
  imperfect 13
  incomplete 8
  most easily and readily codified 65
  strategic, deceitfully releasing 54
information flows 54, 89
  horizontal 221
  vertical 221
information overload 7
infrastructure 226
inimitability issue 19, 20
innovation 14, 22, 70, 154, 221
  commercial leverage given by 94
  continual/continuous 216, 219
  discouraging mergers to ensure 160
  focus on 193
  fundamental aspect of 218
  important role of 228

265

Index

incremental 220, 224
institutional 15, 214
interactive 214, 217, 223
key to 16
managerial 224
organizational 214
policy 181
regional 4, 214
social organization to generate 227
sustaining 216
technological 224
innovative industries 193–7
insider information 152
insiders 108
instability 77, 78
institutional environment 39
  boundary between firm and 45–6
institutional investors 135
institutional pluralism 15
institutional thickness 75, 82, 218
institutionalist perspective 89, 96, 218
institutionalization 74, 76, 90, 224
  accounting profession 124 n.
insulin 204
intangible services 237
integration 53
  forms of 229
  locational 72
intellectual property rights 51
intensification 132, 134
interactions 53
  firm-environment 89
  inter-firm 36
  selectively exclusive face-to-face 153
  see also social interaction
interconnectedness 51
interdependence 42, 43
  management of 43
  place-specific untraded 227
  socially constructed networks of 89
Interferon Sciences 199–203
inter-firm relationships 8–9, 53, 67
  close 61

internal combustion engines 79
internal contradiction 74
internal markets 63
  capital 66
  emergence of 21
  labour 66, 215
internalization costs 65
international trade 216
internationalization 4, 48, 105
Internet-based businesses 237
interorganizational phenomena 228
interpretation 225
  uncertainties of 17
intra-firm relations 49
  close 61
inventiveness 16
inventories 11
investment:
  corrosive effect on longer-term
    strategies 152
  fashions in strategies 153
  impossibility of predicting or
    ascribing probabilities to
    outcomes 2
  longer-term, suppressing 156
  low 22
  new high performing assets 134
  poorly performing,
    discarding 128
  suboptimal 156
  transaction-specific 7
  unsteady flows 203
investment bankers 151, 153, 155,
  160, 164
  strategies dictated by 156
Ioannides, S. 240–1
Ireland 104
'irrational exuberance' 152 n.
isolating mechanisms 14
Italy 123, 219
  southern, social capital
    formation 226
  see also Third Italy

266

Index

Japan 105–6, 202, 222
Jensen, M. C. 119, 127
Jensen-Butler, C. 227
Jessop, B. 173, 174, 175, 176
jewellery 64, 76
job creation 87
Johnson, B. 16, 215, 221
Johnson & Johnson 198 n.
judgement 22
  bad 98
  entrepreneurial 15
just-in-time transactions 224

Kalmarism 221
Kansas 201
Kenosha 150
Kirzner, I. M. 22, 241
Klein, B. 66
Klein, P. 7, 8, 22, 37
Knight, F. H. 20
know-how 18, 49, 226
knowledge 18, 19, 89
  commercial 94
  contextual 226
  diffusion of 219, 221
  disembodied 226, 227
  efficient mechanisms for creation and transformation of 16
  evolution of 16
  expert 250
  exploitation of 219
  firm-specific 108
  importance of 63
  local, place-specific 4
  mutual 225
  perfect 13
  proprietary 65
  scientific 94
  shared 16, 51, 63, 225
  situatedness of 16
  sticky, codified 226
  strategic, deceitfully releasing 54
  technological 39
  unintentionally leaked across firm boundaries 51
  utilization of 219
  see also tacit knowledge; *also under following headings prefixed* 'knowledge'
knowledge-based theory 244 n.
  control of knowledge in 23
knowledge creation 220
  fostering 61
  potential to promote 230
knowledge flows 54
knowledge-intensive activities 52
knowledge leakage 17
knowledge transactions 17
knowledge transfer 18
  evolving, path-dependent processes of 17
  fostering 61
  mechanism for 70
  seen as central to success or failure of firms 13
Kogut, B. 16, 17
Kohler, A. 135
Kondratieff long waves 193
Kovacic, William 161
KPMG 132
Kroszner, R. S. 44

labour 138, 185
  coercive controls over 125
  excess expenditure payments to 126
  firm's right to exploit 120
  harmony of interests between capital and 177
  high calibre 200
  intensification practices 132
  possibility for negotiated involvement of 222
  skilled 47, 194, 198, 203
  structural class relationship between capital and 169

267

Index

labour market:
　empowerment 221
　flexible 215, 216
　improved skills of the individual traded on 222
　internal 66, 215
　low-end 216
　middle class, professional 215
　social regulation of 222
　unstable, insecure 215
Labour party/government (UK) 182, 183, 184, 187
　leaders 181
Lagendijk, A. 237
Lancashire 179
Langlois, R. 37 n., 42, 65, 245
language 125, 225
　common understandings among users 120
　shared 107
Laughlin, R. 125, 129 n., 141
Lave, J. 16, 52, 110
layoffs 159, 203, 237
　mass 178
　'payoffs for' 162
Lazonick, W. 216, 219, 222, 227, 229
leadership 95
　compatible styles 107
lean production 63, 219
learning 10, 11, 20, 23, 87, 88, 89
　'catch-up' 220
　central to success or failure of firms 13
　collective 195, 221, 222, 227
　constant 224
　evolving, path-dependent processes of 17
　fostering 61
　importance of 63
　incremental and cumulative 12
　interactive 217, 218, 221, 223, 229
　joint 224

　mechanism for 70
　meso-level 223–6
　micro-level 221–3
　potential to promote 230
　reciprocal, socially based 93
　situated 16
learning economies 215–21
　flexible 222
　globalizing 227
　policy strategy aiming at promoting 226
　post-Fordist 214–15, 227, 228
learning organizations 215–21
　macro-level 226–9
learning regions 227, 228
Leborgne, D. 222, 224
Lee-Metford guns 79
legal firms 40
legitimacy 123, 129, 173, 200
legitimation crises 173, 174
Leland, John 68
Leonard, S. 39
leveraged buyout 155
Lewis, J. 178
Lewisham 74
liabilities 138
liberal ideology 177
liberal market economies 216, 221
liberalization 216
licensing 203, 204, 207, 209
limited spatial analysis 197
Lipietz, A. 222, 224
Lipparini, A. 223, 224
litigation 205
Litton 156
living standards 216
　working class 173
Loasby, B. 3, 7–8, 20
local authorities 180, 227
local economic systems:
　local boundary between firm and 46–8
　subsidiaries embedded in 4

268

location 197, 199
  significance of 243
Lockheed/Lockheed Martin 150, 155, 157, 159, 162
London 129
  overconcentration of new industry 185
  see also City of London 107, 108
London Stock Exchange 135, 137-8
Long Island 159, 164
Loral 155
Lorenz, E. 225
Lorenzoni, G. 223, 224
Los Angeles 157, 159, 161 n., 163, 164
Louisiana 159
Lovering, J. 165
low-tech industries 219
loyalty 222, 225
  buyer 14
Lundquist, J. 154 n.
Lundvall, B.-Å. 16, 215, 221, 225, 226, 227, 229
Lyon region 225

McDermott, P. 23
McDonnell Douglas 159, 162, 163
MacKinnon, D. 176
McKinsey & Company 154 n., 161 n.
Madsen, T. 13, 14
Magma Copper Company (US) 132 n.
'make or buy' question 55, 65
Mäki, U. 246
Malmberg, A. 40, 41, 44, 48, 50, 51, 118 n., 243, 244
management buyouts 101, 103, 104
management teams 9
managerial competence 15
  high 16
managerial control 111
  separation of ownership from 88
managerialism 18, 109
  discourse of 89
Marchionni, C. 246

March, J. G. 5, 9, 10, 92, 122 n.
market capitalization 135
market failure 16, 18
  theories of the firm need to move beyond 14-15
market-makers 74, 75, 79, 80
market niches 102
market power 153
market pressures 64
  firm as refuge from 89
market segmentation 14, 193-4
marketing 204, 207
  foreign rights 206
  global 201
  niche 199-203, 209
markets:
  boundary/distinction between firms and 55, 67
  establishment, maintenance and regulation of 177
  external 152
  financial firms engage in extensive manipulation 152-3
  geographically differentiated 47
  global 219, 222
  hierarchies versus 87
  military 163
  new 95
  potential 205, 209
  volatility of 194
  world 222
  see also factor markets; financial markets; internal markets; product markets
Markusen, A. 41, 42, 44, 93, 152, 162 n., 195, 249
Marshall, A. 119, 225
Martin, J. 39, 53
Martin, R. 246
Marx, Karl 150
Maryland 157
Maskell, P. 6, 37, 65, 89, 118 n., 239, 240, 243-4

Index

Mason, P. 106
mass customization 63
mass production 72, 77–9
  advocates of 75
  flexibility given way to 79
  fragmented demand
    undermines 194
  historical alternatives to 62
  shift away from 61
Massachusetts 157
Massey, D. 20, 194
Masten, S. E. 55, 247–8
Master and Servant legislation 73
masters 177
  see also small masters
Matsusaka, J. 156
Meckling, W. H. 119, 127
medical complexes 195
Medicare formulary 209
mega-mergers 150, 151, 163
  and 'pure play' prescriptions in
    aerospace 153–7
'memes' 17
mergers 97, 130, 134, 140
  boom in 105
  costs of 161, 163
  defence 160, 161, 162, 163
  frequent waves 153
  growth produced by 135
  Wall Street-instigated 159
  see also mega-mergers
Merrill Lynch 155
metal trades 64, 69, 81
Mexico 198 n., 202, 205
Meyer, J. W. 123–4, 125, 126
micro-operations 70, 81
middle class 215
Middle East 104
middlemen, *see* small masters
Midwest 198, 199, 201, 204
Miliband, R. 171 n.
militancy 181
military spending 154

Mill, John Stuart 119
Miller, P. 124 n., 125, 129 n.
Mills, Brad 132 n.
mining industry, *see* BHP
mission statements 134
Mjøset, L. 217
modernization 179–81
Moen, E. 241
monetary reward 8
monitoring 36
monopoly 20, 74
  commercial aircraft 163
Moore, J. 6
Moore, R. 177
Moran, P. 3, 8, 9, 14–16, 20
Morgan, G. 241, 242
Morgan, K. 222
Morgan Stanley 138, 151
Moss, D. 69
motivation 8
Mountain states 157
multinational corporations 93
  understanding growth and
    evolution of 4
mutual understanding 67

Napoleonic wars (1805–15) 69, 72, 74
NASDAQ 137
National Government (UK) 182, 183
national interest 185
National Patent Development
  Corporation 199
natural resources 130
  world's premier supplier of 137
Navy aircraft contract cuts 158
NBS (National Business Systems) 240,
  241, 242
NEC 39
NEDA (North East Development
  Association) 186, 187
NEDB (North East Development
  Board) 181–2, 184, 186
  wound up 183

Index

Nelson, R. 5, 9, 11–12
neoclassical theory 4–5, 66, 87, 89, 90, 119, 152
  concept of human capital 218
neo-Fordist tendency 216
neo-Foucauldians 176
neo-Gramscians 175, 176
neo-Taylorism 221
Netherlands 104
networks 40, 46, 87, 110
  boundaries between firms within 48–51
  clusters of 228
  competence 228
  cooperating firms 221
  cultural 121
  embedded 65
  family 100
  governance structure of 223
  institutionalist, embedded 90
  inter-firm 49, 228
  inter-organizational 36
  intra-firm 228
  less well-developed 109
  local, firms need to be quasi-integrated into 63
  loose coupling within 223
  processes operating within 14
  social 121
  socially constructed 89
  'statuses' within 96
  third-party referral 101, 108
  trust 4
  vertically disintegrated structures 48
New Brunswick 201
new entrants 95
new firm formation 4, 194
new industrial spaces theory 4, 193, 194, 195–6, 210
new industries 185
new international division of labour 216
New Jersey 198, 199, 200, 201, 203, 206

New South Wales 132
New York 129, 154 n., 157, 198, 199, 200
Newcastle (Australia) 132, 134
Newcastle and Gateshead Chamber of Commerce 180
Newdegate, Sir Richard 68
niche marketing 199–203, 209
NIG (Northern Industrial Group) 183–6, 187
Nobel Interests 77
Nokia 35
Nonaka, I. 225, 228
non-economic factors 63
Nooteboom, B. 22, 36, 54, 95, 96, 246–7
Nordic countries 242
  see also Scandinavia
North East England 176–86
Northumberland and Durham Coal Owners' Association 179
Norton, B. 118 n., 120
Norway 217, 218, 222, 226
NPV (Net Present Value) enhancement 137
Nunn, Sam 154 n.
Nutropin 205–6
NYSE (New York Stock Exchange) 137

obligations:
  contractual 74
  debt 127
  shared and common 218
Oden, M. 157, 162
Offe, C. 172–3
Office of Economic Security (US) 160, 161
Oinas, P. 38, 49–50, 237, 244, 245
Ok Tedi copper/gold mines 138
oligopoly 193 n., 198
Ollila, Jorma 35
O'Neill, P. M. 120, 131
opportunism 6, 7, 8, 16, 65

271

Index

oral contraception pills 198 n.
organization theory 221, 227
organizational capability 15, 23
  building 27, 229
organizational institutionalism 45
organizational slack 10, 11
organizational types 20
Osaka 202
Osterloh, M. 8
O'Sullivan, M. 222, 227
Otto, E. 79
Ouchi, W. 8
'outside' directors 108
outsourcing 102
ownership concentration 20

Packalén, A. 50
Papua New Guinea 138
Parke Davis 198 n.
Parker, E. 193
parsimony 5
partnership strategy 225
Patchell, J. 224
patents 14
paternalism 62, 177
path-dependence 10, 17, 106
  evolution 12
  heterogeneity reinforced by 14
  process of change 12
  significance of 6
patronage 107
Pavitt, K. 12
Penrose, E. 5, 9, 10, 11, 13, 18, 20, 22, 242, 245
Pentagon 160–1, 162, 163, 165
'Pentagon City' 157
performance:
  commercial 104
  enhancing 4
  past 11
  stock 152
  systematic differences 13
performance narratives 85–145

performativity 87
Perry, Bill 160, 161
petroleum 137
petty bourgeoisie 109
Pfeffer, J. 106
pharmaceutical firms 197–8, 193, 200, 201, 202, 203, 206, 208
Picciotto, S. 172 n.
piece-rates 71
Pinch, S. 244
Piore, M. 66
place-based clusters 4, 14
  embedded networks of 15
Polanyi, K. 45
political struggle 169
politics:
  modernization 179–81
  reaction 177–9
Poovey, M. 123, 124
Port Kembla 132
Port of Tyne Commissioners 180
Porter, M. 16, 216, 219, 222, 223, 226, 227
portfolio investment 101, 127, 129
portfolio management model 133, 134
post-Fordism 214–15, 216, 219, 223, 227, 228
Poterba, J. 151
Poulantzas, N. 171 n.
Powell, W. 7, 96
Power, M. 125, 129 n., 141
power 44, 49
  'capillary' notion of 175–6
  inter- and intra-organizational inequalities 97
  proscribed 112
  state 176
  technical and positional 98
  unequal 89
  use of 51
power elites 108
power relations 46, 170
  shifting 18

stabilization of 99
strategic codification of multitude of 176
unequal 50, 91
powerfulness 4, 91, 96
powerlessness 4, 91, 95, 96, 215
  unrecognized 97
premium payments 76
prices:
  fair 73
  proxy 81
  share/stock 135, 156
Priem, R. 5
problem-solving 20, 222
problem-stimulated search 10
procurement spending 154
product markets 47, 173
production 69
  advanced 196, 201
  basic unit of 222
  capitalist relations of 171
  commercial, expanded 201
  flexible 63, 194
  high volume 203
  innovative, technologically-based 72
  local systems 47, 73
  moving and consolidating 158
  rational landscape of 65
  redesigned 123
  regional systems 39
  see also lean production; mass production
production capacity 150
production function 6, 8, 66, 89, 90
professional associations 110
profit 11, 94, 97, 248
  alertness to opportunities 22
  associated with deep employment cuts 163
  excessive 157
  higher expectations 151
  manufacturing 152
  negative 133

short-term 153, 157, 159
top 100 biotech firms 200
windfall 159
profitability 127, 178, 200
  maintaining 97
progestogen 198 n.
property rights 6, 14, 42, 243, 247
  delegated 248
  intellectual 51
  transfer of 55
property sell-offs 163
protectionism 179
proteins 204, 205
protestant ethic 217
proto-firms 71
proximity 63, 194, 225, 228
Prussian government 77
public utilities 180
Puerto Rico 198
Purdue Pharma 201
'pure play' 153–7, 161, 164, 165
Putnam, R. 218
Putterman, L. 44

quality 225
quasi-firms 21, 63, 67
quasi-integration 63, 66–7, 223–4

R&D (research & development) 197, 199, 200, 208
  financial risks of 224
rail companies 180
Rand 161
Rappaport, A. 126 n.
rates of return 132
  acceptable 151
Rathe, K. 21, 22
rational choice 8, 12–13, 20
rationalism 6, 89
  ahistoric, timeless 5
rationality 243
  crises 175
  market 87

273

Index

rationalization 105
raw materials 47
Raytheon 156, 163
RBV (resource-based view) 10, 11, 13–19, 20, 65, 89, 90, 65, 67, 89, 90, 96, 242, 244 n.
Reagan administration 154, 164
realism 5
receivership 104
recession 101, 102, 106
reciprocity 9, 49, 62, 109
   socially constructed networks of 89
recombinant process 204, 205
recontextualization 17
redistributive welfare policies 173
redundancy payments 101
regional development:
   acknowledging financial firms and state in 164–5
   endogenous 227, 229
   new programme of 181–3
   role played by sociocultural and institutional structures in 218–19
regional development agencies 101
Regional Development Boards 181
regulation 92, 174
   codified outcome of 110
   system-forming 91
   see also social regulation
Reinmöller, P. 225, 228
reinterpretation 17
relational contracting 67
   group contracting as 70–4
relational view 18, 19, 23, 121
relocations 157, 159, 162, 163, 185
rent-seeking behaviour 13
   competitive 19
rents:
   above-average 10, 13
   sustainable 13
repeat business 9
reputation 51
   difficult to establish 203

   influence and 108
   tarnished 74
   threat of losing 50
Resnick, S. A. 120
resource allocation 22, 177
   strategic, intra-corporate 50 n.
resources:
   activity-specific 89
   capital 71
   control of 42
   excess 10
   exploitation of 9
   financial 100
   general mobilization of 220
   new, development of 9
   scarce 49
   shared 47, 51
   shifted to areas where returns can be maximized 128
   substituted 9
   transfers of 66
   unique 216
   world's largest company 117
   see also RBV
restructuring 106, 165, 203
   economic 149
   fad-driven 157
   geographical 149, 152
   industrial 152
   regional 152, 160
   spatial 157, 160–3
retained earnings 152
rewards 177
Richardson, G. 67, 242
Ridley, Lord 181, 183, 184
risk minimization 100, 101
risk sharing 194
rivals/rivalry 13, 14, 193
Roberts, J. 247
Robertson, P. L. 42, 65
Roche Holdings 206–7
Rose, N. 174
Route 128 area 39, 195

routines 11–12
Royal Commission (1938) 184
royalties 205
Rugman, A. 10, 13, 14
Russia 78
Rutgers University 162

Sabel, C. 62, 225
Sacramento Valley 206
SAIC Corporation 157
St Louis 157, 159
Salomon Brothers 155
San Francisco 203, 206
San Manuel copper facilities 134
sanctions 177
Sandofi-Winthrop McPherson 201
Sargent, William 73
Sarin, A. 156
Saul, S. 74
savings 161, 162
Saxenian, A. 39, 41, 54, 93, 195
scale economies 199, 202, 205, 208
scandals 94
  accounting 123
Scandinavia 6, 217, 218, 227
  see also Denmark; Norway
Schlicht, E. 52–3
Schmitz, H. 224, 225
Schoenberger, E. 99, 121 n., 150
Schrader, D. E. 118 n., 119
Schumpeter, J. A. 9, 22
Schwartz, Bernard 155
Scotland 179
Scott, A. 165, 195, 241
Scott, D. R. 122 n.
Scott, W. 43, 45, 47
search behaviour 11, 12
  problem-stimulated 89
Searle 198 n.
Seattle 164
selection environment 11
selection practices 52
selection techniques 109

self-interest 7, 75, 81–2, 127
  management 127
self-promotion 82
semi-autonomy 42, 43
semiconductors 195
Sennett, R. 215, 216, 222
Servaes, H. 156
'shareholder revolt' 152
shareholder value creation 133
shareholders 117, 127
  accrual of sharemarket-based capital gains 128
  powerful 155
  superior returns for 135–7
  see also SVA; TSR
shipbuilding 180
Shipowners' Association 179
Shleifer, A. 159
short-termism 105, 151
significant ties 109
Silicon Valley 39, 93, 160, 195, 215
Simon, H. A. 52, 122 n.
sliding scale arrangements 177
small firms 48, 99, 106, 109, 199
  biotech 208, 209
  defence-specialized 164
  importance of cooperation between 227
  manufacturing 62
  networked 70
  process innovation in networks of 193
  waged labour tied to 76
Small Heath 77, 78, 79
small masters 69–70, 76
  negotiation between contractors, artisans and 73
Smallwood, Dennis 161
SMEs (small- and medium-sized enterprises) 88, 99–104, 154, 219
  growth, significance and susceptibilities 62–3
  managing coalitions in 111

275

Index

Smith, Adam 119
Smith-Doerr, L. 96
Snider rifles 78
Snyder, W. 54
social benefits 81
social capital 217–18, 221, 222, 229–30
  access to 49
  alternative interpretations of 223
  building 214, 228
  industry-specific 47
  not all cultural settings possess or produce 226
  sources of 18
social cohesion 217, 225, 228
social contacts 23
social interaction:
  close 65
  emergent products of 90
  patterned 52
social justice 217
social networks 36, 39
social norms 218
social regulation 73, 91, 173
  constructing a new mode of 176–86
  labour market 222
social relations 39, 45, 171
  concrete, ongoing systems of 46
  contradictory 173
  diverse 18
  firm embedded in spatial structures of 223
  intensive 51
  local 243
  pre-established 51
social struggle 169
socialization 71, 88, 108
  coalition members 98
  into accepted practices 111
  mechanism for 70
socio-economic perspectives 89
software 195
  international entrepreneurs 94
solidarity 217

Sony 237
Soskice, D. 216, 218, 242
South Africa 130
South Atlantic states 157
South Hampshire 99–102, 109, 111
South Wales 93
Southampton 102
southern Africa 117
Special Areas 181, 183
stability 49
Starbuck, W. H. 94
start-ups 100
state 169
  political firms and 147–68
  role of 159, 160–3, 165, 173, 176, 177
  State Derivation debates (1970s) 170, 171 n., 172
state intervention:
  necessary 183, 184
  old 'Liberal' fear of 185
  selective 179
steelworks, *see* BHP
stereotypes 72
Stern Stewart and Co 126 n.
Sternberg, R. 193
Stewart, G. B. 126 n.
Stigler, George 119
Stinchcombe, A. 20
stock markets, *see* Deutsche Bourse; Euronext; London; NASDAQ; Sydney; Wall Street
Stonecipher, Harry 163
Storper, M. 39, 41, 47, 51
strategic coalitions 88
  formation and reproduction of 109
strategic decision-making 40, 48, 50, 106, 242
  coalitions 110, 111
  commonality in approaches to 107
strategic planning 22
strategic-relation theory 175
strengths and weaknesses 10
  commercial 104

strikes 73, 177
structural contingency model 23
structuralism 87, 89
structuration 243
subcontractors 67, 199, 203
  collaboration with 223
  long-term relationships between firms and 225
  networked relationships between contractors and 66
subjectivities 99
subordination 91
subsidiaries 104, 202
  embedded in local economic systems 4
subsidies 162
Sugden, R. 40, 48
Summers, L. 151
superior returns 14
suppliers 47, 69
  collaboration with 223
  external 65
supply 10
  matching with demand 95
'supporters' 52
surplus values 117
  firm's right to appropriate 120
survival:
  firms dependent on each other for 46–7
  prospects of 129
SVA (shareholder value added) 118, 125, 130, 133, 138, 139
  management narratives based on 126–8
  maximization of 132, 137
  moves to enhance 134
Swedberg, R. 45, 95
Sweden 216
Switzerland 206, 216
Sydney stock exchange 135, 137
symbolic communication 17
Syntex 198 n.

tacit knowledge 16, 221, 226
  sharing of 225
takeovers 97, 101, 155
  boom in 105
  growth produced by 135
  hostile 153, 159
  protection against 127
targets 11, 66
tax breaks 159
taxation 173
  fair rate of 130
Taylor, M. 3, 8, 16, 18, 21, 23, 39, 89, 90, 91, 96, 97, 98, 100, 105, 107, 108, 118 n., 238, 239, 242, 245
Taylorism 123
technological change 61, 70, 72, 193, 220
  fostering 67
technological districts 227
Teesside 179, 180, 181
theory of the firm 21, 51, 55–6, 61, 91, 97, 235–54
  behavioural 92
  dynamic 64
  neoclassical 89
  omission of entrepreneurship from 22
  see also complete-contracts; evolutionary theory; incomplete-contracts; knowledge-based theory; RBV; transaction-cost view
Third Italy 39, 66, 218, 226
  rapid economic development 227
third-party referrals 100–1, 107, 108
Thrift, N. 21, 39, 40, 41, 42, 45, 46, 48, 49, 50, 96, 175
time significance 6
time horizons 22
time-specificity 93, 97, 106
timelessness 92, 93
Times, The 108, 109
TNCs (transnational corporations) 4, 23
Tokyo 129

277

Index

Toyotism 221
trade unions 181, 184
  major 176, 183
  pliable 177
  representative and cooperative minded 217
trading volumes 135
transaction-cost view 6, 7, 16, 19, 20, 22, 89, 90, 196
  functionalism at the heart of the argument 8
  fundamentally static 9
  inconsistency to theory 8
  reasoning 87
  specific attempt to incorporate entrepreneurship into 23
transaction costs 66, 81
  agglomeration functions to lower 194
  importance of 65
  minimizing 196
transnationalisation 41
triangulation 149, 163
trust 49, 51, 62, 67
  building 9, 221, 225
  extended 224
  institutional 225
  lack of 226
  mutual 225
  possibility of creating 225
  substitute for formalized control system 63
  threat of losing 50
TRW 164
TSR (total shareholder return) model 126 n.
Turopolec, L. 122 n.
Tyndall, G. 122 n.
Tyneside 179, 180

UBS Warburg 138
uncertainty 10, 48, 76, 119, 128
  competitive 89
  high 22
  judgmental decision-making under 22
  Knightian 20
  satisfying behaviour base on 13
  transactions that involve 7
'undermen' 73
unemployment 181
  aggregate 215
  chronic 178
  short periods of 215
United States 104
  aerospace industry 150–7
  defence spending 195
  drug-producing industry 197–9
  industrial-military complex 93
  investor behaviour 151
  military industry capacity 160
  redistribution of production capacity 150
University of California, San Francisco 203
unpredictable technology 203
untraded interdependencies 4, 89
upgrading 217, 224
upper echelons theory 106, 107
utility 98

Vacaville 206
value chain collaboration 228
value creation 10, 14, 15, 123, 133
values:
  cultural 238
  moral 81
  shared and common 218
Van Gils, H. 244, 245
venture capital 75, 160, 197
Verbeke, A. 10, 13, 14
Vernon's product cycles 193
vertical disintegration 195, 207, 223
  severe 194
vertical integration 37 n., 194, 223
  break-up of firms 128
  large corporate structures 48

Index

Virginia 157
Vishny, R. 159
volatility 139, 140, 194

Wadeson, N. 65
wage bargaining 179
wage cuts 177
waged labour:
 biological and social reproduction of 171
 converting owners of micro firms into 81
 tied to particular small firms 76
Wales 179
Walker, G. 13, 14
Walker, R. 18
Wall Street 153–4, 155, 156, 159, 160, 161, 163, 164, 165, 199, 200
 'mood of' 209
 see also NYSE
Ward, D. M. 78
Warwickshire 68
Washington, DC 157, 162
wealth 104
 appropriating 109
 pursuit of 4, 111
wealth creation 87, 94, 95, 101, 103, 109
 fashionable ways to 106
 shareholder 117
 vehicles of 3, 98–9
weapons systems 157

Wearside 179, 180
Weeks, J. 5, 7, 16, 17, 18
Wenger, E. 16, 52, 54, 110
WestLB Panmure 138
White Paper on Employment Policy (UK 1944) 185
Whitley, R. 42, 43, 52, 241
Whyalla 132
Whyte, W. F. 122 n.
Wildavsky, A. 122 n.
William III (of Orange), king of Great Britain & Ireland 68
Williams, D. 69, 70–1, 75
Williamson, O. E. 6, 7, 8, 52
Winter, S. 5, 9, 11–12
Wise, M. J. 74
Witt, U. 21, 22, 240
Wolff, R. D. 120
Woolcock, M. 218
working class:
 living standards 173
 powerless and vulnerable 215
World Bank 165
write downs 133

Yeung, H. 18, 19, 23, 118 n., 239
Young, M. S. 122 n.
Yu, T. F.-L. 42

Zadeh, Norm 153
Zander, U. 16, 17
Zeitlin, J. 62